The

Germans

BY HERMANN EICH

Translated from the German by Michael Glenny
(published in hardcover as *The Unloved Germans*)

The Germans

A SCARBOROUGH BOOK
STEIN AND DAY/*Publishers*/New York

FIRST SCARBOROUGH BOOKS EDITION 1980

The Germans was originally published in hardcover
as *The Unloved Germans* by Stein and Day/*Publishers.*
Translation © Macdonald & Co. (Publishers) Ltd., 1965
Copyright © 1963 Econ-Verlag GmbH, Dusseldorf and Vienna
ISBN 0-8128-6057-8
Library of Congress Catalog Card No. 65-14399
All rights reserved
Printed in the United States of America

Stein and Day/*Publishers*/Scarborough House
Briarcliff Manor, N.Y. 10510

CONTENTS

I

COMPLICATED SIMPLIFICATIONS

No one would seriously contest that there is very little truth in such commonplaces as 'artists are careless' or 'women are fickle'. Similar generalisations, however, are in common use about nations or peoples —'the inscrutable Chinese', 'perfidious Albion' and so on. They are thoughtlessly bandied about at all times and not only in time of war or as results of official propaganda. We call these ready-made judgments stereotypes; they are remarkably widespread and firmly rooted, even among schoolchildren. Karl Aschersleben, writing in a German educational journal in April 1962, described an interesting experiment on this subject. He wrote forty-five adjectives on the blackboard and asked children from the upper forms of a number of primary schools to distribute them, to the best of their ability between the Romans, the Germanic peoples and the Huns. The result corresponded exactly to the views normally propagated by the standard school text-books. The Huns were described by more than half the children as cruel, the Romans as warlike and the Germanic tribes as brave. The dubiousness of such concepts became even more obvious with the subsequent questionnaire based on peoples of the present day. The Russians were unhesitatingly qualified as cruel. In the German popular imagination they have clearly assumed the role occupied over fifty years ago by the 'hereditary enemy', the French; in neither case were there any proper grounds for the validity of such a sweeping verdict.

Those alien races whom people have come to regard as hostile are arbitrarily labelled with all the worst human characteristics. On the other hand we tend to treat ourselves and our own people more kindly than others, at least in relation to foreigners and in times of national glory. Then self-adulation knows no bounds. When, however, the country's fortunes are reversed there is at once a suspicious trend towards self-accusation and a tendency to despise what was once admired, to admire everything new and foreign.

The question as to whether a nation can ever alter its character has been posed many times. But if a man can change radically, why not a race? If a Saul can become a Paul, may not an evil nation become good? The Germans have a special interest in proving that a nation can undergo a fundamental change; if they do not they will remain forever marked with the stigma of the Hitler era. Yet Paul was only the other face of Saul and the crimes of the Third Reich can only be said to represent one aspect of the German national character. The period of extreme nationalism, with all its manifestations of inhumanity, is more properly attributable to the clash of good and evil instincts, such as occurs in every individual, than to a total moral collapse. In the latter case there would be no possibility of salvation, as we learned after 1945 and after every period in which evil had the upper hand. Even Goethe remarked in 1813, in a conversation with the young Professor Luden, that the Germans were "so worthy as individuals, so wretched in the mass". One might retort that an omelette made of good eggs cannot be wholly ruined. Goethe himself was plagued by those very contradictions so often attributed to the Germans. One will come nearer to a just assessment of a nation by recognising its contradictory nature rather than by branding it wholly black or wholly white.

Schopenhauer considered all talk of 'national characteristics' to be nonsense. Human limitations and failings merely take a different form in every country and we then, he maintained, call this national character. Unless we are prepared to make drastic over-simplifications, it is impossible to pronounce judgment on a whole nation and we should abandon the attempt; but this runs counter to our instinct to achieve self-knowledge (which Schopenhauer himself was prepared to deny least of all). He is in fact the source of some of the harshest verdicts passed on the Germans by a German.

The only authority who considered that the Germans revealed their inmost nature without guile was Publius Cornelius Tacitus. To the Romans, beaten but still full of hubris towards the victorious barbarians, Tacitus' idealised picture of their northern neighbours was meant partly as an example and partly to remind them of the 'Teutonic peril'. He did so, unlike the modern method of chauvinistic propaganda, by exaggerating their virtues and their martial valour. Perhaps the ancestors of today's puzzling and contradictory Germans really were more straightforward and easier to understand. "Every nation," wrote the Heidelberg psychologist Willy Helpach in *The German Character*, "is in a perpetual state of transformation." There is "nothing fixed about these people, either physically or mentally". To be unloved (*unheimlich* in German) is a negative characteristic: it implies the active arousal of antipathy and fear. On the other hand the German word *gemütlich*, a synonym for everything sympathetic and attractive, has passed into several languages as an entirely positive concept. The German phenomenon is therefore full of contradictions. What is their origin? What is the truth about this contradictory nation of whom it has been said that they have two souls but no face?

"In the eyes of others the German has no face; hence arises mistrust, disquiet, failure to understand us, a poor opinion of us, even hate and scorn; but this must be borne, as it is our fate," wrote Hugo von Hoffmansthal. Most German faces were "blurred", hardly a single one seemed to announce itself clearly and definitely. "There is so much written on them and all without definition, without greatness." The French, too, have long reproached the Germans with having thoughts as blurred as their appearance. The Frenchman's lively gamut of facial expressions mirrors his thoughts and feelings; the German face is not to be trusted. Paul Claudel considered that the Germans—"lost between Slavs and Gauls"— had no physiognomy. Indeed this very absence of a recognisable physical type seems paradoxically to be the Germans' distinguishing characteristic. Even after allowing for the resemblances produced within similar social and professional strata, age-groups and geographical regions, more than any other European people the Germans evade any attempt at type-classification.

The lack of a definite facial type is not of course in itself a reason for despair. On the contrary this lack of a norm can with some justice be said to indicate an unusually high degree of individuality among the members of the population. This would seem to be confirmed by a remark made by Theodor Heuss, who was asked on one of his many journeys as Federal President where he had found the 'typical' German. "I have never met him," was the reply. The answer could equally well have been "I have met him everywhere". Every head of state would no doubt give a similar answer, at once sensible and non-committal, to this naïve enquiry as to their national prototype, for the 'average citizen' of any country has never been anything more than a caricature. It is therefore particularly interesting that in the cartoon iconography of international caricature there is no longer even a figure to represent the 'typical' German. The 'typical' figure of France is still Marianne, that fiery young woman who so inspired the revolutionaries of 1848 and has remained as popular as the Revolution itself. The 'deutsche Michel'[1] who has now no more than the name in common with his great exemplar, the Archangel Michael who once adorned the banner of Kaiser Otto the Great, never properly typified the expansion-minded German of the Reich but only symbolised the simple, well-meaning 'Little Man'. A symbol of hard times, the haggard 'Michel' with his tasselled cap hardly fits into the present-day world in which so many have re-assumed a paunch and a double chin. The physical persona of the typical German seems, in fact, to be much more subject to fashion and to the pull of events than does any other national type. A follow-my-leader tendency and a passion for the ideal has turned him into a kind of quick-change artist and that not only in caricature. He has enthusiastically modelled his face, his haircut and his clothes after the hero of the day. Some of these heroes were dubious enough but some were the sublime creations of great artists.

The Knight of Bamberg,[2] created about the year 1230, was often held—and by many still is held—to be the ideal German. His manner is regal, his gaze that of a free man, his features noble. A tender melancholy enhances an impression of perpetually youthful beauty. No German looks like this; but he would like to. His female counterpart is Uta von Naumburg, about twenty years younger (1250), the German woman at her Sunday best: the dignified mother, the gay and tender wife, slim of figure. She wears the crown and she knows it, she has an aura of the unapproachable. Generations of German women have longed to look like her. Since the latest major swing in taste dating from 1945 this type has been as little in demand as the other extreme, the generous, voluptuous woman, the 'Germania' of the 19th century.

Since the wars of religion, some people in Germany even claim to distinguish between a Protestant and a Catholic facial type. The knowledgeable maintain that they can easily detect the religious denomination of their vis-à-vis from watching his expression. This alleged ability is traceable to a well-known historical event. Due to the maxim—'cujus regio ejus religio'—established by the Peace of Augsburg in 1555, according to which the religion of the ruler deter-

---

[1] German national cartoon figure, equivalent to John Bull.—Trans.
[2] A famous equestrian figure in Bamberg Cathedral.—Trans.

mined that of his subjects, there emerged a Protestant ascendancy in the north and east and a Catholic preponderance in the south and west of Germany. This explains the tendency to ascribe catholicism to Germans with darker features, those with lighter complexions to the Protestant faith.

During the 18th century male bearing and costume throughout Europe produced a remarkable uniformity in appearance, from private soldier to grand seigneur. The faces seemed as interchangeable as the wigs. Mercenary armies provided racial mixing on a scale unknown since the barbarian invasions. Andreas Schlüter earned himself a place in history by creating in his statue of the Great Elector in Berlin a new ideal German male. In future, however, the rulers of the dynasty of Bradenburg-Prussia were to alternate almost regularly between the virile and the ascetic. That most 'Prussian' of kings of Prussia, Frederick II, preferred the language and wit of the French to the German mentality; his ancestors numbered 79 Germans and 97 Frenchmen. Those kings who really behaved as 'Prussians', Friedrich Wilhelm I and Friedrich Wilhelm III, were considerably less popular with their subjects. Only the last monarch of the house of Hohenzollern succeeded in attaining the status of a symbol of the German national character although, as we know, he failed to keep it up. Gone are those 'Kaiser Bill' moustaches from the German face; gone too from the German scene are most of his pithy views on art and morals.

Whilst the kings of France left their stamp on the culture of their times, the two highly dissimilar German rulers of the twentieth century both made the mistake of wanting to mould the people in their own image. Hitler carried on the Kaiser's concern for the German race in his own peculiar way. It was a matter of producing an ideal race as Tacitus had once described it: "Since they [the Germanic tribes] have not sullied their blood by marriage with strangers . . . thus they all, despite their great numbers, have a similar appearance: blue eyes of defiant gaze, reddish-blond hair and tall in stature." The Romans themselves were the first to destroy this image of German racial uniformity, although in the wishful thoughts of many Germans it remains undestroyed to this day.

On this basis, as though granting a favour, Hitler and his racial experts attempted at last to bestow a standard national face on the Germans of the Third Reich. His conception of it is to be found in

Mein Kampf: "No, there is but one sacred human right and this right is at once a sacred obligation, namely to ensure that the blood remains pure in order that by preserving the best of humanity the species shall be enabled to attain a nobler stage of development. A racially pure state will therefore have as its first task the raising of marriage above its present state of being a permanent source of racial defilement and to consecrate it as an institution whose vocation it is to create likenesses of the Lord and not monstrosities that are half-man, half-ape." Hans F. Günther's book *Rassenfibel* had paved the way for Hitler's theories. It divided the Germans into five races, illustrating the various distinguishing characteristics. The nordic race stood at the top of the scale of valuation, the eastern Baltic race at the bottom. According to Hellpach, Günther's teaching made more converts to National Socialism than all the inflammatory speeches of Party officials.

As early as 1885 Nietzsche, in *Beyond Good and Evil*, was deriding attempts to ascertain the ideal Germanic type by cranial and body measurement. The Germans to him were "a people made up of a gigantic mixture and interpenetration of races". Nevertheless fifty years later the great undertaking was begun. Pedagogues averred that from earliest schooldays the tall, blond, pale-eyed pupils were more advanced than those who were short, dark-haired and brown-eyed. Racial boards saw to it that important jobs were reserved for nordic-type men. The darker variety of German would have to be content with more modest posts—although the very man who had placed himself at the head of the so-called nordic race was himself one of the swarthiest of breeds. Today the purely biological experiments in breeding carried out by the racial fanatics is no more than material for the more dubious sorts of magazine fiction. The moulding of a National Socialist breed through propaganda and education had a markedly greater success. For this experiment the darker type proved to be just as suitable as the blonde.

Today the Germans are once again ready to profess their racial diversity. The intermixture of racial types, accentuated since 1945 by the great westward influx of refugees from the east and by population movements to and from country and city, is the primary impression gained on any trip through Germany. Where a 'pure' breed has been maintained, such as in Frisia and Upper Bavaria, it has become a tourist attraction. In north-west Germany the tall, blue-eyed and fair-haired type is still more common than in the south-west and the average height still becomes noticeably lower the further south one goes. On the left bank of the Rhine the Roman heritage is very noticeable in the preponderance of dark eyes. In alpine districts blue eyes appear again, particularly in women. Traces of Slav origin show themselves in the prominent cheekbones of people from east of the Elbe, yet the differences are receding with every decade. It seems therefore that the 'blurred' German face, which the French claimed to find as they gazed over the Rhine even fifty years ago, will become even more featureless.

Social origin marks people no less than racial origin and makes national typology in the northern hemisphere more difficult. Irrespective of frontiers, workmen bear their ineradicable external characteristics, just as do soldiers or sedentary workers. Particularly with young people the tremendous international levelling process has erased many national differences. Teachers amuse themselves by laying bets with colleagues as to whether they can distinguish the Germans from the French and the British in photographs of student-exchange groups. Whoever is bold enough to try can easily lose a bet in this way.

Not until the forty-plus age-group do national peculiarities begin to emerge more noticeably. In Germans, for example, bone structure begins to display a certain heaviness, the features tend to fullness and movement becomes slower. A foreigner first recognises a German by his gait. The difference between the Latin and the Germanic gait is obvious when German and Italian soldiers file past in succession. The former march, the latter—to German eyes—mince. A Frenchman, sitting at a café on the Champs Elysées and watching a German sauntering by has an immediate impression of something ponderous, slow. The German pace is heavy. The movement of the limbs occurs, by French standards, in slow motion. Friedrich Sieburg noticed, after years spent in France, that wherever one of his compatriots appeared a disturbance was set up. To the lively Frenchman the very sight of a sedate German makes him think of the East; Siberia, he feels, begins at the Schlesischer Bahnhof in Berlin, as the former French ambassador to Germany François-Poncet once put it. A German on the other hand imagines the Russians as being even more heavy-footed, regardless of the fact that they are the most agile dancers in the world.

The graceless German mode of locomotion annoyed Nietzsche too: "They have no feet, only legs," he mocked in *Ecce Homo*. The poorest Venetian gondolier had more elegance in his movements than a *Geheimrat* from Berlin, he claimed—an assertion which at that time not even the Berliners would dispute, as any connection between elegance and culture was fortuitous, even in the late nineteenth century. No prejudiced foreigners but German men of genius themselves have extended this ponderousness of gait to the whole man: "It is the nature of the Germans that they act heavily and everything which they touch turns to lead," wrote Goethe. In *Doktor Faustus* Thomas Mann enumerates the characteristics which are ascribed to the Germans: "A certain squareness, rhythmic clumsiness, immobility, grossièreté"—attributes to be found even in such a great musician as Bach. How, then, can we take it amiss of the American authoress Katherine Anne Porter when in her novel *Ship of Fools* she gives this classic description of the German passengers: "They looked boorish and clumsy and ill-assorted beside the Spaniards. . . . Nothing but a common heaviness showed to which nation they belonged. The Spaniards on the ship amused themselves, to appreciative laughter, by imitating the stiff, clumsy manners of the Germans."

There does therefore seem to be a generally accepted means of recognising the Germans, demonstrated daily by the souvenir merchants of mediterranean holiday resorts when they unerringly address a German in the right language. They also, of course, speak to Scandinavians and Dutch in German and can probably detect no difference between these peoples except that the Germans are always in the majority—yet another example of the curious logic by which people judge foreigners. Thus the image of the German *en masse* emerges with some clarity: he is an inelegant, unattractive creature with a double chin and bull neck, fleshy or big-boned. His eyes are tiny, his mouth chiefly designed for enormous consumption of fodder and now as in the past the German is renowned for his beer-drinker's paunch, although his average beer intake (94.7 litres per head in 1960) lags well behind that of the Belgians and the Australians (128.7 litres and 101.3 litres per head respectively) and although John Bull, that stocky personification of England, is just as often shown with his "fair round belly".

In the Communist press the ponderousness of the cartoon German has been transformed with harshness and cynicism. The German is shown as notoriously warlike: even civilians wear steel helmets, even the citizen of the Federal Republic has two swastikas instead of eyes in his face. Monocle and duelling-scars are still the trademarks of German arrogance as they were in Tsarist times. By contrast the German woman is shown in both eastern and western press as a dim, innocent Gretchen with thick plaits and hair parted down the middle, diamonds on her sausage-like fingers: the very negation of charm.

A German has some difficulty in recognising himself in contemporary foreign caricature. The type-drawing seems off-target or at least inadequate. Again it is evident that the outward appearance of the Germans is far more varied than with most other nations. The ambivalence of contrasting, indeed mutually exclusive emotions and qualities is perhaps the keyword which most readily gives access to an understanding of their nature: "A German is a combination of murder and music", as someone said in a French film of the 'nouvelle vague', a genre which seems to have specialised in 'unmasking' the Germans. Biassed though this definition may be, it does contain an element of truth in its attempt to show the German as made up of contradictions, his actions preposterous, his behaviour 'impossible'.

The deeper the insight into the German character the harder it is to make valid statements about it. In 1923 Carl Jacob Burckhardt considered it to be an insoluble problem to explain to the Americans "the nature of the Germans; at once sentimental yet scientifically and technologically so gifted and so hard-working, this nature which so easily turns to scientific barbarism". Yet to assert that the German character is indefinable (the conclusion reached by Nietzsche) is no solution either. Before Nietzsche, Ernst Moritz Arndt had enumerated those adjectives which make the German character so elusive to define: they were ebbing, flowing, floating, yearning and changing. No foreigner, he considered, could grasp their character "because they could never find the terms to define it". And that, for him, was an end of the matter. For foreigners, such admissions of perplexity are evasions or worse—narcissistic play on their own 'interesting' complexity. One should therefore avoid the German fondness for abstraction and stick to tangible evidence.

Between 1950 and 1960 foreign visitors to Germany were amazed to find, in spite of the division of the country and the plight of the refugees, how rosy German faces had become again. The gaiety of the Germans in that period was felt by many to be inappropriate. After 1960 travellers' tales contained more and more mentions of the deep seriousness of expression which had come over the German face again. The harassed, miserable and uneasy German in the midst of prosperity has become a favourite subject of photography, with captions which emphasize his expression as one of restless avarice or deep-rooted self-doubting anxiety. "Germany, the land where hardly anybody laughs"—this summed up the outside observers' view of Germany even before the erection of the Berlin Wall.

Thus cheerfulness and gloom are equally prone to arouse resentment. On the 2nd February 1923 Rainer Maria Rilke declared that the Germans were unfortunate in not having found a look which corresponded to their particular misfortune: "In the moment of their defeat the Germans might have touched and shamed the whole world with a collective act of true change . . . then, or so for a moment I hoped, the blinkered and prejudiced German face might have assumed once more that lost expression of humility which is such a positive feature in Dürer's drawings." Humility—that is what is missing, even after the second German catastrophe of the century, in those who precipitated it. This apparently unchangeable German, with his evil, distorted face as though forever frozen in the trenches of the last war, still stares at us in foreign films, television shows and plays, the embodiment of human baseness, speaking in nothing but grunts. German actors are engaged to play the parts and for princely salaries they mime the 'unloved German' as the script demands.

Which of the German racial types does the foreigner see in his mind's eye when he talks of the 'average' German? Gabriel Monod, a Frenchman who fought in the Franco-Prussian war, in his book *Germans and French*, published in 1872, carefully distinguished between Prussians, Bavarians and Saxons. It is unimaginable that a German of the same period should have treated, say, Bretons, men of Lorraine and Provence as fundamentally different peoples. Monod regarded the Prussians as the real Germans. He found them crude, though not incapable of a spontaneous gesture of kindness. Unfortunately there were Prussian officers who had beaten women or their own subordinates. Jewellery and silver cutlery were best kept out of their sight. According to Monod the worst looters were the Bavarians and the Prussians from east of the Elbe, whilst Brandenburgers, Saxons, Hanoverians and Rhinelanders treated the French population more kindly.

The Bavarians were considered specially rapacious. Bavarian officers were often more humane than Prussian officers, although the goodwill that this produced was counteracted by the undisciplined behaviour of the rank and file. Monod awarded the highest marks to the Saxons: they frequently showed their natural kindness and were loudest in announcing their detestation of the war. Only the larder was in any danger from the Saxons.

Until 1914 the traveller in Germany was still aware of clearly demarcated types such as Rhinelanders, Saxons, Silesians or Swabians as he journeyed through the country, Baedeker in hand. He judged them with a correspondingly greater degree of differentiation than the summary view which foreigners took of Germany after Hitler's *Gleichschaltung*. The particular characteristics of the various German peoples and countries faded in the lurid glare of the Greater German Reich. The outside world saw, to misquote a famous saying of Wilhelm II, only Germans and no longer Prussians or Bavarians whenever they were incensed about Germany. When the Americans, British, French and Russians marched into their zones of occupation in the spring of 1945, their generalised anti-German feelings made at first no distinction between the various races of Germans. The Germans are all alike—so they had been told and so they maintained. The Bavarians for the Americans, the Rhinelanders for the French, the Westphalians and Lower Saxons for the British and the Saxons for the Russians all became 'the average German' and these peoples have imposed a particular bias on the public image of Germany as now held by these four nations. The millions of refugees saw to it that the image never became too uniform and at one and the same time emphasised, along with diversity, the fundamental similarity of Germans more markedly than ever before.

Tacitus, the indispensable primary witness to the German character, laid similar emphasis in the *Germania* on the unifying factors, after duly recording with an almost German thoroughness the peculiarities of the various German tribes. The Teutons lived in what was for him a land of gloomy forests, treacherous swamps and raging storms. Surely no one would voluntarily leave Italy to settle down in inhospitable Germania—an opinion as well-founded now as it was then. Opinion polls have shown that the thousands of workers who migrate northwards from the Mediterranean countries, impelled only by the most dire necessity, never achieve any rapport with the countryside and frequently none with the local inhabitants. The picture which Tacitus painted nineteen hundred years ago is as valid to this day for his fellow-Italians as it was at the turn of the century for the French, who generally acclimatise themselves more easily.

The image conjured up by the word 'Schwarzwald' (Black Forest), which is very hard for the French to pronounce, was for them the epitome of everything that was weird about Germany.

Tacitus found the Germans at once savage and good-natured. The women exceeded the men, if that were possible, in bravery. If the battle-line wavered they bared their breasts as a reminder of what their fate would be in Roman captivity: rape. No one, in Germania, he said, joked about vice and seduction. A high moral standard achieved more there than good laws did elsewhere. The Germans, however, had their faults: Tacitus did not bore his readers by describing only paragons of virtue. Those same eyes that would flash in a passage of arms, eyes whose steely blue ferocity alone was said to have put whole Roman companies to flight, could also turn blank. They were clearly happiest on the proverbial bearskin doing nothing. (But only for a while. Soon they would feel the need to set off again a-plundering.) "For an inactive life is hateful to the Germans . . . A remarkable contradiction thus lies in their character: they love idleness yet find the calm of peacetime unbearable."

Three hundred years after this scarcely qualified paean in praise of the Germans, the tribe of the Vandals began to earn them a bad reputation. They came from the Oder region. Under their dreaded lame king, Geiserich, the Vandals stormed Rome in June A.D. 455. Their fortnight's occupation of the city earned them the name of barbarians, even though they were Christians. There was no blood-bath and no wilful arson; according to Pope Leo I, Geiserich had forbidden his men to indulge in violence. But they plundered the city and carried off the greatest treasures of the palaces of Rome. The indignation of the Romans over the action of the Vandals is factually unjustified. Rome herself had given the world a sorry example in the sack of Corinth, to name only one instance. Whilst the plundering campaigns of her own armies were naturally represented by skilled Roman pens as glorious feats of arms, the Vandals had no complaisant historiographers to whitewash their deeds: it was literate Rome which formed world opinion. As early as this, guilt was a question of viewpoint and the skill of the publicist. Furthermore the Vandals, as Arian Christians who did not acknowledge the Pope, were considered heretics. Geiserich had already given the Catholic clergy rough treatment when he took Carthage. The Roman landed aristocracy hated the invaders because they had confiscated all estates and put their former owners to work on them as slaves. Clergy and aristocracy, the ruling classes in every monarchy, determined the historical view taken of the Germanic tribes right up to modern times.

In 1519 Pope Leo X called the Vandals and the Huns scourges of humanity. The expression vandalism seems to have been coined in 1799 by the Bishop of Blois, when he denounced the destructive violence of the Jacobins in a letter to the Convention. To this day it only needs a plaster bust overturned in a public park or a flower bed to be trampled anywhere from Mexico to Siberia for the Vandals to be invoked in evil comparison.

Wilhelm II clearly gloried in equating the barbarian hordes with the Germans and made sure that this would never be forgotten. In 1900 he spoke the fateful words: "As the Huns under their King [Etzel] made a name a thousand years ago that even now seems terrible in fable and story, so shall the name of Germany . . . be affirmed in such a fashion that none will ever again dare so much as to look askance at a German . . ." Only the first half of this arrogant wish was to be fulfilled: Huns and Germans became synonymous for their detractors.

Undoubtedly the Prussians, the people which created the Reich and produced monarchs like Wilhelm II, made a notable contribution to the general dislike now suffered by the Germans. Prussian drill, when the Soldier King, Friedrich Wilhelm I, used to chase his tall grenadiers over the sandy soil of Brandenburg, served to alienate the peoples of less rigidly disciplined lands. Life in that spartan country lacked the gaiety and douceur of milder climes. In the raw air of the Prussian capital was bred the tone of voice of the Prussian bureaucrat, which was not exactly remarkable for its kindliness. The Berlin bark all too easily drowned the cheerful Berlin humour. Konrad Adenauer, in a moment of exasperation over the Berliners' attitude, even imputed to them a dash of the heathen. It is a proof of the changeability of foreigners' views that the blockade and the Berlin wall have turned the Berliners into the outside world's favourite Germans. Berlin, incidentally, was the birthplace of that reactionary fanatic Michael Kohlhaas (executed in 1540 and subsequently immortalised by Kleist) who seems to confirm Bernard Shaw's pronouncement that the Germans, with their boundless obstinacy, have the gift of turning any good cause into a bad one.

For a long time foreigners have equated Prussia with the 'junkers'. Churchill and Stalin both counted the junkers among the principal culprits of the last war. During the Weimar Republic left-wing politicians were convinced that the junkers east of the Elbe were doing their utmost to bring down the republic and restore the Hohenzollern monarchy. It was of course no secret that the great landowners lacked enthusiasm for the Weimar state. Again in 1960, in William L. Shirer's anti-German best seller *The Rise and Fall of the Third Reich*, the junker appeared again as a "specifically Prussian product"—Shirer saw them as an arrogant master-race, uneducated and uncultured. He overlooked the fact that a large number of the members of the anti-Hitler resistance was drawn from Prussia and from that same Prussian landowning aristocracy.

The Prussian character is more complex than many foreign critics suppose. The words to the tune of the Potsdam carillon *"Üb immer Treu und Redlichkeit"* ("Be ever true, be ever upright") were more than a mere phrase. Theodor Fontane, himself half French, mourned the old Prussian virtues of thrift and reliability. To him the Prussian way of life was in no way notable for aggressiveness, servility or intellectual poverty. It was not until the reign of Wilhelm II that the Germans in general showed their inability to control the feelings aroused by power and greatness: they expressed themselves not only in national pride, as with the French, or in attitudes of superiority like the British, but in manic illusions, reckless material greed and shallow hedonism.

After the Prussians it is probably the Bavarians, allotted to the Americans under the occupation, who have most influenced the German image. Even foreigners have frequently taken advantage of the antipathy between Bavarians and Prussians and have played the one off against the other. The Bavarians have tended to come off best, particularly as they have sided with Prussia's enemies in several wars and—by no means to be underrated—because they are predominantly Catholic. Nevertheless the Bavarian soldier acquired a bad reputation in the war of 1870–71: the horrible story of French children spitted on Bavarian bayonets is one of the earliest products of modern atrocity propaganda. With the Bavarians changed to Saxons, the impaling of children in the Franco-Prussian war found its way into Heinrich Mann's novel *The Subject*. The Bavarian fondness for strong language, along with *Lederhosen*, hartshorn buttons and their markedly guttural pronunciation, all combine to support the impression of German coarseness. The strong aesthetic sense of the Bavarians which lies behind their rather boorish façade remains unperceived by the superficial observer. A noisy minority determines the verdict on them all, in itself inherently unfair since foreigners' experience of Bavarians is almost invariably restricted to the tourist resorts of Upper Bavaria.

It is the Bavarians who are blamed for the terrible '*furor teutonicus*', whereas it is held to be the Saxons, the unwilling occupants of the Soviet Zone, who are said to have contributed the much pleasanter trait of *Gemütlichkeit* to the German nature. The Saxon is characterised in a well-known saying as being unable to bear contradiction: he always agrees with you at once. The old Munich satirical magazine *Simplicissimus* used to show in its caricatures, besides the beer-soaked Bavarian, a skinny Saxon jingoist complete with bearskin and ancient Germanic horn urging on the Kaiser to an ever more expansionist policy. This particular brand of Saxon patriotism was probably no more than a form of protective compensation against the accusation of being provincial and too pacific. We know at any rate just how forcefully the last king of Saxony, Friedrich August III, expressed his compliance: when asked in November 1918 whether he was prepared to abdicate he replied, "You can wipe your own bottoms from now on." In Goethe's time the Saxons were considered gallant and Leipzig was called Little Paris. As late as the 1920's well brought-up young English girls were sent to Dresden to learn good German and good manners in one of the expensive finishing schools. At the same time Saxony was known as the citadel of Communism, which produced amongst others Walter Ulbricht. At the party congresses of the East German Socialist Unity Party, the Saxon dialect is a sort of 'official language'—although its *Gemütlichkeit* is gone.

During his visit to the Federal Republic in September 1962 General de Gaulle referred again and again to the particular links between France and the Rhineland. In common with the French the Rhinelanders have the art of making the best of life. The French consider the Rhinelanders to be half Frenchmen who would be best annexed to France—a suggestion which was mooted more than once after both world wars. Their separatist tendencies overcome, the Rhineland today can now be seen in the happy role of a bridge across which Germans and French can shake hands. The Rhineland has seldom been given to patriotic excess. The song "The Watch on the Rhine" was written by a Württemberger who lived in Switzerland. People who live on a frontier tend to favour compromise and are consequently somewhat suspect to their more extremist fellow-countrymen. During the Hitler regime the rhenish ex-servicemen's associations protested vigorously against the accusation that steadiness under fire had never been a marked characteristic of their regiments during the last war. Sceptics call them garrulous and unreliable, pointing to that dragon-slayer from the Rhineland, Siegfried, who was unable to keep the secret of Brunhilde's wedding night. With his cheerful bustle, and his loud addictions to wine, women and song, the Rhinelander has done much to create the Germans' reputation for noisiness.

This view, however, fails to take the Westphalians and Lower Saxons into account. In the words of Freiherr vom Stein[1] a Westphalian would rather answer you tomorrow than today, whilst the Rhinelander answers before the question is out of your mouth. Hermann Löns thought that one needed a chisel to prise open the Lower Saxon's lips, just as he was said to walk the whole length of a train to avoid contact with another human being.

This broad spectrum of regional characteristics which a German may possess—as much as any person belonging to a widely differentiated homeland—has seldom caused anyone, at least since 1945, to falter when pronouncing on the Germans or to take any care in distinguishing between their numerous types and characteristics. Whoever imagines in succession a cheerful, cheeky Berlin waitress, a Bavarian mountain innkeeper, a Saxon schoolteacher and a Friesian fisherman will hardly find it possible that anyone could pass fair judgement on 'the average German'. How easily superficial observation leads to misleading views and ineradicable prejudice is shown by the mutual assessment which the various German peoples, who are supposed to know each other well, have made of one another. The Rhineland chatterbox, the Westphalian blockhead, the clod of Lower Saxony, the brutal Bavarian, the Swabian mania for doing business at all costs and the '*Saupreiss*'[2] are typological commonplaces which we have carelessly used for years despite their manifest unfairness.

In his political testament Frederick the Great described the East Prussians, Pomeranians and Silesians with varying approbation. He defended the East Prussians against the accusation of cowardice, but called the Pomeranians undiplomatic. The Silesians were subjected to successive castigation as wasteful, title-struck, lazy and

---

[1] Prussian statesman 1757–1831.—Trans.
[2] 'Prussian swine' in Bavarian dialect.—Trans.

unsoldierly. When even a sovereign bandies about such questionable judgements, no one need wonder at the summary verdicts pronounced by foreigners. At all events the image of the unloved German is the product of excessive simplification.

It is also a simplification to regard the West German, the citizen of the Federal Republic, as the only 'legitimate' German. Foreigners from both West and East exhibit a remarkable unanimity in finding only the Germans from this side of the Iron Curtain unlovable. The other Germans tend to be simply counted as mindless ciphers and unfortunate citizens of a Communist satellite state by the opponents of that ideology and as honest adherents of the cause of peace by the partisans of the Marxist-Leninist line. It is a West German, not a Brandenburger, Saxon or Thuringian, that a foreigner calls to mind whenever his thoughts turn to modern Germany. The German Democratic Republic has exploited this one-sided attitude and since its inception has shifted the onus of responsibility for Germany's prestige and of reparation for the misdeeds of the Third Reich on to the West German state.

According to their Constitution, the Germans of the Soviet Zone are forbidden to take part in working towards a free Germany. The Federal Republic is therefore held to be acting on their behalf; it also represents the whole of Germany in the reparations made to Israel and the settlement of debts owed by the former German Reich. Practically all the reproaches aimed at the Germans are borne by the Federal Republic alone; the West has been inclined to exclude the other Germans from its strictures. They are after their fashion a source of concern to the West, but more as Communists than as Germans. Because they are poorer they can count on more indulgence than the affluent West Germans. Many a western politician has made it clear that the neutralised and subjugated Germans beyond the Elbe are preferable to the free citizens of the Federal Republic with their pretentious demands and their vigorous role as economic competitors.

Meanwhile the highly disparate rulers of the two German states continue obstinately to insist that it is they who represent the true Germany and accuse each other of perpetuating the National Socialist dictatorship by other means. For many West Germans their compatriots in the East live in outer darkness, an uncivilised world. A person coming from 'The Zone' is furtively examined to see whether his suit is clean and whether he has any manners. Conversely, particularly since the erection of the Berlin wall has greatly reduced the chances of escape, the anger of many East Germans has turned not only against the Communist authorities but also against the dwellers in the 'golden west', who are suspected of being only too glad that the burdensome flow of refugees should finally dry up. They feel abandoned and have developed a kind of solidarity of 'differentness' bred of defiance and pride. A certain degree of comprehension of this attitude has even emerged in the West: we look almost with shame towards the G.D.R., where people—even if only in secret—still think about and discuss essential moral issues. The people over there, it seems, have remained kinder and more humane. Even so there can hardly be a single West German who would change places with a fellow-German living under Ulbricht's regime.

Statistics have shown that at the moment the West Germans would not like to change places with anyone. A national poll organised in July 1962 by the Allensbach Institute of Public Opinion with the question: "Supposing you were offered the chance of becoming an American or a Swiss tomorrow, would you prefer to become an American/Swiss or would you rather remain a German?" showed that only 5 per cent of the adults questioned wanted to become Americans and only 12 per cent would have liked to be Swiss.

"Foreigners only dislike Germans because they do not know them." This lapidary phrase of Johann Georg von Zimmermann, who in the 1780s was one of the most famous physicians and most controversial philosophers in Germany, is not only typical of the carelessness with which people were accustomed to shrug off the verdicts of others but is also an excellent example of how often intelligent minds accept the most superficial conclusions whenever it comes to formulating, defending or censuring national character. Even in those days the solution of the problem of the Germans was not as simple as Zimmermann imagined. But he was no more wrong than those foreign authors who have nothing but contempt for the Germans.

Due to its position in the centre of the continent Germany has forever lain in the path of all travellers, of all merchants and soldiers who have wanted to move from one end of Europe to the other. No country in the world has been so travelled-over as Germany, none has suffered so much damage in time of war and yet been so favoured at other times. This ambivalent position of the Germans in the world has had less effect on other peoples' image of the German than might be imagined from reading the numerous descriptions of foreigners' travels in Germany. The relationship between peoples does not depend on how well they know each other; it is much more dependent on politics and the passage of events. Today they may be friends, tomorrow enemies. The alternation of war and peace between neighbouring states bears sad witness to the ease with which human emotions can be manipulated: *raison d'état* has always won whenever a citizen has had to decide between his national consciousness and his friendly feelings for another people. The rulers themselves have never hesitated to change their attitude as soon as the political situation called for a switch from hatred to fraternization or the reverse. In this respect the statesmen of our time tend to indulge in a kind of voluntary schizophrenia. Much as the Germans have reason to be grateful for the way the politicians of the post-war world have officially changed their minds about them, they are nonetheless unpleasantly aware that those same politicians will at once adopt a very different tone towards the Germans whenever they may deem it expedient.

The few kind words which have been said in literature about the Germans (such as Mme de Staël's *De l'Allemagne* (1810)) produce a slightly comical effect nowadays, and the Germans have been praised in ways that they often find painful: if even a dreamer hardly likes being labelled as one of a 'race of dreamers', far less will the soldier relish inclusion in a 'harmless people' or the convinced civilian in 'the most martial race on earth'. At least half the plus-marks which have been awarded to the Germans over the years have been rejected by the Germans themselves and they have obstinately striven to refute them. Lately they have even carried this to the point where the outside world can no longer with any truth call them the most industrious and hardworking people in Europe. It will of course take some time before this fact has been noised abroad: the average man's view of another country generally lags behind reality by anything from a decade to a generation. Cartoonists in particular tend to remain firmly out of date: because their drawings are so much more vivid than dry-as-dust editorials, many people abroad still have the impression that the Germans of today run around armed to the teeth and clad in resurrected or even freshly-made Nazi uniforms. For very many people the clock stopped in 1945; some of them are those responsible for stopping it and who never tire of pointing out that it is beyond repair, whilst others believe them because they cannot face having to change their views.

Many people form their conception of the Germans entirely by indirect means, through the so-called mass-media, or at best through serious books and the accounts of friends and relatives. There is nothing unnatural about this way of forming opinions, but its danger is that the opinions of those unable to gather their own experience of foreign countries is open to manipulation by the media which claim to present them with a picture of the world; propaganda is in fact capable of nullifying the most direct personal experience. For what the visiting eye-witness sees can be a mere chance impression which counts for nothing, and may well be no more than the exception which proves the rule. Thus the biassed catchword will defeat individual observation and organised 'enlightenment' wins against private knowledge every time. The voice of the press is louder than the voice of feeling, the jingo journalist more telling than the most inspired poet—but once the poet adopts the language of demagogy then his employer can count on double the success. The hymns of hate poured out by poets and novelists have always been the most repulsive feature of any campaign of national incitement.

In every country the majority of the literati have always been ready to shoulder arms on command. A writer's decision to serve the state and the prevailing regime is not in itself reprehensible. The trouble only begins after a purely political piece of writing has achieved its aim. It is not blown away by the blast of war as an anonymous leaflet or radio commentary might be: it remains in the corpus of that writer's work, disfigures the belles-lettres around it and even if it is expunged from the *oeuvre* some busybody will be sure to dig it up again sooner or later. The greater part of such tendentious writings that will be cited in this book are not meant as an attack on the authors but as a warning against the power of the written word which was forced out—or so we must assume—in some 'critical' hour and which later they would have preferred to have left unsaid. Thomas Mann, Ilya Ehrenburg and many other great figures of contemporary literature have to answer the accusation of having descended to the level of political incitement. It is possible to argue in support of the need to use tendentious colouring when describing other nations, but nothing can turn even the most expedient lie into truth.

The sentence of damnation which since 1945 the Germans have—almost too resignedly—accepted, is still in force, although when considering the last war it should be said that a struggle of such global dimensions is hardly likely to produce a valid image of national character, even in its most horrible manifestations. It only demonstrates that people—and not only the enemy—completely abandon their positive values and can so distort their own nature as to be incapable of even recognising themselves.

Whether an individual's image of a whole people can be a favourable one is also in the end a question of temperament, of the times, of the society from which one comes and of the society encountered in the foreign country. Before the Italian philosopher Giordano Bruno had yet made the acquaintance of his neighbours north of the Alps, he considered that "drink-sodden Germany is the home of vulgar ambition, pretention, downright arrogance, brutal repression, petty tyranny, servility below and oppression above". On leaving the University of Wittenberg in 1588 he said: "Wisdom has built her dwelling here in Germany. Divine, yea divine is the spirit of this people." Yet a stay in Germany was enough to cure many others of a hitherto favourable view of the country. How many intellectuals who made the pilgrimage from all over Europe to meet the Goethe whom they had worshipped from afar were disappointed by their chilly reception and returned home wounded by the rude manners of the Germans, who could yet write so sensitively. The more superficial the acquaintance the greater the generalisation in views. It is therefore unjust to draw conclusions about the people as a whole from the behaviour of tourists abroad. Nowadays, when travel is no longer the privilege of the well-to-do, they may well be a so-called representative sample of the population, but they do not behave abroad as they would at home. The soldier and the holiday-maker are hardly the best representatives of their country, even when they appear as liberators or bearing tempting quantities of foreign exchange. Both types frequently assume the right to behave spontaneously, i.e. recklessly. One should therefore not pay overmuch attention to complaints about these kinds of visitors abroad, as long as they are not causing demonstrable mischief.

In 1962 the former German Ambassador to London, von Herwarth, contrasted the stereotyped disapproval of German girls visiting cathedrals in their indecently short shorts with the successful experiment of sending 10,000 German *au pair* girls to Great Britain.

These 'ambassadresses' made a good impression on many English families and made them revise their previous views on Germany. This may seem an absurdly insignificant counterbalance to the previous grounds that the British had for their adverse view of the Germans, but in matters of international understanding even the smallest plus-mark must be given its due.

Another cause of delay in the rehabilitation of Germany is the fact that the admittedly monstrous crimes of the Nazi period are largely regarded as crimes of the political right wing and therefore, in accord with the mood of the times, there is small prospect of their being either forgiven or forgotten—in contradistinction to the general attitude towards communist misdeeds. For, as Ernst Jünger wrote in *The Occupation Years*, world politics have "for years had a leftward tendency, which for generations has influenced peoples' sympathies like a Gulf Stream". National Socialism is held to be pure barbarism, whereas Communism, even in bourgeois circles, still retains that messianic aura given to it by Karl Marx. No German accused of war crimes would ever arouse the sympathy shown for the Spanish communist leader Julian Grimau when General Franco carried out his delayed sentence of death for actual or alleged crimes during the Spanish Civil War. The leftward orientation of world opinion even goes so far as to embrace the curious theory of just and unjust wars, according to which Stalin's attack on Finland was an excusable act of self-defence against the aggressive intentions of Hitler, whereas every war in which 'right-wing' Germany took part is denounced as a war of pure aggression.

To obtain the fairest evaluation of what foreigners think about Germany, one must take the opinion-monger's own situation into account, which should include his geographical, social and political location as well as the factors of time and personal circumstance. This nation of unpleasant contradictions has itself given rise to a richly contradictory repertoire of firmly-held opinions. It has facilitated the making of snap judgments but has actually hindered the formation of sound views about itself. It is not only the errors and crimes of the Germans that have been responsible for other people's predominantly unfavourable attitudes but to a great extent also the permanent willingness to curry favour with others by loud exclamations of *mea culpa*. The German will gladly accuse himself— if by so doing he can create a climate of extenuating circumstances. Foreigners consequently find it easy to incriminate the German with his own statements; indeed much that is most passionate in German literature reads like nothing more than a bill of self-indictment. Well-meaning experts who have classified the Germans on Eichendorff's model as ineffectual *Taugenichts*[1] or as examples of *Simplicius Simplicissimus*[2] have in doing so tried to absolve them from the responsibility for a part of their deeds and grant them the benefit of the doubt as being 'unfit to plead'. There is, however, nothing in the least flattering about such an opinion.

German publishers are in turn no less zealous than the litterateurs in their enthusiasm for spreading the 'unvarnished truth' about their compatriots. There is not a book of the *I Hate Germany* type which—except during the Third Reich—did not find a conscientious or indeed a grateful publisher, regardless of whether the arguments used were sound or nonsensical. From Hölderlin's diagnosis, "Corrupt to the marrow, abusive in every degree of exaggeration and petty spite", to the epics of self-castigation produced by the younger generation of contemporary writers there stretches a Wailing Wall, along whose length an endless litany of Germanic self-hate is poured out with varying degrees of real and false emotion—which seems to be a specifically German disease, a fashionable disease imparting a delicious sort of pain that flourishes today as never before. It is worth mentioning here that the author, as soon as he announced that he was going to write a book about Germany's image in the rest of the world, was offered material from all sides by his own countrymen with touching eagerness—ninety per cent of it anti-German. Those who offered pro-German material made a point of emphasising that they "normally never had much good to say of the Germans".

"There must be a strange magic in this word 'German'," said Bismarck in the Prussian Diet in 1864. A century later this magic has lost nearly all its potency, even in Germany itself. The German of today is a Minotaur who sees himself as evil and unwanted and therefore rages at himself; the outside world, however, still believes firmly in the old legend that the Minotaur demands human sacrifice.

[1] *Taugenichts* – 'Ne'er-do-well.' The gay but feckless hero of the *Diary of a Ne'er-do-Well*, romantic novella by Joseph, Freiherr von Eichendorff (1788–1857).
[2] *Simplicius Simplicissimus* – naïve central character of 17th-century picaresque novel by Grimmelshausen (1622–1676).—Trans.

2

"THE GERMANS ARE . . . OR ARE THEY?"

In modern war not only does weapon triumph over weapon but words are deployed against words. A good slogan is half the battle. This viewpoint can be traced as far back as Alexander the Great. In 1870 Napoleon III despatched his troops to the Franco-Prussian War as 'Saviours of Civilisation'. They were beaten by the Prussians on the field of battle, but they won the propaganda war. The year of Sedan is the turning-point when, in the rest of the world, the popularity of the Germans changed to detestation and their 'simple honesty' into a dangerous threat.

At first the victorious Germans were applauded, even if without quite the fulsomeness of Carlyle's letter to *The Times* of 11th November 1870 in which he wrote: "That noble, patient, deep, pious, and solid Germany should be at length welded into a nation and become Queen of the Continent, instead of vapouring, vainglorious, gesticulating, quarrelsome, restless, and over-sensitive France, seems to me the hopefullest public fact that has occurred in my time."

But this benevolent view of the victors faded rapidly. After the expulsion of Napoleon III the French Republic took the first place in the sympathies of the United States, which until then had been reserved for an ill-defined image of Germany, a country that did nobody any harm. By 1875 it was already customary to call the German Reich a repressive police state and France the land of intellectual liberty, a comparison which Nietzsche appropriated in his essay *The Twilight of the Idols*. Gradually all Europe joined in the anti-German campaign so effectively opened by France—the same land from which a few decades previously the most glowing image of German virtue had been disseminated, the image of the German as a model of good behaviour. Madame de Staël had described this paragon with touching affection in her extensive book on Germany without evoking any noticeable contradiction from her fellow-countrymen. A generation later some of the greatest Frenchmen, such as Jules Michelet and Victor Hugo, were to endorse her opinion.

After 1871 those seeking to represent the Germans as depraved were obliged to deny the traditionally favourable view of them, which had held good for centuries, or else to try to undermine it with contrary evidence, which can always be produced when needed. Another way was to contrast the newly-founded German Reich with the classical Germany of poets and thinkers and to shake one's head with disappointment at the way in which a nation can change for the worse within eighty years.

Since a historically documented admission of guilt has become one of the forms of reparation which, together with money, machinery and coal is exacted from a defeated opponent, history has become as much a subject of skilled manipulation as has so-called public opinion. In this way heroes became villains overnight—and vice-versa. Dates are deleted from the records, other dates are produced. Documents are given a different interpretation, old frontiers called in question and still older ones declared valid; everything that a nation has valued is reduced to nullity. The bad conscience and sense of penitence of the vanquished are supposed to become a permanent condition, since if they recognise their miserable state as being a just punishment they will be more obedient to the directives of the occupying power.

That such a procedure is not without justification in certain cases is proved by the situation of Germany after the defeat of 1945. The view of history which had held for twelve years had been manifestly shorn of its validity on that 8th May 1945: that it was based on falsification there can be no doubt. The Nazi historians had interpreted Germany's past exclusively from their own standpoint; Hitler, for instance, had had postcards printed showing him ranged in the company of Frederick the Great, Bismarck and Hindenburg.

It is an irony of fate that this sham continuity was appropriated by the victorious Allies and given out as historical truth—preceded, as it were, by a minus sign. For them too Hitler was the culmination of a thousand years of history, but a contemptible history. It seemed to be in the interests of the new masters of Germany to utilise such disparate phenomena as a prehistoric cadaver preserved in the moorland soil of North Germany, an aphorism of Walther von der Vogelweide, a fragment of Luther's table talk, one of Bismarck's speeches in the Reichstag and a marginal note of Kaiser Wilhelm II's to prove the generally disgraceful character of the German people which would inevitably have one day produced a monster such as Hitler.

The principle was not new. In 1870 French historians and publicists had already set to work ransacking the history books for evidence of the personal and political weaknesses of the Germans: they were to be convicted by their own past. After a great deal of touching-up they were presented with an image of their own historical development compounded of aggression, cruelty and stupidity. This form of proof, however, was incomplete as long as it failed to separate the Germans from those great figures who had given their stamp to the great classical period of German culture. There was indeed no lack of attempts to prove that Bach, Goethe, Kant and Beethoven were citizens of the world who had been fortuitously assigned to Germany. French scholars liked to maintain that Goethe belonged to the whole world and the chance that he was born in German Frankfurt was one of the quirks of history. The fact is that for all his uniqueness, all the typical faults and virtues of the Germans were to be found united in Goethe. In his years of despair over Germany Thomas Mann, who well knew what nonsense it was to separate Goethe and the Germans, was prone to equate classical Germany with German history as a whole, which was for Mann nothing less than diabolical. In his *Doktor Faustus* Goethe appears as in some sense a forerunner of Hitler. Most critics of the Germans are of course aware that the formula according to which the Germans are by nature worse than other nations can be refuted, or at least shown as highly questionable, by the eighty-year period of German classicism.

Goethe and his Weimar circle allay the reproach that throughout the 19th century the German mind developed a tendency to peevish intellectual self-sufficiency. Goethe was the very opposite of a German cultural nationalist; mankind meant more to him than the nation and his humanism and universality, which took precedence over all forms of national limitation, was his most sincere canon of belief. His deference towards non-Germans was at times carried to the point of embarrassment. He always spoke of Napoleon as "my emperor" and he rarely went out of doors without wearing his Legion of Honour. He demonstrated an admirable indifference to the ebb and flow of political fortune when after Napoleon's defeat he received a victorious Austrian field-marshal in his house at Weimar still wearing the cross of the Legion of Honour.

The breadth of Goethe's interests is shown most vividly in his sympathies for two parts of the world with which his contact was of necessity purely intellectual—China and America. On 31st January 1827 Eckermann observed his friend reading a Chinese novel. There had been a flourishing Chinese literature, Goethe had remarked, when our ancestors were still living in the woods. From Weimar Goethe followed the development of the United States with great interest. He informed himself minutely of their geographical situation and made his Wilhelm Meister, together with other worthy and far-seeing Germans, emigrate to the new continent. Anger at the false romanticisation of past glory and petty academic squabbles induced him to make the much-quoted remark: "Things are ordered better in America." For him North America was synonymous with progress and he always preferred it to what he felt to be the gloom of mediaeval Germany, the favourite subject of the German romantics. Five years before his death Goethe was discussing with Eckermann the desirability of cutting a canal through the Isthmus of Panama.

The image of the ideal German was formed by the visitors to Weimar. Madame de Staël began her journey through Germany in October 1803. At first she was disappointed. Conditions seemed to her oppressive and provincial. Her heart was not touched until one day she heard glorious music being played in one of the smoke-blackened taverns. Thus arose the first, stubbornly persistent cliché about the Germans—the split image with music, philosophy, profundity of thought, Goethe and Bach on one side and on the other coarseness, stuffiness, frowsiness and the reek of beer.

Externally the Frenchwoman from Geneva found the Germans crude and boorish. "Stoves, beer and tobacco smoke create around the common people in Germany a hot, heavy atmosphere which they are loth to quit." She was struck by the contrast between the elevated level of the intellectuals and the crude manners of the common people. The stiffness of German society increased her nostalgia for Paris.

But then Germaine de Staël was seized by the "poetry of the German soul". She wished that a share of German enthusiasm could have been found among the Frenchmen of her time, who were, she thought, too superficial, too cold and unromantic. She described the thrill at meeting the groups of poets and writers at Weimar; she found no signs either of German cruelty or of repressive militarism.

Her praise embraced German women, unable though they were to compete with French elegance. Their complexion was delightful, their blonde hair admirable and their voices thrilled with delight. She was specially loud in praise of the fact that in Germany love was considered more important than marriage—the reason for the sensible and permissive attitude towards divorce. Goethe attested that Mme de Staël had "breached the Chinese wall of antiquated prejudices which divided us from France". Goethe often seemed to the French-woman to be too stiff; she did not like him "until he had drunk a bottle of champagne".

When Goethe read her book *De l'Allemagne*, in which he himself was portrayed as the outstanding intellectual figure of Germany and amongst the greatest in the world, he considered that this charming lady was publishing such an exaggerated picture of German upright-ness that one could only advise one's foreign friends, in case they were deceived, not to leave their baggage unattended when in Ger-many. Otherwise this intelligent woman's views on German honesty were accepted without a qualm in the literary world of the time. Only Napoleon had cause to be infuriated by the book. He was not once mentioned in it and therefore branded it as "un-French" and even called its authoress "a whore—and an ugly one, too". His Minister of Police thought that the French had no need to model themselves on other nations and banned the book; Mme de Staël had indeed planned it as a piece of revenge for a humiliating rebuff which she had received at the Emperor's hands: she had offered herself to him as his mistress and had been refused. Later Heinrich Heine wrote in his *Thoughts and Musings*: "As to her relations with Napoleon—she wanted to render unto Caesar that which was Caesar's; when he did not wish it, she declared war on him and rendered it twofold unto God."

Thus the Germans profited from the fact that Germaine de Staël wished to punish Napoleon for his wounding behaviour towards her by a challenging book in praise of the Germans. But their reputa-tion gained equally from appearing to be so completely harmless and self-absorbed; the drawbacks for the Germans themselves of their division into dozens of small states were a source of comfort to other countries. People envied the Germans without wanting to change places with them.

In every family there is always one member who without being able to point to any concrete success is frequently being held up to the others as a good example. This was approximately the role which the Germans played in the family of nations at the time. Typically, Balzac made all the decent characters in his *Comédie Humaine* Germans. What splendid people they are, the French reader would say; but never forgetting to add—the poor fellows!

Weak nations generally find that the world judges them more kindly than those that are strong and powerful. A swing in the friendly attitude towards the Germans was bound to occur as soon as they began to disturb their neighbours by competition and pretentions to power and to elbow their way towards "a place in the sun", as a slogan of the time put it. The tasselled nightcap of 'Michel' the German changed into a spiked helmet and the world observed with resentment that he was now demanding to have his say everywhere without being asked.

The nation which, united almost overnight, began to cut across the interests of others, could no longer expect to be looked upon with the benevolent eye of a Germaine de Staël. As the land of poets and thinkers set about entering into world trade, building a fleet and forging weapons, its stock in the market of world sympathy dropped like shares in a stock-exchange collapse. People began to discover the dangerous characteristics of the German paragon. He could not retain universal approval for long when once he reached, not for the lyre or the pen, but for the sword or the bulging notecase.

After the proclamation of the Kaiser in 1871, German industriousness became sweated labour in the view of the outside world, loyalty became militarism, love of good food and drink became gluttony and drunkenness and the poets and thinkers became ridiculous intellectual snobs. The vices and weakness which were attributed to the Germans from this date onwards can be listed under six headings:

1. The German is rude, boorish and cruel.
2. He is a blinkered nationalist.
3. Politically and economically he is by inclination insatiable.
4. He is a militarist and a trouble-maker.
5. The German mentality is too servile ever to make a reliable democrat.
6. The German has a mania for work. He has no idea how to enjoy life.

One is prompted to ask whether there is any good to be said for the Germans. If we are to be fair a table should also be drawn up of the positive characteristics which are attributed to the Germans. This has also frequently been done both at home and abroad and the virtues described with as much exaggeration as the vices. In *The German Character*, Willy Hellpach assembled what in his view were the good points of the German national character, also listed under six headings:

1. Creative energy.
2. Thoroughness.
3. Orderliness.
4. Sincerity.
5. Firmness.
6. Loyalty.

It remains open to question in which of the two sets of six points the Germans prefer to see themselves—those listed by the prosecution or the six (in part distinctly questionable) virtues given by Hellpach. For Nietzsche Hellpach's six characteristics correspond more or less exactly with what he called the insipidity and lack of positive definition of the German nature.

Finally it should be pointed out that the Germans' own opinion about the English, the French, the Americans, Russians and other nations with which the course of history has brought them into close contact is no more accurate or unprejudiced than the foreigners' view of them. The standard German attitude to the Italians, for example, is that they may be quite good at *amore* and can sing nicely but are politically unreliable. The French are thought of as poor soldiers, somewhat untidy or careless. The British are as proud of their insular situation as if they had created their islands themselves and they only count themselves as part of Europe when they see some advantage from it: as individuals they are well dressed but boring. . . . It is pointless to enumerate any more of these clichés with their stereotypes—Fritz, Kraut, Piefke[1] and Boche, Ivan, Poilu, the Tommies, the Yanks, the Wops, John Bull, Marianne and Uncle Sam—antiquated figures of historical typology, created for simpletons and meaningless at any level other than generalisation. One's objections to them can always be halfway sustained; still they stand as an unalterable symbol for the whole nation, yet on closer scrutiny

[1] Piefke=Austrian derogatory slang for a German.—Trans.

they are as meaningless as the equally much-abused national heraldic animals—the eagle, the lion, the bear.

It has been shown that most of the reproaches levelled at the German people have not been without justification, but that alongside them there clearly exist errors, mistaken views and prejudiced opinions which can be easily refuted. Many characteristics have, in much of the population, long since reverted to their opposites. The widespread rejection of rearmament and the lack of national consciousness—now even regretted abroad—are signs that the sermons which have been preached at the Germans since 1945 have had far-reaching effects.

CRUDITY OR CRUELTY?
The German Boor

Friedrich Nietzsche, railing at his country from abroad, considered the German mentality in all its ponderousness and tedium to be a product of German breweries and German cooking—the stodgy soups, the meat boiled to shreds, the "puddings, heavy as paperweights". Add to these the "positively bestial" capacity for drink of the Germans and one could then understand "the source of the German mentality —their bloated intestines". One of the reservations which even Mme de Staël had about the Germans was their propensity to talk, smoke and drink beer.

When it became customary to search the history books for witnesses to the more dubious aspects of the German character, attention was drawn to the somewhat uncomplimentary passage in Tacitus' *Germania* where the Germanic tribes were said to "turn night into day" with protracted drinking bouts accompanied by games of dice. In the days when the Germans were in general favour, foreign scholars, in concert with their German colleagues, had demonstrated that the ancient Teutons were by no means to be regarded as idle tosspots. There was a simple explanation for their addiction to drink as described by Tacitus: in those days there were no inns; for festive occasions each family would therefore prepare their sweet-tasting drink, mead, brewed from twelve parts water, one part honey and various herbs. Mead, however, deteriorated quickly and had to be drunk as soon as it was made to prevent it from going to waste. German intemperance was thus explained away as German thriftiness.

Charlemagne was obliged to legislate in order to induce his subjects, of Germanic as well as of Latin race, to moderate their drinking. He forbade the dangerous custom of toasting. Since refusal to drink in reply to a pledge was a mortal insult, inconvenient people could be eliminated by alcohol poisoning. Even the church, which in many regions held a monopoly of brewing up to modern times, was repeatedly forced to threaten with hellfire all those who as beer-drinkers were at the same time their best customers. In the cities the guilds were responsible for upholding decent behaviour when drinking and they expelled members who drank immoderately.

It seems to be clear that the Germans have always been topers. Ulrich von Hutten reported from the Diet of Augsburg (1518) that he could always recognise foreigners because unlike the Germans they were not drunk every day. Two years later he wrote in his note-book after a visit to a tavern: "What quaffing, what belching, what spewing . . .!" Martin Luther also remarked on the general "spirit of guzzling and swilling". He feared that "this perpetual thirst will be the bane of Germany unto judgment day", writing in 1541. The Italian Girolamo Soranzo, ambassador at the court of the Emperor Rudolf II in Vienna, considered, at the same period, that the Germans lived such short lives because they aggravated their lust for drink by their overheated stoves.

Bismarck on the other hand felt that "the bane of Germany" was rather too great a tendency to abstinence and a lack of spirit. He recommended his compatriots to drink a quarter of a bottle of champagne every morning, the better to start off the day's work. The broad masses of the people did not acquire a taste for champagne and fine wines until the Franco-Prussian War of 1870-71. The German soldiers looting wine-cellars became a favourite theme of anti-German propaganda. The champagne cellars of Reims, it was said, were drunk dry by the victors as if by a "herd of thirsty pigs". This tone was maintained after the war; Father Didon, a witty French observer of the Bismarckian Reich, devoted pages of *Les Allemands* (1880) to describing the wild, beer-sodden, swaggering German students. Beer became a sort of tangible symbol of the German out-look: the huge beer-mugs, filled and re-filled in rapid succession, typified German lack of moderation in everything. Didon des-cribed an occasion when the band struck up a military march in a beer-hall: the students' eyes went moist and took on a sinister gleam.

Nietzsche had already pointed out the connection between German beer and muddled German thinking. The connection between alcohol and music was an even richer field for exploitation and has always been regarded by foreigners as central to the German character. Power-lust, intoxication, self-surrender and an urge to follow-my-leader, unpredictability and greed are easily combined by the effect of both beer and the roll of drums. Many visitors to Germany after 1871 dismissed the Germans under the general heading of little more than loud-mouthed drunkards and only worth treating as such; people recalled the slightly naïve advice of Tacitus that others should encourage the Germans' weakness for alcohol: "Such weaknesses of character might well destroy them sooner than war."

The Pied Piper of Hamelin with his seductive pipe-music; Frederick the Great—general and flute-player; Richard Wagner and his world of teutonic opera; Hitler and his Munich beer-cellars, his fanfares and his marches—they might all be said to have a connection with the effect on the Germans of music and alcohol. In Thomas Mann's *Doctor Faustus* German music is "of the devil" and is the very opposite of enlightenment, progress and democracy. The composer Leverkühn's pact with the devil in this novel is symbolic of the Germans' fatal subjection to the forces of darkness. Thomas Mann considered that the root of all Germany's ill-fortune lay in the figure of Faust-Leverkühn. The German, incapable of coming to terms with the world, takes refuge in the boundless realm of sound.

On the lower plane this mixture of music and alcohol produces a peculiarly German form of sentimentality, which is expressed in many maudlin folk songs, whilst at a higher level the German abandons himself, intoxicated by music, to "the manifold, the formless, the inexhaustible—to a certain German violence and exuberance of the soul." After hearing Wagner's *Meistersinger* Nietzsche considered this to be a typical German characteristic. In *Beyond Good and Evil* Nietzsche declared that his fellow-countrymen were "a people of yesterday and the day after tomorrow": they had no today. In *The Wagner Case* he added that it was highly significant that Wagner's rise to fame coincided with the rise of the German Reich.

German taverns have long been breeding-grounds of a German vice, which is connected with alcohol and a certain kind of music—boorishness. At any rate the critics of Germany have had little difficulty since 1871 in showing that calm, unobtrusive behaviour and good manners were not among the most marked traits of the Germans. After the great switch of opinion on Germany from positive to negative, many foreigners were no longer prepared to accept German noisiness with all its accompanying effects as a harmless element of the famous German *Gemütlichkeit*.

In July 1520 Erasmus described the conditions in a German inn. When the scholar politely asked the innkeeper for a wine that was slightly less sour and a more comfortable bed he was thrown out with curses. In the growing mass of post-1871 anti-German literature similar examples were cited endlessly. The French, who in 1870 considered themselves the victims of German aggression, represented the war as a contest between Teutonic coarseness and Latin refinement. Previous encounters with the German foe were recalled: it was then exactly fifty-five years since Jahn, the father of the *Turnverein* movement,[1] had, after the entry of the German troops into Paris, walked down the Champs Elysées—to the amusement of the passers-by—as a proud victor, clad in a flowing shirt of coarse linen, his hairy chest bared. Anti-German books now cited him as the prototype of the German boor.

Jahn's behaviour certainly goes a long way to explain many of the objections felt towards the representatives of a certain German tendency. With his parallel bars and his knees-bend on the heath outside Berlin, Jahn had hardened the muscles of Germany's youth for the final battle with Napoleon. Hating everything foreign, he preached an exaggerated form of teutonism which must have seemed comical not only to foreigners. Alcohol, at least, had no place in his theories: he preferred well-water. At the Congress of Vienna Jahn, as described by Varnhagen von Ense, went out of his way to befoul the parquet floors with dirt which he carefully brought in from the street on his boots, in order to demonstrate his contempt for the throng of well-bred diplomats. On such occasions he always wore his hair in long waves. Heinrich Heine called him an "ideological adolescent" and even Treitschke, normally enthusiastic over anything earthy and Germanic, considered him a "noisy barbarian".

Jahn in fact is the incarnation of that German leaning towards a conscious rejection of the 'refined' behaviour of other nations. This 'teutonism' was manifested, to the scorn of both German and foreign critics, in those lumpish monuments to 'Germania' with her

---

[1] Gymnastic clubs of patriotic intent, founded in 1811 to train Prussian youth to free their country from Napoleonic rule; later widespread throughout Germany.

armour-clad bosom, in drinking vessels copied from ancient Germanic mead-cups and in a kind of poetry, at once maudlin and defiant, in which coarse soldiers' slang and sentimental versification combined to produce a unique blend of jingoistic *kitsch*.

In his book on Germany Father Didon noted that the coarse German language, which lacked the range and nuances of French, was itself an obstacle to a civilised conversational tone and served to stress the general German tendency to coarseness. Goethe seems to have been of the same opinion when he wrote in *Faust*: "If you speak politely in German, you are lying". In *Wilhelm Meister*, however, the contradictory genius declared: "French is the language of society, well fitted to be the universal tongue so that all may lie and deceive one another as much as they wish." Here he was, of course, expressing naïve popular opinion rather than his own view. He liked to make fun of the passing anti-French phase with ironical mock-serious expressions which he put into the mouths of the philistine bourgeoisie. "A true German cannot abide a Frenchman, but he loves to drink their wines," says the drunkard Brander in the Auerbach's Cellar scene, after Mephistopheles has magically produced him a bottle of champagne. In another passage Faust is praised by Mephisto: "You talk almost like a Frenchman," meaning almost as cynically and shamelessly as a Frenchman. "To swear like a Frenchman" was, according to a song in *Des Knaben Wunderhorn*, a much-used phrase during the Napoleonic wars but the only expression of this kind which has been preserved to this day is "to speak plain German to someone". It is no compliment to the Germans that whilst this phrase ostensibly means "to tell the unvarnished truth", in reality it has generally come to mean to hector.

Many foreigners find it significant that the mood is always heightened in German theatres whenever Götz von Berlichingen delivers his shocking invitation[1] to the imperial envoy.

Even though it has been proved that this or a similar remark exists in fifty-five other languages this classical utterance is typically German since in its time it expressed the decisive switch from political subjection to open rebellion. As a cringing subject—whom we shall meet elsewhere—the German (and of course not only the German) was for centuries forbidden to express his opinions freely. The local princeling merely exorcised free speech with the rod. Götz' savage

---

[1] An obscene expletive which has made the name "Götz von Berlichingen" into a euphemism for the actual phrase, similar to "Cambronne" in French.—Trans.

retort to his imperial persecutor corresponded exactly to a German urge for catharsis. The need to compensate for an enforced servility by uncouth behaviour towards others is one of the most crucial German character traits. A person who has been bullied all his life gets his revenge whenever he can. A serf is forced by bondage to thump the table and shout at his equals in the tavern. A mal-treated soldier becomes a petty tyrant when he in turn is promoted. Custom decreed the posture of subjection towards the sovereign and the subordinate official imitated the ruler's most cherished privilege, that of bullying his subjects.

In *Beyond Good and Evil* Nietzsche expressed his anger at a "mannish woman", namely Mme de Staël, daring to solicit the sym-pathy of Europe for the Germans by picturing them as well-meaning and weak-willed boobies. Nietzsche considered that Napoleon, who, like the Genevese authoress thought of the Germans as simple-tons, came to his opinion of Goethe ("Voilà un homme!") simply because he was amazed to meet a real man instead of a simple fool. This is a rather bold interpretation of the emperor's remark; at any rate Napoleon continued to believe in the general ineffectiveness of the Germans even when resistance began to ferment in supposedly subject Germany, the country whose people to his mind were simply "not murderous enough" to follow the example of the Spaniards and to launch a bloody insurrection against the French army. On 2nd December 1811 Napoleon wrote to the anxious Marshal Davout: "Judge for yourself what you have to fear from such an honest, reasonable, calm, meek people that is so far from any form of out-break that during our campaigns in Germany not a single man of our troops was murdered." Later Ernst Moritz Arndt was to extend this judgment: if a German army in France had suffered a setback equivalent to the defeat of the Napoleonic army in the Russian winter, "not a mouse of a German" would ever have seen his native land again. In Arndt's opinion they would have been slaughtered to a man by the violent French.

The Wars of Liberation against Napoleon passed without the Germans, for all their noisy posturing, losing their reputation for being harmless. The 'Biedermeier' period[1] saw a full-scale return to German *Gemütlichkeit*. Its character has been exactly seized in the drawings of Caspar David Friedrich and Ludwig Richter. The

---

[1] An expression used roughly to denote the 1830s–1840s; stylistically comparable to early Victorian.—Trans.

German was frequently described as a compassionate soul. Chateaubriand, in his *Mémoires d'outre-tombe*, held that the French had inherited the cruelty of the Gauls, that it was only "latent under the silk of our stockings and our cravats" whereas the compassion of the Germans extended even to animals, so often ill-treated in Latin countries.

To put the horror of the Third Reich in proper perspective it is important to realise that although the Germans have for long, and often justifiably, been accused of being boorish and dull, they have not in previous centuries had the reputation of being cruel and inhumane as well. Indeed other nations have repeatedly made fun of the Germans for being so innocuous for all their noisiness.

The French historian Alexis de Tocqueville remarked sarcastically that revolutions never took place in Germany because the police would forbid them. Lenin is supposed to have said that a workers' uprising was impossible in Berlin because before seizing the railway stations the revolutionaries would be certain to queue up to buy their platform tickets. It is a demonstrable fact that the German revolutions of 1918 and 1933 were carried through with comparatively little bloodshed.

In other, particularly Latin, countries, such lack of enthusiasm for full-blooded revolution would be considered shameful. It was not exactly flattering to the Germans when Siegfried von Kardorff, a Reichstag deputy of the People's Party, laid the blame for the destruction of the Weimar Republic on the "bar-parlour politicians", who obscured and corrupted the average man's political judgment with their beery nonsense and mindless clichés such as "The November Criminals".[1]

For lack of really serious uprisings a disproportionate significance has been given to any sort of brawl caused by high-spirited youths or small pressure-groups. On the one hand the public immediately felt itself threatened, on the other hand they were delighted that the nation was at least showing some sign of life. The police, normally not an overworked body of men, generally showed a marked keenness to wade in, truncheons flying, to remind the population of the citizen's proverbial 'primary duty': to keep quiet. The unnecessary severity of the German police towards harmless rowdies has

---

[1] Right-wing catch-phrase denoting the Social Democratic German government which signed the Armistice and brought about the Kaiser's abdication in 1918.— Trans.

always been seized upon by foreigners as further evidence of the notoriously heavy German hand, a view which persists to this day.

Heinrich Heine in his treatise *Religion and Philosophy in Germany* pointed to some of the sinister depths in the German character. The German, he considered, was by nature sluggish; but one should not be deceived: brutal Teutonic aggressiveness had only been tamed by christianity. Should this check ever be removed "then the savagery of those ancient warriors will rear up again with the senseless urge to run berserk famed in song and saga". The venom of German hate, wrote Heine in another passage, "would fill the Great Vat of Heidelberg to the brim". Whilst this may be taken as prophetic of the horror which was to re-emerge in Hitler's Germany, it is equally significant that Heine had to go back to the pre-Christian era for evidence of a German tendency to barbarism.

After the last war allied occupation officials such as the Englishman Michael Balfour (*Four-Power Control in Germany*) came to the conclusion that many Germans turned into murderers under Hitler because of an urge to suppress their own weak nature and prove to others and themselves that they were made of the stuff that measured up to the 'great' epoch in which they lived. At the same time foreign psychologists found it particularly significant that from 1933 to 1945 German policy was often consciously directed against any form of tolerance or humanity. Harshness and manliness, it seemed, were not so much lauded in Nazi Germany because they were present in excess but because Hitler was always complaining of a lack of them. His derision at unmanly weakness was meant to force the time-servers to suppress their humanity. Even in the case of Eichmann there was evidence of the distortion and suppression, under the dictation of an evil and stronger will, of a character that was not basically inclined to cruelty. The terrible process of psychological compensation through the substitution of evil for good in their natures, which was accomplished in so many Germans after 1933, obviously needed as a prerequisite an all-pervading system of coercion which utilised to criminal ends the German tendency towards unquestioning obedience to superiors. When the orders from above and the concomitant need for compensation ceased at the end of the war, the Germans, not without considerable feelings of remorse, reverted to their true nature. Once again they became—as under Napoleon—"not murderous enough" to carry out the assassinations and acts of sabotage which the occupation forces, at first barricaded behind thickets of barbed wire, obviously expected.

Left to himself the average German, for all his occasional tendency to rage and shout, is not prone to deeds of bloody violence. He was not even capable of producing an underground partisan movement, as was finally shown by the miserable failure of the Werewolves— a movement which only wreaked its havoc in the imaginations of Goebbels and a few Allied generals. After the blood-lust of the war the new, or rather the old German docility clearly produced an impression of confusion and ambiguity in outside observers. Even after the First World War Churchill felt justified in saying of the Germans that in victory they would leap at your throat, in defeat they would lie whimpering at your feet.

Whoever examines post-1870 German history in the way that foreigners generally do will undeniably stigmatise the Germans as churlish, greedy and noisy. Cruelty, however, which many would like to adduce as a natural extension of boorishness and lack of manners, is not a specifically German characteristic. Even the monstrous crimes of the Third Reich were not the work of a naturally cruel *people*—of which more later. In this case the German has been guilty much more of thoughtlessness and indifference. Foreigners, however, have always felt this accusation to be too mild and they have used harsher words.

Carlo Levi, author of the famous novel *Christ Stopped at Eboli*, probably had a truer insight into the Germans than all the prophets of German barbarism. In his book *La Doppia Notte dei Tigli*, written after his stay in West Germany, there is the lapidary sentence: "The Germans go about with eyes obstinately closed". One might add that in doing so many Germans are not even dreaming but—to use a fashionable expression—they have simply 'switched off'.

". . . ÜBER ALLES IN DER WELT"
German Nationalism

After the German victory over the French in 1871 Dostoyevski wrote that never had anyone witnessed such an outburst of nationalistic bombast as in the new imperial Germany. (A few decades previously Heine had already remarked that there was something cramping about German patriotism: it made one's heart shrink like leather in the cold instead of being something warming and expansive.)

It is, of course, undeniable that nationalism in the sense of an exaggerated national consciousness has always existed in Germany. Nevertheless when foreigners began to accuse the newly unified Germany of being not only coarse but given to nationalistic delusions, many Germans were genuinely and not unjustifiably amazed. Though there obviously were certain cases of hidebound nationalism, the German has equally often, if not oftener, exhibited an extraordinary, at times positively treasonable, generosity of outlook.

Let it be remembered that at the very time when Bismarck was demanding a cessation of power politics in favour of politics of national interest and claiming to exercise only the latter—admittedly "in the consciousness of our strength"—every European great power had its nationalistic slogan. In England it was called 'splendid isolation', in France 'la grande nation'; yet the British were, after all, doing no more than point out a fact of geography and the French, like the Americans constantly reminding others of their devotion to the Rights of Man, could always point to the historic achievements of their forbears. The German exponents of great-power politics had no such facts to fall back on. In a speech to the Reichstag in 1888 Bismarck gave a somewhat strained reason for the superiority of the Reich, attributing it to German education. "And where no other nation in the world can copy us," he said, "is in the peculiarly high level of general education in Germany, a level to be found in no other country." This particular claim to hegemony might have sounded touching or even ridiculous to Germany's anxious neighbours had not Bismarck's theme in this speech been a demand for increased expenditure on armaments. Abroad, the identification of the standard of education with militarism was held against Bismarck. It very much seemed as though the Germans intended to spread their enthusiasm for education all over the world, if necessary by force, especially as they now—again in Bismarck's words—"feared God and nothing else in the world".

'God' and 'the world' are syllables which come readily to the Germans whenever they speak of their own interests. Calling on the greatest physical and metaphysical concepts known to man, far from inducing a sense of humility, was a means for the Germans of boosting their feeling of national superiority. Universal virtues such as loyalty, honesty and decency, even female beauty were given the label 'German' by poets and speech-makers, as though they were a German prerogative.

Hardly had Germany come into existence when its name was being given a mystic tinge. A 'secret' Germany, an 'inner' Germany were conjured up and finally declared by Hitler to be the promised 'Thousand-Year Reich'. Fichte was profoundly convinced of the necessity of an 'eternal' Germany for the continued existence of the world when in 1808 he exclaimed in his fourteenth *Speech to the German Nation*: "If the German people goes under then all mankind goes with it without hope of a revival." This was a form of nationalistic excess which was justified in that hour of rebellion against foreign domination and which only had any validity as long as those exceptional circumstances lasted. But because German politicians of a later age made enthusiastic use of Fichte's speeches, it is hardly surprising that suspicious foreigners cited them as proof of Germany's aggressive nationalism.

As a prolific coiner of nationalistic phrases the Prussian state historiographer Heinrich von Treitschke aroused considerable attention—and dislike, even among his fellow-countrymen. He elevated the Germans, whom he rigidly distinguished from the other "sub-germanic nations", to the rôle of "bearers of culture" and admonished them "wherever we are the masters never to yield an inch of German culture to alien forces". Earlier, Emmanuel Geibel, professor of poetry and aesthetics at Munich, had expressed the pious wish in a poem written as an epigraph to *Germany's Calling* (1861): "May the world yet feel the healing power of the German character." Abroad hardly any attention was paid to him, but from the foundation day of the German Reich onwards he drew nothing but unfavourable comment and was later regarded as the historical forerunner of all the aggressive Nazi songs, of which the terrible

"For today we have Germany,
Tomorrow the world. . . ."

was the loudest and the most feared. What no foreigner and hardly a single German realised was that the author of the poem had made no more than the modest claim that "Tomorrow the world will *hear* Germany."[1] The change to *belongs to* was made by the over-enthusiastic singers, who probably had no idea what they were supposed to be claiming; nevertheless it was a sound of ill-omen for foreign

[1] In German the difference between the words 'belong' and 'hear' is only one syllable. The original version read: "Denn heute *hört* uns Deutschland." = "Today Germany *hears* us"; and the altered version "Denn heute *gehört* uns D'land." = "Today Germany *belongs* to us" etc.—Trans.

ears. We have heard the last of this battle song. What has been kept, or rather restored to favour is the German national anthem, composed on 26th August 1841 on the then British island of Heligoland by Hoffmann von Fallersleben, a professor from Breslau. There can hardly be a foreign book written on the German problem since the foundation of the Reich which has not quoted, in the original language, the challenging chorus of this song—usually without the slightest attempt to examine the actual circumstances in which it was composed. From then onward *Deutschland, Deutschland über alles* was taken as an irrefutable proof of German aggressiveness and megalomania. In reality August Heinrich Hoffmann von Fallersleben lacked practically every normal attribute of a militant nationalist. Until 1840 he was chiefly known as an author of mildly agreeable devotional verse. In writing these resounding lines about the Germany of his day—a country made weak by division and disunity—the democratically-minded university professor was clearly doing nothing more than consoling his injured conscience. He would certainly never have published his song if anyone had prophesied to him that one day the entire non-German world would come to regard it as the very embodiment of German truculence. Hoffmann had no intention of setting the world on fire: he had trouble enough in opposing the muddle created by the mass of petty German states and the reactionary, pseudo-constitutional princely regimes which controlled them. For the politically offensive sentiments expressed in his *Unpolitical Essays* he was relieved of his office in 1842 without a pension and refused entry into several states of the German Union. Later he came to terms with the authorities and retired with full pension rights.

Anyone who sets about dissecting the French national anthem, *La Marseillaise*, written and composed by a captain of engineers Rouget de Lisle, with the same degree of prejudice, would find in this revolutionary marching song little but extremism and bloodthirsty aggressiveness. The Frenchmen of today who sing "Aux armes, citoyens!" take these words, in spite of all their internal political problems, no more literally than those Germans who hail their country "Over All" to Haydn's tune. In practically every national anthem in the world the mother-country is celebrated in similarly emphatic terms. Until the Franco-Prussian war the present German national anthem was practically unknown and even in 1914 it stood only third in popularity among patriotic songs to "Die Wacht am Rhein" ("The Watch on the Rhine") and "O Deutschland, hoch in Ehren" ("Oh Germany, high in honour"). Until 1918 the national anthem was "Heil Dir im Siegerkranz"[1] ("Hail to thee in Victor's wreath") which was originally written in 1790 by a Schleswig pastor Heinrich Harries for "the Danish subjects to sing on His Majesty's birthday". It was not until 1922 that President Friedrich Ebert, a Social Democrat, raised Hoffman's song to the dignity of the German national anthem; this was obviously not done out of any attempt, beaten as Germany was, to lay claim to great-power status but rather as some form of consolation for a nation suffering the consequences of a lost war.

After seven years' suspension the words and tune were re-instated as the national anthem by Federal President Theodor Heuss, although with the proviso that on official occasions only the third verse was to be sung. Henceforth the Germans were only to claim "Unity and Law and Freedom" instead of the wish to be "Over All". Even so the argument continued, in Germany and abroad, as to whether it had been right to instate this song as the national anthem. During the Third Reich it had been sung too often and always in conjunction with the "Horst Wessel Song" of the S.A. It was hard to forget this connection between the two songs. The chairman of the F.D.P., Dr. Erich Mende, having sung all three verses at a congress of student associations in Berlin on 6th January 1962, had to submit to being told by the Hamburg spokesman of the Liberal Student's League that to sing all the verses was an anti-democratic act.

Foreigners, as soon as they hear the anthem being played, still feel a breath of Germany's aggressive sense of mission. When Chancellor Adenauer said in Rome on 22nd January 1960 that he believed that God had given the German people the special task of being "the West's guardian against the powerful forces working against us from the East," foreign journalists reacted in angry exasperation to this barefaced piece of German messianism. The excitement caused by Adenauer's apparent resurrection of the 'Bulwark against bolshevism' theory was partly explicable by its earlier use by Hitler, even though it was an inescapable fact that postwar politics had in fact given the Federal German Republic the role of shield-bearer for several other western states. The sober realisation on the one hand that militarily speaking the West German army is essential to the defence of western Europe and on the other a lingering antipathy have created in the West that bitter-sweet

[1] Sung to the same tune as "God save the King."—Trans.

feeling which characterises relations between the Federal Republic and its Atlantic partners.

Whatever may be said of today's West Germans, they are not nationalists or patriots in the conventional sense. There was a time when the whole population of a German town would stream to join the solemn celebrations held to mark the victory over the French at Sedan. Today it is hardly possible to induce the public to appear in reasonable numbers at memorial services held for those who lost their lives in the East German uprising of 17th June 1953. The national misfortune of the Berlin situation has to be trumpeted aloud day in and day out simply to keep it from vanishing from the West Germans' memory. The parties complain of the lack of political interest in the younger generation which gleefully mocks every political miscalculation and is supposed to be only waiting for the revelation of some scandal involving party officials, ministers and generals to give a new impetus to its tendency to protest and to opt out of politics.

The "nationalist neurosis" mocked by Nietzsche, the fiery speeches on solemn occasions of the type of Wulicke (the headmaster in Thomas Mann's *Buddenbrooks*) are extinct. Friedrich Glum, professor of history at Munich, was well aware that he was preaching to deaf ears when he opened his book *The Rise and Fall of National Socialism* (1962), based on his distinguished series of lectures, with the words "A healthy sense of national identity is something natural. It was therefore felt to be perfectly normal at the time when National Socialism was on the rise. . . . Healthy nationalism is to be found all over the world. . . . But in Germany the word has many meanings, which include both the sound and normal sense of national identity and the dangerously exaggerated forms of nationalism." The difference is more apparent in the adjective than the noun: 'national' is not necessarily 'nationalistic'.

Ernst Moritz Arndt wished every German to be able to regard "All Germany" as their homeland, a viewpoint which is represented today not only by the various east German refugee associations; but the average German is not inclined to take risks on this score. If there can be said to be a 'national' urge of any kind, it is for a peacefully united Europe. A patriotic poet of our time, from whatever western nation he may come, is expected to call for "All Europe" as one homeland, giving no special preponderance to any one country and even leaping the geographical barrier to include the U.S.A. in the new 'nation'.

The contention that the Germans are often prone to an exaggerated cosmopolitanism and admiration of all things foreign is as old as the criticism of their blinkered nationalism. Even in Luther's time admiration of foreigners had turned into a tendency to ape them. No nation, he considered, so readily accepted foreign loan-words into their language: the Germans admired them as one might brightly-plumed birds in the desert. In 1600 an author by the name of Junghaus von Olnitz wrote: "Furthermore the Germans have the evil habit of imitating others like apes and fools. . . . If they can but babble a few words of another tongue they will flock to the company of Spaniards and French." Once in Italy a Johann becomes a Giovanni, in France a Jean, in England a John. As a foreigner the German finds himself more interesting. Bismarck complained that the tendency to enthuse over other countries' national aspirations at the expense of one's own was a form of political disease apparently limited to Germany. Indeed the Germans, themselves vainly searching for a form of libertarian constitution, did show great sympathy with the struggles for liberty of the Americans, Poles and Greeks (although no more than did Englishmen and Frenchmen). During the eighteenth and nineteenth centuries the Pan-Germanists and the jingoists carried on a permanent feud with the xenophiles and those who despised petty-bourgeois nationalism, without either side clearly gaining the upper hand. Klopstock's warning against "over-rating foreigners" and Lessing's attempts to curb the imitation of everything French in the theatre of his time by putting in its place a national German drama were deserving and well founded. As the Germans had yet to become a nation they should first have given careful thought to what it was that united them. The German character only began to suffer when the foundation of the Reich brought about the unification of all the minor States, and nationalism, deprived of its internal expression, began to leak into the outside world.

It is yet another manifestation of the Saul-Paul complex in the German character that both its xenophilia and its patriotism contain the seeds of a violent revulsion. The German's enthusiasm for others is easily roused but he likes to see his feelings reciprocated. If he feels himself rejected he will revert to an injured pride and hurl it back at the ungrateful foreigner. The years since 1945 have shown up the German's susceptibility to foreign influence, for good as for ill, in its most extreme form. Their defeat was so complete that only through dependence on foreigners could the Germans hope for any sort of revival. Undoubtedly it often contained an element of calculation, but it produced simultaneously a genuine enthusiasm for things foreign that lay in the best tradition of Goethe's and Herder's sympathetic absorption in other nations' ways of life and culture.

At the climax of the Wars of Liberation against Napoleon Goethe ostentatiously adopted a cosmopolitan stance in order to remind people of the great supra-national ties which ought to bind the nations together. According to his *Annals or Diaries* of 1813, during the Battle of the Nations at Leipzig he consciously devoted himself to the remotest subject of which he could conceive, namely a study of the Chinese Empire. Since his youthful *Götz von Berlichingen* he had long ago outlived the patriotic mood of 'Storm and Stress', which had now taken over the reins of politics. Not for a moment did intellectual Germany cease to look beyond the frontiers—and the bond with the spirit of France was never broken even in the turmoil of war.

A proof of the changing values placed on German nationalism and of its own changeability is given in this quotation, dating from 1873, from a Russian weekly magazine *Grazhdanin* ("The Citizen"): "We have long and often enough scoffed at German patriotism, but in reality we should envy them their love of country since it lends them the strength to make constant progress. Admittedly the intellectual life of Germany today often shows signs of savage teutonism which reveals not so much the nation's self-regard but rather a form of morbid amour-propre, but in all this there is a positive side. The Germans at the moment are happy . . . and at this one can only rejoice."

This was written by Dostoyevski, who has been subsequently accused of an almost pathological rejection of everything to do with the western world, a few years after he had expressed his revulsion at the nationalistic braggardism in which the Germans indulged at the time of the foundation of the Reich. Thousands read this article about the Germans with its generous plea for sympathy with the Germans in their hour of national euphoria. It sounded as if the neighbours in the west had suddenly changed. In reality only the author of the article had revised his opinion of them, although this period actually witnessed an improvement and consolidation (albeit temporary) of relations between Germany and the Russian Empire.

A PLACE IN THE SUN
German Expansionism

There is no mystery as to why a small, weak country should have more friends in the world than a large, strong country. It was reserved for the Germans to discover to their amazement that a nation can boast of its intellectual achievements without forfeiting the sympathy of others but arouses immediate irritation as soon as it makes a claim for a juster share of this world's goods. The Germans, accused as early as the first half of the nineteenth century of extravagant demands and more lately of being positively insatiable, found it particularly hard to reconcile this reproach with their own traditional sense of being under-favoured compared with other nations.

Even Goethe had this feeling. He told Luden at Jena in November 1813 that only his scientific studies offered him any consolation for the feeling of being deprived of the proud consciousness of belonging to a nation that was "great, strong, respected and feared". During World War II Thomas Mann found it worthy of note that Goethe (talking to Eckermann in 1829) touched a sore point when he remarked that the English with their practical commonsense were laughing the Germans to scorn and "winning the world" whilst the Germans plagued themselves with the solution of philosophical problems. Both before and after 1800 it was fashionable for Germans amongst themselves to scoff at their ineffectiveness and challenge each other to change their ways. In his hymn *To the Germans* Hölderlin compared his people to a child with delusion of grandeur—riding a rocking-horse and waving a whip: "full of great thoughts but unable to act". In similar mood Heine wrote in *Germany—a Fairy Tale*:

> *The French and the Russians are lords of the land,*
> *The sea belongs to the Britons*
> *Whilst we lay claim to rule*
> *The airy world of dreams.*

For most of the first half of the last century the Germans, in the eyes of both foreign and German observers, were regarded at least in politics as impractical and inexperienced; they sought in the clouds what lay at their feet, said Schopenhauer. But then came the change from dream to reality. Its advent was proclaimed with a monstrous flood of words. Hoffmann von Fallersleben's *Deutschland, Deutschland über Alles*, extracted from the context of his *Unpolitical Songs* and quoted by every patriotic speechmaker was at first a purely oratorical claim. Since in the cramped circumstances of mid-nineteenth-century Germany the good things of this world were still few and far between, a greater, happier and stronger Germany was to be summoned forth—at any rate in words and proclamations. Foreigners, however, took all this windy German rhetoric seriously and labelled it variously Pan-Germanism, imperialism or simply unfair competition.

At the Paris Universal Exhibition of 1867 the firm of Krupp aroused the greatest interest by exhibiting a gigantic block of cast steel. The French public looked on the steel monstrosity with mixed feelings. As an internationally-minded businessman Krupp was selling his weapons to all comers; yet there was the obvious danger that in case of war his firm would limit itself to supplying the German army. This colossal lump of steel had the effect of a milestone in the development of Germany along the road from the land of dreams to the real world.

The orators in St. Paul's Church[1] had come to realise that words without deeds were useless. No German Reich was going to be founded on programmes and declarations alone, however resounding; even before the victorious Franco-Prussian war many Germans showed signs of turning to concrete action. Victory over France seemed for many more the signal for an explosion of acquisitive energy: the surge of unbridled capitalism in the 1870s with hideous great banks shooting up like mushrooms, wild speculation in railways and gigantic factories showed that even as a business man the German was a compulsive fantast—although no longer a harmless and well-behaved one. German industrial life was characterised by a mixture of Prussian efficiency and American hustle: there was no more time left for the poets and thinkers and the businessman became the predominant German type.

If an excess of intellectual speculation had once been the Germans' besetting sin, there now grew up a positive antipathy to the abstract and the metaphysical. The country which had once gained the respect of the world through its intellectual achievements wanted henceforth to impress by its industriousness and the quality of its goods. Like the 'swot' among schoolboys, the hustler in economic

---

[1] The venue of the abortive All-German Parliament after the 1848 revolution.

life is seldom liked. The Germans made the mistake of believing that they could win goodwill and respect through zeal. Foreign industry felt itself challenged, whilst those who had admired the Germany of the romantic movement now showed their disappointment that the Germans, just as any other country, were suddenly interested in nothing but money and profits. A beautiful and reassuring image was shattered, but the Germans seemed little affected by the anxiety of their neighbours, who would have much preferred the Germans to continue philosophising and leave money-making to others.

Critical remarks from neighbouring states on the consequences of the German victory of 1871 made it quite clear how much foreigners would have preferred it if the Germans, instead of creating a unified Reich, had remained a congeries of small states. Indeed, the Germans only became aware of the scale of their achievement through the envy which they began to detect around them. To Ernest Renan's accusation that the new German Reich was a mindless concentration of power, the Germans contended that for the past century they had made enough contributions to the realm of the mind and that for a change they proposed to devote themselves to material benefits. It was only now that the harmless verses of a Geibel or a Hoffmann von Fallersleben began to acquire sinister undertones. *Deutschland über Alles*, loudly intoned on Sedan Day, was now something more than the modest call to unity which von Fallersleben had put into verse.

Thanks were given to God for having, as Wilhelm I put it in his victory telegram after Sedan, so visibly blessed German arms. God was, as it were, engraved on the shiny new nameplate of the German Reich as a sleeping partner. "Bend the knee before that Great Ally who has never yet forsaken the Germans!" demanded Wilhelm II in 1903, in one of the Kaiser's lesser-known pronouncements. The Reich, which saw itself as the Kaiser said on another occasion with "Enemies all around" lying in wait for it, had recourse to constant and loud self-affirmation, as though otherwise no one would have believed in its magnitude and glory—not even the Germans themselves.

A tendency to magniloquence was noticeable even in Bismarck. On 29th September 1864 he declared before the Budgetary Committee of the Prussian House of Deputies that Prussia should wait for the suitable moment to rectify her frontiers and should be prepared for a successful role as the unifier of Germany. Then followed the much-quoted passage: "The great questions of our time will not be decided by speeches and majority resolutions—that was the great mistake of 1848 and 1849—but by iron and blood."

Bismarck's "iron and blood" speech is often cited as proof of German ruthlessness. The fact is that practically every nation followed the same policy when they set about the work of unification—Italy and the U.S.A. were both united by blood and iron. 1871 only served to justify Bismarck's prediction. It is significant, however, that a brutal-seeming political truth, even though all the Powers have made use of it at one time or another is forever quoted in its *German* context.

In contrast to Frederick the Great's laconic tradition the Prussian state, as forerunner of the unified German state, was restored after Napoleon's victories with the aid of an agonised flood of verbose appeals to patriotism, a process described by Hellpach as "an exhausting delivery with forceps". It required an enormous outpouring of speeches, pamphlets and proclamations to provide Prussia, humiliated by Napoleon I, with a new national self-confidence. How differently did the Austrian character react under similar pressures! Austria recovered from the defeat of Königgrätz with gaiety and elegance, surviving the blow with the aid of its enviable capacity for muddling through. A "blood and iron" speech in Austria would have been scarcely conceivable. In Austria a spade is not always called a spade; they are not so blunt and are more skilled in the art of not treading on others' toes.

In 1917 Hugo von Hofmannsthal made the interesting experiment of juxtaposing the differing characteristics of the Prussians and the Austrians. Having defined both peoples' attitude to authority (in Prussia the crown was the supreme authority; in Austria the crown was the repository of supreme confidence), he came to the following conclusions about the opposing attitudes of the Prussian and the Austrian as individuals:

Prussian	*Austrian*
Lays down the law.	Prefers to be vague.
Self-righteous, pretentious, schoolmasterly.	Bashful, vain, witty.
Loves crises.	Avoids crises.
Business and professional interests predominate.	Private interests predominate.
Compulsive overstatement.	Extreme irony.

From the comparatively modest forms of Prussian self-assertion there then developed in imperial Germany, the 'German taste for the colossal', as the French called it. The Wilhelminian era loved its trappings on the grand scale. The ponderous cupola of the Berlin cathedral and the gargantuan slab of the Reichstag building, whose glass lantern had to be placed lower than originally planned since it would have ranked as lèse-majesté to have exceeded the height of the imperial palace, gave off a splendour which owed little to aesthetics. The 'glorious era' promised by the Kaiser was depicted ad nauseam in stone and mortar.

Foreigners only noticed the posturing, the clanking of spurs and the arrogant behaviour. But just as Bismarck, with his delicate digestion and his unexpectedly high-pitched voice, was not the colossus which his cuirassier's breastplate seemed to make him, so a great deal of weakness and insecurity was concealed behind the crude manners of the Kaiser's era. Big words were not infrequently used to boost the speaker's own lagging courage.

A generous dose of theatrical verbosity was also a characteristic of the Pan-German League, which in the years before World War I gave foreigners many a pretext to criticise and depreciate the Germans. In the summer of 1890 a nationalistic protest movement had arisen in Germany over the cession of Zanzibar in exchange for Heligoland, which until then had been British. (Incidentally, if the protest movement had been successful, Germany today would possess neither Zanzibar nor Heligoland!) Bismarck—after his dismissal—devoted an entire chapter of his memoirs to this exchange, which he considered a bad bargain. An after-effect of the Zanzibar protest movement was the foundation of the Pan-German League, and even this Wilhelm II felt to be too faint-hearted in its views. The League, which was not dissolved until 1939, never achieved a membership of more than twenty thousand. Its capacity for making a noise, however, was so considerable that to many a prejudiced foreigner it seemed to represent the voice of all Germany—and was constantly cited as such by hostile propaganda.

It was the League that gave a new meaning to Hoffmann's *Deutschland über Alles*, which the Pan-Germans hoped to turn from political dream into reality. They wanted to gather up all the Germans in the world and set up the Germanic bloc in competition with similar British groupings. In Europe the Pan-Germans envisaged a self-sufficient German economic union and abroad an extended German colonial empire—hence the indignation over Zanzibar. The proclamations of the League were so phrased as to be quotable by every anti-German as proof of Germany's greed and expansionism—usually oblivious of the fact that it was almost always an affair of words and not deeds.

"We are", wrote the Pan-German Fritz Bley in all modesty in his book *Germany's Position in the World* (1897), "undoubtedly the best warrior nation [Kriegsvolk] on earth, we are the most skilled in all branches of knowledge and the fine arts. We are the best settlers, the best seamen, even the best merchants. . . . It is in us that God, who has quickened man with his living breath, is thinking."

In another passage Bley defined the intellectual level of the Pan-German thus: "Higher education is the pigtail which must be shorn off at the scalp if the German is to grow his fresh, curly blond locks again." It was grotesque to represent "a bow-legged race of be-spectacled, feeble-minded pedants" as the German intellectual élite. Instead, it seems, raucous vocal exertion and seas of print were to be the means of creating a national greatness which more fortunate nations, not such latecomers on the scene, had long ago created without such tortuous exertions.

Wilhelm II brought to a fine art the aggravation of other countries by violent speeches. Whereas Bismarck generally calculated the effect of his words in advance, the Kaiser, once launched on a speech, gave way to his diffuse and ebullient emotions. The root of the trouble may have been traceable to a congenital physical defect: at the birth of Wilhelm II Field Marshal Wrangel had shouted to the rejoicing crowd that he was "a splendid new recruit". Two days later is was discovered that the "recruit" was already physically unfit due to a partially withered arm.

The arm, which was to be useless for the whole of this life, drove the Kaiser to make statements designed to conceal his congenital weakness and make him appear as a personality of boundless strength. He loved to be photographed, carefully concealing his shortened arm, in full dress uniform or in the costumes of his ancestor Frederick the Great and to perpetuate this image of himself in the recently invented newsreel film. As a joke of the day had it, the Kaiser put on his admiral's uniform to go to a performance of *The Flying Dutchman*.

Even his upturned moustaches seemed to be straining after effect. The court hairdresser took out a patent on it and sold hundreds of

thousands of his special moustache-nets under the brand name "*Es
ist erreicht!*" The eyes always a-glint, the shining sword, the sergeant-
major-like notes in the margins of state papers, the parade-ground
tone carried into the auditorium of the court theatre—all betrayed a
forced, unnatural style. A basically insignificant physical defect had
to be perpetually compensated for by a show of strength and
all Germany loyally joined in with the emperor's exercises in
compensation.

Bloodthirsty speeches rather than bloodthirsty action were
characteristic of Wilhelm II. Hot-blooded, as Bismarck so accurately
described him in his *Thoughts and Recollections*, he was constantly
guilty of tasteless turns of phrase: "You must shoot your mothers
and fathers if your Emperor commands you to!" or: "I shall smash
anyone who opposes me!" Most of his utterances ended with an
exclamation mark, emphasising the theatricality of his tone.

The acme of the Kaiser's rashness was reached in his "Huns"
speech of 27th July 1900, already quoted above. The German
Ambassador in Pekin had been murdered by the Boxers. Germany
contributed troops to an international punitive expedition. Seeing
off his troops to the front, the Kaiser shouted to them: "No quarter
will be given!" No prisoners were to be taken—an unheard-of
order in view of the Red Cross Convention, then already in force
for a quarter of a century.

The British historian Chamier, an admirer of Wilhelm II, wrote
later that the "Huns" speech had probably been misunderstood.
In saying "No quarter!" the Kaiser had merely meant that no pity
was to be expected from the savage Chinese foe and the German
soldier must therefore be prepared for merciless fighting. But it was
the very misfortune of the Kaiser's speeches that they could always
be interpreted ambiguously, allowing the Kaiser's enemies naturally
to choose the meaning most damaging for him and for Germany.

Having horrified the whole world with this speech, Wilhelm II
then received with great kindness the Chinese princes who were
sent on an expiatory mission to the European capitals to crave
pardon for the murder of the German ambassador. A caricature
in *Simplicissimus* showed the princes sticking out their tongues at
the assembled German notables and the caption made Reichs
Chancellor von Bülow say of this Chinese gesture that it meant
roughly "I humbly beg your pardon!"

Once again a wild gesture by the Kaiser had evaporated into

nothing. But whilst the world remembered the "Huns" speech, the friendly reception of the Chinese princes in Berlin was written off in three lines.

Posterity remembers the last German emperor above all for his lack of balance. He was the son of Princess Victoria of England.[1] As a German he wanted, like so many Germans, to be accepted on something like equal terms by the British. He imitated them by inaugurating and carrying out a world-wide German foreign policy. As a minister of state, von Bülow had shown the way in a Reichstag speech of 6th December 1897: The time, he thought, was past when the Germans conceded to one of their neighbours supremacy on land, to another command of the sea and reserved the heavens for themselves. The Germans wanted to have their say in East Asia: "In a word—we do not want to put anyone in the shade, but we too demand our place in the sun." A famous phrase was coined. The German urge for a place in the sun, however justified it might seem, aroused as much vexation among those who already had their places as a new arrival in an already full railway compartment.

But of course German foreign policy at the close of the nineteenth century was by no means made up exclusively of mischief and caprice. The population had increased by leaps and bounds: the population increase between 1890 and 1914 was 16 million, until finally the total population of the Reich reached nearly 70 million. Production rose at the same rate. In coal output Germany rapidly reached second place in the world, and in output of iron it even headed world production. In thirty years the German merchant marine increased in size three times. The value of foreign trade shot up from 7.6 milliard marks in 1890 to 22.5 milliard marks in 1913. The leading industrial nation of continental Europe achieved greatpower status almost automatically. Morally it did not sound very convincing when other states, who had used the same methods in their own ascent to world power, began to be outraged at Germany's vigorous expansion. Most lamentable of all, however, was the lack of skill shown by the German leadership of the day. A lasting place in the sun could only have been gained and kept with the aid of the right allies. The best places were already taken: no one was likely voluntarily to cede so much as standing room. But it was then that German clumsiness in the choice of allies began to be apparent: the

[1] Eldest child (1840–1901) of Queen Victoria.—Trans.

latecomer should have realised that alone or in weak company he would always be vulnerable. The right course would have been to proceed with discretion; instead of this the Wilhelminian establishment behaved tactlessly and carelessly, for reasons less of ill-will than of stupidity. Instead of proceeding with tact, the nouveau-riche felt obliged to demonstrate his achievements to everyone. The Germans demanded a say in everything. The others, who finally banded together to isolate and crush the noisy competitor, were certainly no better than the Germans. It was simply the 'accursed lot and duty' of the German government to adjust the expansion of the Reich to the existing European balance of power. The policy which Hitler was finally to bring to such a depressing climax, namely to be at odds with almost the whole of the rest of the world, was already being launched under Wilhelm II.

The rivalry with Great Britain ended in a catastrophe for Germany. The question of guilt is less interesting than the ever-recurring German inability to gain another country as its constant ally. The long series of offences which the two cousins, Wilhelm II and Edward VII caused each other and each other's people began on 3rd January 1896 with the Kaiser's telegram to Kruger, President of the Transvaal. The Kaiser had hesitated before sending the unnecessary telegram. His advisers out-voted him and in consequence the British were infuriated to read the Kaiser's congratulations to the Boers who had succeeded entirely on their own resources in throwing out the English marauders.[1]

Overnight the Kaiser became one of the most detested figures in Britain, the Germans' scorn having been added to the humiliation of defeat by the Boers. National pride was wounded. The telegram was all the more pointless because it was unable to alter the Boers' fate: no military aid was forthcoming from Germany. When the Union of South Africa was finally created between Boers and Britons, any grateful memories of the telegraphic encouragement from Berlin were no doubt effaced. Typically, German effrontery had once again expressed itself in mere words.

The maritime rivalry with the British (with Wilhelm II crying: "Neptune's trident belongs to us!") arose from the same urge to be finally recognised as a Great Power by Britain. "A world-wide foreign policy is the need of the hour," cried the Kaiser at the launching of the *Wittelsbach* on 4th July 1900. The ocean was to

[1] This refers to the Jameson Raid.—Trans.

play an essential part in Germany's greatness. Then came the interview with the *Daily Telegraph* on 28th October 1908. The scarcely credible fact about it was that the Kaiser meant it in all sincerity as a conciliatory move. In this published conversation between the Kaiser and a British colonel, Wilhelm II tried to create the impression that the Boers had been defeated by a plan which he had personally devised and handed to the British General Staff—those same Boers with whom the Kaiser had sided in his telegram. On this occasion the German people, their Emperor insinuated, had been the spoilsports: he, of course, was pro-British but had been unable to act otherwise in face of the anti-British mood of German public opinion. Finally he demonstrated his mastery of the art of infuriating several nations at once by referring to the "yellow peril" threatening from Japan and the secret intentions of Russia and France to wage war— on England!

Today it seems scarcely comprehensible that the German nationalists, as represented by the Pan-German League, regarded the Kaiser as a weakling. Perhaps they had recognised the truth that his magniloquent phrases were, for him, self-justifying and were not signs of a genuinely aggressive urge. Even the influential publicist Maximilian Harden, in his magazine *Zukunft* through whose columns he had brought about the downfall of several of the Kaiser's friends such as Prince Eulenburg, accused the Kaiser—whom half the world regarded as an aggressive Teuton—of indecision and weakness.

In July 1905, when Reichs Chancellor von Bülow was threatening to resign, the monarch, who never lost an opportunity to stress his closeness to God, announced in his own hand on 11th August 1905 that he would commit suicide: "The morning following the submission of your letter of resignation would find the Kaiser lifeless! Think of my poor wife and children!" In some backwater of a petty state such posturing by the sovereign would have been touching. For an empire and an emperor which extolled German manliness on every occasion it was impossible.

The Kaiser himself was often mortified by the subsequent effect of his words. He was always resolving to moderate himself. He is remembered as a man who wished to do good but was himself his greatest impediment to doing it. One is tempted to say that his mentality and his political tactics—if they were tactics at all—were half a century ahead of his time. Only now have we reached the epoch of statesman's tirades as instruments of policy, of terrifying challenges to battle hurled from one hemisphere to another: only now have we learned that nothing irrevocable actually occurs as long as the exchange is limited to insults. In the case of Imperial Germany, however, the rest of the world still equated words with deeds.

THE DRAGON'S TEETH
German Militarism

That the Germans are dangerous seems to have been proved irrefutably once for all by the two world wars. That they were started by Germany is one of the articles of faith of both the eastern and the western worlds[1]—and is practically unshakeable. The stigma of twofold guilt has undoubtedly been drawn on itself by a country that even in peacetime has always evinced a distinctly martial spirit. Yet there is a difference between provocative speeches and gestures by a nation's spokesmen and the question of whether a whole people can really wish to start a war and have this on their conscience. It was the appearance of German soldiers on all European and most overseas battlefields which produced the impression that the soldier's calling was the German's favourite occupation and that he was taught the arts of war from childhood onwards. Once again foreigners were able to call on a host of reliable witnesses to this and as so often they begin with Tacitus.

The *furor teutonicus*, the age-old, elemental aggressive mania of the Germans, was recorded by the Roman poet and historian Lucan at a time when Germanic tribes such as the Cimbrians and the Teutons, in their search for land and food, invaded Upper Italy and terrified the Romans with their savagery. When the fighting reached the waggon-train stockades, the Germanic women would throw themselves into the mêlée, hair streaming and uttering piercing cries, as a final reserve force. Women and men stood up in battle "as though of iron". The magic effect of warlike panoply seems to have had its effect on the ancient Teutons, although on this point Tacitus contradicts himself. "They have no desire to flaunt their accoutrements of war," he writes in one passage but in another he writes: "Any matter, be it public or private, is settled in full martial panoply." The truth probably is that even a thousand years ago there were some who were uniform-struck and others who regarded armour as no

[1] With certain eminent exceptions as far as World War I is concerned.

more than one form of working dress, to be exchanged for their more comfortable everyday clothes once the job was done.

In both world wars the *Song of the Nibelungs* served foreign propagandists as an early proof of German bloodthirstiness. Wagner, amongst others, had revived the legend of the Ring of the Nibelungs with every conceivable device at his command. It was thought typical that Hitler was so enthusiastic about these operas, in which everything is immoderate in scale and obedience and contempt of death count for more than happiness and decency. The Christian element is nothing but whitewash. Hagen throws a chaplain into the water to test the truth of a prophecy—a man is used as a guinea-pig, as was done later in the concentration camps of the Third Reich. The same Hagen lays Siegfried's corpse at Kriemhild's threshold and decapitates her child. Kriemhild shows no pity even towards her own brother. The glorious hero Siegfried is left to stumble blindly to destruction. A reading of the *Nibelungen* revealed to Clemenceau, France's wartime prime minister, the German death-wish: "Read her poets—death on horseback, death on foot, death everywhere. The Boche loves war for its own sake and because every battle ends in heaps of slaughtered flesh."

For foreigners the German penchant for drill, obedience, marching and all warlike pursuits was first demonstrated in Prussia. "War," declared Mirabeau on his return from the Prussian court, was "the national industry" of that state. Winckelmann, founder of German classical studies, came to the same conclusion. He fled from Prussia because art and science were incapable of flourishing in a country which was nothing but "one great barracks". He would, he said, rather be "a circumcised Turk than a Prussian". Observations such as these were frequent and have given Prussia the reputation of a country bent on aggression, where recruits were bullied and all human dignity suppressed. The reality was less fearful, not least because similar conditions perhaps prevailed in most other countries at the time.

In June 1640, with a few thousand regular soldiers and deserters from other armies, the Great Elector had laid the foundations of the Prussian military establishment. On his death he left behind thirty thousand trained soldiers. Prussia's territories were widely scattered: from the Rhine to East Prussia her lands had to be secured against her acquisitive neighbours, consequently the need for a strong army was self-evident. Friedrich Wilhelm I, known as the soldier-king, used a harsh recruitment policy to bring the Army up to a strength of eighty thousand. It became the fourth largest army in Europe, although in population Prussia stood only in thirteenth and in area in tenth place. For four decades Prussia actually became a military state, until France eclipsed her in this rôle—without, incidentally, the French acquiring a universal reputation for aggressive militarism. In his essay *The New Society* (1919) Walther Rathenau rightly pointed out that the British and French had never felt the need to provide such elaborate justification for the mere existence of their armed forces as had the Germans. The universal image of the German soldier is as an aggressor: of the British, French or American soldier as a defender.

Gerhard Ritter, a professor at Freiburg University, in his book *Statecraft and Warfare* written in 1954, has striven to clarify the vague concept of 'German militarism'. Although anything but a supporter of Hitler, it is noticeable in Ritter's work that he wrote the first volume of the book when influenced by the German victories of 1940–1941. At any rate the historian judges Frederick the Great with a certainty which not everyone may share, as being free from the vices of militarism. Ritter excuses the purely aggressive war of 1740 as an expansion of the national territory justified by the times. Frederick had never relied on arms alone and his incursions into war had always been complemented by a lively diplomacy. War was still a political instrument; war aims had not yet become boundless. Ritter distinguishes Frederick the Great on the one hand from Ludendorff and Hitler on the other, the latters' thought and actions in war being purely military.

Bullied in youth by his father who used to kick him and pull his hair out and even mercilessly forced him to watch the execution of his friend Katte, Frederick the Great was, for all his liberal tendency in the realm of intellect, destined later to demand a similar degree of obedience from his subjects, even if it had to be assisted by whipping —a practice common in all armies at the time. After his father's death Frederick strove to create a balance between Prussian tradition and his own ideas. His day was divided between giving orders on the parade ground, ruling the country and playing the flute. He did at least abolish the use of torture and coined such remarks as: "I am tired of ruling over slaves." It is to his credit that he shared the perils of war and the hardships of campaigning with the rank and file. He impregnated his five million Prussian subjects with the notion that service is worthier than gain. Since sentiments like these have become unfashionable Germany has been markedly less fortunate in her public servants.

With his nickname 'Old Fritz' the lonely king became popular with his humblest subjects. With his character, oddly compounded of coldness and humanity, there are not many Germans who see him in retrospect principally as a soldier or a militarist. During the Weimar Republic it was by no means the worst Germans who hoped that the Prussian virtues of thrift, simplicity and social welfare of which the great king had been the prime exemplar might lend strength and stamina to the tottering republic. Social Democrats, such as the Prussian Prime Minister Braun, made no attempt to conceal the fact that they were proud of being Prussians: a pride which had nothing to do with the military element in the Prussian tradition.

Contemporaries—with the exception of a few individuals such as Mirabeau, already quoted above, (who had noted in 1788 that Prussia was "not a state that had an army but an army that had a state")—found conditions in Prussia to be fairly normal. In those days national power was exactly reflected in the size of the military establishment. How little Prussia can have resembled "one great barracks" was proved by Napoleon's easy victories over the Prussians. When Napoleon, with no better moral credentials than had Frederick II in his attack on Silesia in 1740, declared war on Prussia, the Prussian barracks were full of foreign mercenaries surrounded by hordes of women and children who were obliged to earn their keep because the modest soldier's pay was inadequate to feed a family. Their willingness to risk their lives against the mighty Corsican was correspondingly meagre. At Magdeburg General von Kleist surrendered without a fight, as did twenty three other Prussian generals with twenty-four thousand men and a succession of fortress commanders, who were court-martialled after the Wars of Liberation. At the outbreak of war in 1813 the Prussian army numbered a mere sixty-five thousand active troops. Compared with a France armed to the teeth Prussia was now a state that had an army and no longer an army that had a state. Whole regions of Prussia were exempted from military service; grants of leave were generous. In order not to damage the country's economy, foreign mercenaries were enlisted.

In 1859 *The Times* of London (quoted by Paul Sethe in *From 1848.*

to the Present Day) mocked at Prussia for wanting to be a great power whilst its troops had been conspicuously absent from all recent fields of battle—including the Crimean War and the war in Northern Italy. The critics of German militarism generally overlook Prussia's avoidance of war between 1815 and 1864. Even the peacetime Prussian in uniform offended those who imagined the whole of German life to be dominated by parade-ground regimentation. Heine, arriving in Prussian Aachen from Paris in 1844, described this impression in his epic poem *Germany*.

At any rate in 1800 Friedrich Wilhelm III felt it quite inappropriate to place any military reliance on popular sentiment. He was extremely vexed at the appeal for volunteers in the Wars of Liberation and was convinced that there was a natural antipathy between the civilian population and the army which still partly relied on the lash to maintain discipline. A call for volunteers smelled to him dangerously of the French Revolution; the king regarded reformers such as Gneisenau and Stein, who strove to make the army a truly popular force and wanted to eliminate class differentiation by equal prospects of promotion for all, as Jacobins in German dress. He was suspicious of any kind of popular enthusiasm. The army was an instrument of the monarchy and not a nation in arms after the style of the French revolutionary army. For this reason the kings of Prussia obstinately resisted any parliamentary interference in military affairs. The 'intoxicating whiff' of revolution must be kept out of the barracks. When the volunteers in the wars against Napoleon had done their duty, their call for a constitution was rejected. The army command did not wish to be dependent upon a parliamentary vote of military credits. The existence of patriotism and a sense of responsibility seemed only conceivable among the upper classes.

In his *History of Germany* Treitschke mentioned a number of significant clashes between civilians and the military caste. In 1823 a grandson of Marshal Blücher stabbed to death an actor who was unwilling to give way in an amorous relationship. In 1844 a lieutenant called Leithold killed a Königsberg lawyer in a duel, the king intervening to forestall the punishment for which popular demand clamoured. In August 1846 troops were employed at Cologne because a fair threatened to develop into a general brawl. In Silesia troops took part in the suppression of the weavers' revolt. In 1847 soldiers were summoned into action against workers protesting against the high price of potatoes. In November 1848 General

Wrangel, seated watch in hand on a chair as the representative of 'superior power', had the Prussian Chamber of Deputies cleared. The army was regarded as a tool for the control of the 'enemy within', felt to be lurking among the poorer sections of the population. In order to prevent too close a relationship developing between the armed forces and the people, regiments were regularly cross-posted about the country and for the same reason soldiers were not generally allowed to serve in areas near their homes. In the period around 1850 the profession of arms was in no way regarded as an honourable service to king and country: well-to-do middle-class families would write to the king of Prussia petitioning exemption from military service for their sons. Students demonstrated for total exemption. With appropriate reticence even Bismarck wrote later that he would have not regretted it had illness permitted him to avoid military service.

Similar crises of confidence and clashes between the population and the army occurred, of course, in other countries during the same period. The healing of this breach generally only occurred in moments of nationalistic upsurge, such as during World War I, when it occurred universally. In Imperial Germany, a state which had come into existence as a direct result of military victory, militaristic tendencies were at first the exclusive province of the political Right wing: they were opposed by the fundamentally anti-military Left, which until the outbreak of war in 1914 never rid itself of the suspicion that the army was no more than the Kaiser's household troop for the suppression of social unrest. But in 1914 "the readiness to mobilise was present in every country. The World War was one of the most popular wars known to history." (Ernst Jünger.) Proof of this is given even more by the inflammatory appeals of writers suddenly turned militant patriots than by the Orders of the Day of military commanders. The Kaiser is said to have been appalled by the outbreak of war; not so his subjects, to judge by the enthusiastic demonstrations of August 1914.

The core of the problem of German militarism has long been recognised as the excessive influence exerted in politics by senior officers of the armed forces. Oversimplified formulae which make out all politicians to be good and all generals bad are quite inadequate to describe the relationship. In Prussia and in Imperial Germany the monarch combined in his person both political and military leadership. Clausewitz, in his famous essays "On War" (1816–30), regarded the political and military elements in the state as a natural unity: war was "a continuation of political intercourse" and not something separate. Tension was only felt as the result of rivalry between political and military leaders, which did not always redound to the moral credit of the civilians.

Freiherr vom Stein considered that the Germans would wait in vain "for that public spirit shown by the English, the French and others to take root in Germany and for the day to come when we need no longer point continually to those limits which the military, in lands where public spirit reigns, may not overstep". Stein wanted to keep the swaggering generals as far removed from the business of politics as possible. His admiration for public spirit was not without its tinge of departmental jealousy and there is no reason to claim that at the time Stein was more peace-loving than the Prussian army command. On the contrary, in his impatience to defeat Napoleon, he constantly accused the military of idleness and indecision. It was in the Wars of Liberation that Marshal Blücher was to utter his bluff old-soldier's indignation at the "dispotism of deplomats"[1]. There arose the expression that the pen ruined what the sword had gained. At Paris Blücher was determined to blow up a certain bridge; when he was advised against it he declared that the diplomats were giving away the conquests won by the soldiers' bravery. The clash between 'ink' and 'blood' is nowhere more vividly expressed than in the arguments between the calculating Chancellor Hardenberg and Marshal Vorwärts. It was generally a question as to who should have the last word and had nothing to do with the quality of humanity or love of peace.

The antagonism between the Prussian prime minister Bismarck and the Chief of the General Staff von Moltke must primarily be regarded as a struggle for supremacy between departments of state. In 1866 Bismarck, in opposition to the generals' thirst for glory and revenge, concluded peace with Austria on extremely mild terms. Whatever the circumstances he inclined to do the opposite of what the generals advised. In the Franco-Prussian war he complained about the 'demigods' of the General Staff who held back from him vital military information. Even in purely military questions Bismarck was determined to have his say: he made it clear that the lifting of the bombardment of Paris was tantamount to high treason. In 1871 against his own better judgment he allowed himself to be swayed by

[1] The incorrect spelling is Blücher's own: "Dispotie der Deplomatiquer".

the military reasoning of the king to detach the whole of Lorraine from France in the peace treaty. German territorial claims based on patriotic sentiment were angrily dismissed by Bismarck as professorial twaddle. And yet France remained a great power even after 1871. She was not obliged to disarm and by 1875 was ready for war again. Anyone wishing to trace the human element in politics will recognise in Bismarck's post-1871 attachment to peace not only statesmanlike vision but also the unwillingness to pave the way for further victories for the already overzealous military.

Forty years later in World War I the politico-military antagonism flared up again between the politician Bethmann-Hollweg and Lieutenant-General von Moltke. The Reichs Chancellor was determined not to lose the chance of a political initiative: the Chief of Staff could only see military necessity. The quarrel between the pen and the sword finally resulted in the army leaders Hindenburg and Ludendorff dominating politics, unwilling to tolerate any rivals. Even the Kaiser had to submit to them.

The Kaiser, certain generals and a number of politicians contributed unwittingly by careless talk and over-audacious interference in civil affairs to the accusation made abroad that the Germans were militarists to a man—"military mad", as Dostoyevski wrote from Berlin. When Bismarck complained of the lack of political consciousness among the Germans, the German people were soon to be divided up, in the barrack-room jargon affected by the young Kaiser, into "sloppy civilians" and "clear-eyed soldiers". In his youth the monarch felt himself particularly attracted by officers. He preferred military attachés as his political advisers. When the German ambassador in London, Count Metternich, reported that an enlargement of the German fleet would strengthen the impression in England that a war was unavoidable, the Kaiser called him a panicmonger. He preferred to believe the forceful despatch of the German naval attaché in London who cut across the ambassador's warning by predicting that German naval expansion would force the British into offering an alliance with Germany. This was exactly what Wilhelm II wanted to hear. He called the Reichstag deputies who opposed military appropriations of the required magnitude "unpatriotic scoundrels". As to the constitution, which contained parliament's entrenched right to fix the level of military expenditure, he declared that he had never read it.

The imperial manoeuvres were the climax of the year for him—not only for him but also for foreign observers who utilised the occasion to collate information on German military activity which they interpreted according to their viewpoint as either threatening or ridiculous. An indispensable accompaniment to the manoeuvres was a great deal of loose, boastful talk about war and its value as a "purifying ordeal" and an "elemental power". Later the sober armaments statistics were to prove the crass discrepancy between this heady talk and the true ratio of Germany's military strength to that of her opponents.

Heinrich von Treitschke had called peace a state of disease and praised the "moral sublimity" of war. In his opinion the desire to banish war from the world amounted to "a crippling of human nature". In the long period of peace between the Wars of Liberation and the German-Danish war of 1864 the General Staff grew extremely anxious; they were unanimous in believing that in peacetime, if not the whole population then certainly the army tended to soften and atrophy. The war minister, Count Roon, declared: "To keep the nation from rotting—that is the task which I consider still capable of solution, although only for a limited period. The canker will attack the army, too, if it does not see some action." The army got what it needed: three wars within a decade, but even a few years later Moltke felt obliged to issue a warning that "the world would sink into materialism" if it were not regenerated in battle. General von Bernhardi did much to lighten to task of foreign propagandists, in their subsequent effects to prove Germany's war guilt, with his verbose books *Germany and The Next War* (1912) and *Our Future* (1914). "Bernhardism" as the expression of the German urge to violence could easily be proved by quoting from the general's books: "Might is the supreme right and the struggle for that right will be decided in the highest court of arbitration—war."

In the Reichstag in 1898 a politician of the Centre Party, to the applause of the House, described the non-commissioned officer as "God's representative" and at the same time a court preacher called military service "the service of God". All this, trumpeted forth in peacetime, could only produce the impression abroad that Germany really had become the "one great barracks", as Winckelmann had described Prussia. Whilst the French politician Léon Gambetta, referring to the lost territories of Alsace-Lorraine, demanded that Frenchmen, following the example of the Romans should "forever think of it and never speak of it," Imperial Germany was by contrast much given to uttering challenging statements. Were others accusing them of militarism? Very well—yes, the Germans were militarists, even in civilian dress. A professor of economics from Berlin, Werner Sombart, went so far as to define militarism as "the closest possible liaison between Weimar and Potsdam—it is Beethoven in the trenches".

In a similarly provocative manner the German delegate, as the first to speak, made fun of all disarmament proposals at the first Hague Peace Conference in 1899. At the second Hague Conference eight years later the German representatives again did their best to appear to be trying to wreck the conference. Several other countries were equally unwilling to disarm, but it had to be the Germans who with their sarcasm defeated the motion for an international armaments control. When the conference ended the German delegates found themselves isolated. Leavetaking was notably cool and as many other delegates as possible avoided shaking the Germans by the hand. This did not worry them overmuch. In the eyes of the whole world and to the considerable amusement of British and French nationalists, the Germans had heedlessly taken a course which saddled them with the guilt of having sabotaged all efforts at international disarmament.

This was the time of the hoax of the Captain from Köpenick, alias Wilhelm Voigt, a cobbler, who for minor offences had spent nearly half his life behind bars. Dogged by the police, he found himself unable to find steady employment after his discharge, was expelled from a number of towns and finally reached Berlin where, in order to emigrate, he planned the forceful acquisition of the passport which the authorities had so far withheld from him. On 16th October 1906, disguised as a captain in a uniform picked up in a junk-shop and at the head of eleven grenadiers which he had taken under his command on the way, he occupied the town hall of Köpenick without the slightest opposition, and had the mayor, his secretary and the cashier marched off into military custody. When asked for his credentials Voigt pointed to his eleven soldiers and said: "Here are my credentials."

The soldiers' unthinking obedience to an impostor and the equally naïve respect shown by the civil servants in the Köpenick town hall to a uniformed criminal were regarded abroad as 'typically German'. The Kaiser was apparently unperturbed by the incident:

he is said to have laughed when the hoax was explained to him. The military mentality had shown its superiority to the civilian mentality and it had proved what a single officer (even though an impostor) and eleven men could do.

Compared to all the resounding speechmaking about the "shining sword", the fighting strength of Germany was much less impressive than any contemporaries supposed. By 1890, even adding the forces of Austria-Hungary, Imperial Germany had already been overtaken in military strength by her subsequent adversaries. The other countries armed discreetly and were delighted to allow Germany's noisy war-like posturing to divert attention from their own arms build-up. The French liked to call their army a "necessary evil" which led to the erroneous impression that the French armaments effort was less than that of her German neighbour. In reality by 1910 the French reserve forces were approximately a quarter larger than the German reserves. In the period around 1910 German expenditure on the army and navy amounted to about 1.3 milliard marks. At the same time 4 milliard marks were being spent on spirits, beer and wine. The per capita expenditure on the armed forces was a bare twenty marks and over sixty marks for alcohol.

The speech-makers who pompously celebrated the Kaiser's birthday with quotations from the classics such as "Life is not the greatest good we have. . . ." and "Dulce et decorum est . . .", etc., only served to intensify the foreigners' suspicion of Germany's unbridled militarism. Soon even the manufacture of arms in the German Reich was taken amiss. An armaments factory such as Krupp began to acquire the reputation of indulging in a criminal activity, although they were doing nothing different from what Schneider-Le Creusot were doing in France and Vickers Armstrong in England. What in other countries was regarded as a perfectly normal strategic and economic activity was branded as criminal in the case of Germany. It was only in the last third of the 19th century that Krupp was engaged primarily in arms manufacture, contrary to the generally incorrect belief held abroad that arms have always been Krupp's main concern. Later, armaments were to form a mere fraction of Krupp's total output. During the Third Reich the firm actually hesitated to manufacture weapons at all. To this Goering remarked that old *Geheimrat* Krupp von Bohlen might once have been in a position to decide to make chamber-pots instead of canons, but now things were different. . . . Krupps were subjected to a remarkably similar kind of criticism when in 1955 they refused the requests of the western powers to start producing arms again.

The strongly theatrical and literary element in Germany's moves to arm before World War I is most clearly shown in the build-up of the German fleet. Hastily created under the nose of the British following Wilhelm II's motto "Our future lies on the water!" the German navy was supposed to be the means of keeping Great Britain out of a war. If failed to do so. When war came the fleet was hardly committed: the Kaiser wanted to keep his gigantic toy intact. Finally, the carefully preserved fleet was supposed to be the determining factor in making peace; instead, it sank itself. The image of a Germany armed to the teeth was shown up as being at least half fiction; yet Germany's habit in military matters of biting off more than she could chew was perpetuated in the Third Reich. Recent research has shown that Hitler's boasting of the ninety milliard marks which according to his speech of 1st September 1939 he claimed to have spent on armaments was an over-estimate of about forty milliard marks.

There is no question that in 1914, whatever estimates may be nowadays made of the actual quantities of weapons, the talk in Germany was of a significantly powerful military machine. The tragedy was that the supremacy and self-confidence of the military establishment had no factual basis. Germany had in reality long been overtaken by her future opponents of World War I; she could not rely on her armaments to force a decision if it came to a conflict. Reason therefore would have suggested an active and flexible policy of diplomacy, but instead the political leadership of Imperial Germany allowed the military to tie their hands with the Schlieffen Plan. This committed Germany—on this point at least she was clear-sighted and free of illusions—to a war on two fronts. The plan, conceived entirely in military terms, did not long survive the awful probability that Great Britain would be drawn into the war as a result of the violation of Belgian neutrality. With France, Russia, England and the United States as potential enemies, the initial military position for Germany and her inadequate allies was the most unfavourable that could be imagined.

In retrospect it is extraordinary, in view of these problems, how little effort the German government made to restrain the bumptious Austrians. The politicians' room to manoeuvre in their efforts to avoid a world war were reduced to an intolerable degree. The soldiers acted in accordance with purely military necessity—or what they thought to be such. Moltke's telegram of 30th July 1914, in which he promised to stand by the Austrians through thick and thin seems incredible today. The hope that this reminder of the military solidarity between Berlin and Vienna would induce the Russians to act with more circumspection was incapable of fulfilment because it over-estimated the deterrent effect of the German army.

Whereas Clemenceau thought that war was too serious an affair to be left to the generals, General Ludendorff maintained on the contrary that wartime politics were far too complicated to be entrusted to the politicians. When in 1918 Kaiser Wilhelm II began to formulate rather more moderate war aims and approved a milder version of the Treaty of Brest-Litovsk, the commanders-in-chief, Hindenburg and Ludendorff, forced him to adopt the harsher version. Only when defeat was inevitable did the military chiefs lose their enthusiasm for unfettered responsibility in Germany. A civilian and not a soldier was appointed to head the German armistice commission. The army kept itself in the background. In his memoirs Field Marshal von Hindenburg fabricated an all too easy excuse for himself. He claimed that the exhausted German front line had collapsed "like Siegfried, from the treacherous spear-thrust of the savage Hagen". Thus was born the legend of the 'stab in the back', which was intended to saddle the civilians with the responsibility for the defeat and to salve the generals' reputation.

To prevent the renaissance of the 'stab in the back' myth, the victorious powers made sure at the German capitulation in World War II that this time the German generals should testify to their defeat by their own signatures. Nevertheless in May 1945 this gesture lacked the real significance which it would have had if it had been used against the Reich of 1918, dominated as it was by the military. In 1945, for a change, it was not the military—under Hitler largely disinclined to embark on warlike adventures—who were responsible for war and defeat, but the civil power as embodied in Hitler. Under Hitler the politicians used the military as their tool and not vice-versa. Paradoxical as it may sound, unbridled militarism was first imposed on the Germans by a civilian, Hitler, who had never managed to reach a higher rank than corporal.

The Austrian-born civilian militarist, Hitler, made a nonsense of the accusation that Germany was ruled to the bitter end by a bellicose military caste. If the Reichswehr, with its lack of sympathy for the Weimar Republic (a feeling which was reciprocated) did remain passive at Hitler's investiture as Reichs Chancellor, secure in the feeling that its commander-in-chief Field Marshal von Hindenburg would refuse to countenance any abuse of power; if indeed, as some maintain, the military even held the stirrup for Hitler to mount, then their attitude both at that time and in the years to come absolved them of the sin most often laid at their door.

It was part of the officer corps which made the attempt, though far too late, to bring down Hitler's regime. The years 1933 (Hitler's seizure of power), 1934 (murder of General von Schleicher), 1938 (dismissal of Colonel-General von Fritsch) and 1939 (outbreak of war) are all dates on which the Army missed its opportunities. At the moment of truth it showed, in fact, too little militarism, if by that one means the army's exertion of a decisive influence on wayward politicians with the aim of saving the country.

National Socialism was totalitarian but not strictly speaking militaristic: it made use of the army but did not depend upon it for its existence. The Party and the state police organs were much more essential to Nazism than the armed forces and rapidly became more powerful than the military establishment. Hitler knew that within the Reich his only potential source of real danger was the officer corps, still bound together by tradition, and that on the other hand he could only wage war successfully if he could rely on the vigour and fighting spirit of the troops. In order to gain the loyalty of both the highly sensitive general staff and of the gullible rank and file he made a point, in his outward appearance, of playing the part of the simple veteran of World War I, wearing nothing but a plain uniform jacket and the Iron Cross. This carefully stage-managed simplicity involuntarily recalled those qualities which the world had always admired in the German soldier.

However great the distaste for German militarism, the German soldier has always won the respect of professional observers. For several decades Potsdam and other garrison towns were the rendezvous of officers of foreign armies seeking instruction. The armies of many Asiatic and South American countries were built up on the Prussian model. The German instructor was a synonym for professional excellence. The virtues of the German soldier were being praised long before Prussian drill came into existence: ". . . namely their stamina under the greatest hardships and their incomparable blind obedience to their officers", as the Venetian ambassador Girolamo Venier wrote in the 17th century. No mention of their patriotism, however, is made at this period: the German fighter did not worry greatly over which side he was fighting for. If well enough paid he would march into battle for any master and offered himself, according to a phrase of the jurist Samual Puffendorf, "for sale almost everywhere in Europe". This mercenary spirit was later to be criticised as sharply as was his exaggerated nationalism as soon as Germany became a unified nation. Yet even the bitterest enemies of Germany confessed to a love-hate feeling for these "thoroughgoing soldiers" who so loved their country. "They are for us as much an example as an object of justifiable detestation . . . there is real glory in defeating opponents such as these"; thus Sylvestre Armand, a French author writing in the 1890s.

But above all it was the famous words of praise in T. E. Lawrence's *Revolt in the Desert* which warmed the German soldier's heart after so much chilling foreign criticism. (The scene recalls the most 'chivalrous' theatre of war in World War II, North Africa, where twenty-five years after Lawrence's experiences the British and Germans clashed again.) On the German desert campaign of World War I Lawrence wrote:

"Exceptions were the German detachments; and here, for the first time, I grew proud of the enemy who had killed my brothers. They were two thousand miles from home, without hope and without guides, in conditions mad enough to break the bravest nerves. Yet their sections held together in firm rank, sheering through the wrack of Turk and Arab like armoured ships, high-faced and silent. When attacked they halted, took position, fired to order. There was no haste, no crying, no hesitation. They were glorious."

After World War I Winston Churchill, half politician and half soldier, vacillated between admiration and abhorrence of the German soldier. Finally in *The World Crisis 1911–1918* he awarded him some ambiguous praise: The German soldiers, he declared, had already done enough for history. Nearly twenty million people had died "before the sword was wrested from that terrible hand".

In the proclamation issued by General Eisenhower on entering Germany in spring 1945 it was announced that the victors would eradicate German militarism which had "so often" shattered the peace of the world. Thus German aggressiveness was to be immortalised as a permanent phenomenon. In May 1954 *Life* magazine, in a special number on Germany, attempted to be rather more specific than Eisenhower's rather vague "so often". Five times in the last ninety years it was claimed, and seventeen times in the last two-hundred years Germany's neighbours had been obliged to go to war with Germany. According to this somewhat naïve reckoning every war which has occurred in Europe within the last two hundred years was caused by Germany. For decades 'Germany' and 'war guilt' have been spoken of in one breath, so that abroad the two words have become almost synonymous. The anthology *Stocktaking—A German Balance-Sheet* 1962 contains a re-examination of the warlike activity of Germany or, where appropriate, Prussia. From this it appears that up to 1914 of the 213 years of its existence the Prussian state was at peace for 168 years. A corresponding study of England, France or Italy for the same period could hardly produce a more favourable set of figures. "Prussia only lost two wars and won seven or eight. This may be the cause of other nations' resentment," commented the Berlin writer Hans Scholz.

Nowadays only obstinately nationalistic historians continue to labour over the attribution of war guilt in the ages of Frederick the Great, Napoleon or Bismarck. It is really only the two world wars which provide the significant evidence for Germany's unhappy reputation. The discussion of German guilt for World War I is now almost closed. In the twenties politicians of all persuasions condemned Article 231 of the Treaty of Versailles which fixed on Germany the sole guilt for the war. All political parties in Germany—although with varying degrees of vehemence—protested at the 'lie' of German war guilt. After the experience of World War II the protests of those days seem to us exaggerated and oversmug. It was certainly absurd for Germans to maintain that World War I had been forced upon an unwilling Germany: it was an excessively naïve formula, although splendid for use at patriotic demonstrations.

Germany must, however, incontestably be prepared to bear her share of the common guilt for the failure of the world's statesmen prior to World War I. No one has yet discovered a better answer to the vexed question of the allocation of war guilt than Lloyd George's description of a world that "slithered" into war. This irresponsible slithering embraces also that part of the guilt which every German should be prepared to accept from history without grumbling.

In contrast to World War I, after the capitulation of May 1945 there did not seem to be any doubt, even in Germany, of the Germans' sole guilt for the second world war. The image of a Hitler who dragged first Poland, then France and Britain and finally the Soviet Union into war, was too unambiguous for assertions of Germany's innocence, after the style of 1918, to have found any support.

From 1951 to 1956—according to three polls made by the Allensbach Institute of Public Opinion—the Germans' view that their country was responsible for the outbreak of war in 1939 came to be held with increasing conviction. In 1951 32 per cent of those questioned admitted this, by 1956 as much as 47 per cent. 15 per cent in 1951 and 20 per cent in 1956 claimed to be "Don't knows"; only 4 per cent in 1951 and 3 per cent in 1956 thought that the war had resulted from the inescapable logic of events. Tending equally to drop—from 12 per cent to 24 per cent—was the number of those who believed that other countries, i.e. those hostile to the Third Reich, might have World War II on their consciences. How great was the astonishment therefore when suddenly more or less reputable historians from the victor nations began, with an enormous array of documentary proof, to cast doubt on Hitler's war guilt.

Two books, which appeared on sale in Germany in 1961, are perhaps suspect as exercises in axe-grinding in spite of the differences between them. One is *The Origins of the Second World War* and is the work of the former Oxford historian A. J. P. Taylor. The other was written by the American David Hoggan and has the intentionally provocative title, *The Enforced War*. Taylor and Hoggan began by trying to throw overboard the apparently incontestable evidence and charges produced at the Nuremberg Trials. Neither of them were prepared to allow any value to the notorious Hossbach Memorandum of 5th November 1937, which was held at the Nuremberg War Crimes trials to be irrefutable proof of Hitler's aim of world conquest: it consisted, they claimed, of another of Hitler's usual monologues which his closest associates had merely wanted to use, by giving more plausible grounds for German re-armament, as a cover for Hitler's policy of calculated risk.

According to Taylor and Hoggan the German army in 1939 was not really capable of waging war. Hitler had only wanted to *frighten* other states, not to conquer them by force. The great surprise for everybody employed on studying the Third Reich after the war was the discovery that until 1943 Germany had actually been far from totally mobilised. Hitler, for instance, never thought of conscripting women for war service. Only after Stalingrad was the attempt made to attain the degree of total mobilisation which, to judge from Hitler's speeches, had supposedly been in operation since the start of the war.

Naturally, in spite of Hoggan's assertion to the contrary, it was not fondness for peace which made Hitler start off with a less than total war effort. He had come to power through a popular vote and despite the scorn which he was later to show for public opinion, did not want to sacrifice all his popularity at once. Like an actor, he could not bear to appear on stage without applause. The war, he knew, was not greeted with enthusiasm by the German people, so he was at pains to show that compared with World War I this latest passage of arms would not be nearly so unpleasant. The shortages of the first war were not to recur, and indeed the first winters of the war were not the demoralising affairs, with the diet reduced to mangel-wurzels, which people remembered from World War I. In the first years of the war the economy was still able to satisfy civilian demand for food, shoes, clothing and furniture. Hitler wanted to remain the beloved Führer who still had something to offer his people, even in war. Outwardly it seemed as if all Germany was arming feverishly. In reality, compared with the determined efforts to arm in England, Russia and later America, the German war effort ambled along at a rate unbelievably slow for anyone who drew his impressions from Hitler's fiery wartime speeches. Up to a very late point in the war Hitler persisted in the belief that he could eliminate his enemies singly with a series of cheap, rapid victories.

In *The Origins of the Second World War* Hitler is portrayed as a gambler whose plans were knocked awry by the war itself. Taylor and Hoggan point out that if Hitler had been really bent on war he would never have spent so much money on his favourite pastime, urban construction. Even the 15th March 1939, the day of the occupation of Prague, which is usually regarded as the point at which British patience finally and understandably gave out, is robbed by Taylor and Hoggan of its significance. The occupation of Prague, they maintain, was practically forced on Hitler once the Slovaks had renounced their union with the Czechs. The British historian sees Hitler as a typical Austrian improviser, utilising the opportunities which the stupidity and short-sightedness of others put in his reach.

Taylor and Hoggan consider that the guarantee, which Great Britain made to Poland in March 1939 as a reaction to Hitler's march into Prague, was a blunder. Poland, in their view, was the wrong country to be given a blank cheque for unconditional military assistance. Whilst Taylor talks of no more than "an automatic development towards war", Hoggan, on extremely sketchy evidence, goes so far as to place Lord Halifax, the British Foreign Secretary and Beck, the Polish Foreign Minister at the head of the list of those responsible for the war. Lord Halifax is shown to have bent all his energies from October 1938 until September 1939 to involving Germany in a major war. Hoggan sees the cause of this in the old policy of the balance of power: the Germans had grown too strong for Britain's liking.

Since the German edition of *The Enforced War* was published by the Journal of the German High School Teachers' Association, foreigners must have assumed that this book was being officially given to German history teachers as a recommended textbook. The president of the German Historians' Association, Professor Hans Rothfels, protested against this at the closing meeting of the congress of historians at Duisburg in 1962. Professional critics, he said, had unanimously rejected Hoggan's thesis that "fundamentally Hitler had always wanted peace". There were points where it could be proved that the author had falsified the evidence. It was particularly noticeable that he had treated many of Hitler's public announcements as absolutely reliable evidence, but had minimised his military directives and secret comments from the time of his seizure of power until the first years of the war. The book was being published, said Professor Rothfels, by someone who wanted to mislead the German public.

Taylor's attribution of war guilt has proved to be questionable for quite a different reason. As this unconventional historian has admitted, it annoyed him that the Germans whom he regards as a thoroughly guilty people should so easily be able to shrug off their burden of guilt by laying it all on the dead Hitler. He finds it curious that such contrasting figures as Winston Churchill and the German nationalists should have agreed in accepting Hitler's sole war guilt. Something, he felt, must be wrong here. Taylor is determined not to let the Germans off so lightly. The thesis of his book is that Hitler only promoted and tried to realise what had long been the aim of all German parties: the destruction of the system created by the Treaty of Versailles.

The assertion that Hitler was only the incarnation of wishes and demands common to all Germans therefore looks more like a reformulation of the ideas of collective German guilt than a lightening of the load of German responsibility for the war. Taylor's book is fundamentally an appeal to the victor powers of the last war to be on their guard against the incorrigible Germans.

It argues a certain maturity in the Germans, beaten in two world wars and subject to twenty years of debate over the question of war guilt, that they remained largely sceptical towards these latest attempts at exculpation. The cries of triumph with which the numerically insignificant German nationalists, anxious to exorcise their past, have seized upon Taylor's and Hoggan's books, found hardly any response in the nation as a whole. Apart from all else, Hitler himself, as Rothfels hinted, provides abundant documentary evidence which contradicts his posthumous defenders. In *Mein Kampf* he unequivocally propagated the notion that Germany should seize territory in the East which he must have known was impossible without war. In another passage he clearly showed that he was aware that: "The lost territories would not be won back by sharp-tongued parliamentary babblers but by a sharp sword, in other words by a bloody struggle."

The former German Foreign Minister von Ribbentrop complained in his memoirs (written in Nuremberg under the shadow of the gallows) that Beck had not made his way to Berlin to negotiate. Such naïveté is positively disarming. Having seen what had happened to the Czech politician Emil Hacha who in March 1939 in Berlin was forced to accept a German protectorate of Bohemia, it is hardly surprising that Beck looked for his salvation to London rather than to Berlin. On paper Hitler affected to be moderate; but after his entry into Prague all confidence in his word had vanished. It is typical of Ribbentrop's character, compound of a mixture of naïveté and impudence, that he could accept that Hitler would never have used the proposed German autobahn through the Polish Corridor to send German tanks rampaging over the Polish countryside. Poland, after all, possessed an area which the Nazis unceasingly referred to as "ancient German soil".

As the war-guilt debate after World War I had become so hopelessly confused, whoever fired the first shot in a new war must at least have realised that for lack of other more cogent criteria, the entire responsibility would fall on him. That the first shot in World War II was fired by Hitler would not be disputed by the most biassed of his defenders. In vain were Ribbentrop's memoirs combed for a sentence which might have proved that twenty years after losing a world war Germany had no other choice but to go to war again. Even if Taylor and Hoggan were right in maintaining that in September 1939, faced by Polish resistance and British support, Hitler was caught in a position with only one way out— there still remains the fact that it was he who was responsible for having allowed that situation to develop.

All attempts at moral escapism are very properly dismissed by a remark made by Romano Guardini in 1948: "It would be cowardly to say that what happened was inevitable: in reality it happened because people wanted it to happen." The saving formula of 'slithering' into war cannot be used a second time, at least not where the German leadership is concerned; but the German people, who in September 1939, in contrast to August 1914, showed no trace of enthusiasm for war, realised too late that thanks to Hitler they had been struck dumb and were excluded from any say in determining their own fate.

THE VIRTUE OF LABOUR
German efficiency

When German competition in world markets began to be unpleasantly noticeable as a result of the economic upsurge of the newly created Reich, foreigners began to accuse the Germans of working too hard. Until then the Germans had been respectfully called 'industrious'; now it seemed that even here they were kicking over the traces. They were said to waste their lives by toiling ceaselessly from morn till night. This enthusiasm for work, spurred on as it was by industrialisation and the first hint of prosperity, seemed to many other peoples, particularly to the Latins for whom life only began each day when work was done, to be almost the most disagreeable of all German characteristics. Whereas the Germans prided themselves on this new-found national efficiency, the world at large laughed at the Germans for sweating their guts out with idiotic persistence and for their determination to give a bogus 'significance' to this most prosaic activity. They poeticised work, made the manual labourer the subject of philosophical speculation and of cast iron statues.

In no other country with the possible exception of the Soviet Union, have so many paeans been composed to sweat and callouses as in Germany. Wagner thought that to be German meant "to do something for its own sake". In her bitter essay *Speaking Frankly About the Germans* (1962) Gudrun Tempel writes: "In Ireland the efficient man who is also a miser is despised. . . . Only in Germany is efficiency sufficient unto itself." Industry and thoroughness can easily lead to unpopularity if they emerge at a time when other nations, as a result of strenuous activity at an earlier stage in their history, have attained a certain prosperity and begin to look down on hustle and bustle as something rather common. The first reaction therefore was to discredit this new, slightly ridiculous but dangerous competitor by propaganda against the quality of his goods.

In the early years after 1871 the hectic German industrialisation did not, indeed, always produce results of high quality. In 1887 Great Britain imposed the mark of origin 'Made in Germany', without which German goods might not be imported into the British Empire. It was expected in London that the high-quality British products would then be easily distinguishable from the German junk and the door effectively bolted against German competition. But as soon as they had surmounted their industrial growing-pains, the German products soon became a synonym for quality and 'Made in Germany', intended as a stigma, grew to become a sign of excellence. Their quality and comparatively low prices opened many a market to German firms where previously British or French businessmen had dominated.

The newcomer who is breaking into an export market is soon obliged, in order to gain attention, to use tougher sales methods than merchants who have been selling their goods for decades in the same market unchallenged by competition. The German export salesman of the Wilhelminian era, described by the writer Hermann Bahr as "the commercial traveller who behaves like Wotan", seemed to the British bumptious and obtrusive, whereas he was only obliged to be pushing in order to wrest his share of the market from the others. According to the philosopher Max Scheler, the export salesman was the deciding factor in the anti-German tendency of the international business world. With his odd clothes and his bad manners he created the worst possible impression. One only had to compare him with the British businessman to assess the damage which had been caused abroad to the image of the whole nation by the clumsy behaviour of so many Germans abroad.

As the myth of shoddy German workmanship was easily contradicted by the satisfied customers, another line of attack was that the German indulged in unfair competition and used any means to get a grip on a new market. The unconcealed commercial jealousy of the British was regarded at the time by the Germans as one of the prime reasons for Great Britain's entry into World War I, although when seen objectively British fury at the massive German attack on world markets was as natural a reaction as were the efforts of a booming German industry to sell hard. One should not underestimate jealousy at the economic success of a competitor country as a factor in the formation of public opinion. The unease was not confined to the industrial and financial columns of the press at which the man in the street scarcely glances. The state and the employers have always taken care that the masses should feel equally hurt and jeopardised. Whenever there was a wave of unemployment or a wages crisis care was always taken to point out that the cut-throat practices of other countries were not the least of the reasons for the distress suffered by the employees—and of course by the employers also.

When after the capitulation of 1945 the Germans were forced to build a new existence for themselves out of the ruins, foreigners' fear of competition seemed to spring to life again very quickly. The Germans, it was said in the years between 1950 and 1955, were making their old mistake of alienating the sympathies of other countries by their furious zeal for hard work, their starvation wages and their unfair competition. But this reaction was short-lived. When the first phase of post-war reconstruction was completed, it became clear that the Germans were determined to enjoy the benefits of plentiful spare time. The rough work was done: people could clothe themselves, eat their fill and live decently again. Anxiety over a return to unemployment or to the miserable conditions of pre-currency-reform days was stilled and, feeling the strength of his position, the German worker began energetically demanding a reduction in his hours of work. Around 1830 the average working week in Germany was 90 hours. By 1961 it had dropped to 44 hours. An international comparison made in 1962 showed that in 1962 Germany had, seventeen years after its total collapse, the shortest industrial working week. It was calculated that the monthly average of hours worked in industry was 189 in the Netherlands, 188 in Italy, 187 in Switzerland, 186 in England, 184 in France, 183 in Belgium, 179 in Sweden and, lowest of all, 178 in the German Federal Republic.

The change that had occurred in the German attitude to work was even noticed by foreign observers. In April 1957 Victor Collins, correspondent of the London *Daily Herald*, undertook a series of articles to test the assertion, which constantly recurred in his own country, that the Germans worked longer, harder and better than their British counterparts. Collins could find no evidence to support the theory of the super-hardworking German and the idle British. He got his first shock when he watched German workmen on building sites and at roadmending. Instead of feverish activity he generally saw, he said, one man working and three men watching him.

In other British newspapers there were humorous references to the German mid-morning break. Around ten a.m. a whole nation would start guzzling enormous hunks of sausage, leisurely washing them down with beer or milk. The notion that the German worked for work's sake because he lacked the talent for enjoying life turned out to be a phrase only applicable, if at all, to times of hardship. The enquiry showed that the German is as prone as anyone to idle. It is no longer possible to maintain seriously that the German is a sort of work-machine that functions with complete devotion to its superiors for the good of its country.

One of the results of the post-war boom was that it became increasingly fashionable to change one's job. The chief reasons were expectation of higher pay and better working conditions. Mobility was particularly high amongst younger workers. For many, a frown from the foreman sufficed to make them leave their job. It became a habit to 'have a cold' at regular intervals as a form of extra paid holiday. At the same time it should not be forgotten that individual employers, with their over-hasty urge to make profits and ill-advised investment have themselves contributed to undermining the moral climate of labour relations.

Hand in hand with the worsening of industrial relations in Germany, deficiencies in the quality of German products became noticeable. In the summer of 1961 several apartment blocks in Heidelberg had to be evacuated as due for rebuilding after a mere two years. Instead of 'cheap and nasty', as German goods were sometimes called in the first rush of industrialisation after 1871, they now began to be 'expensive and nasty'. American businessmen visiting Germany have pointed out that many an American nowadays prefers to buy his camera and binoculars from Japan instead of from Germany; with many German products price and quality are now out of all reasonable proportion.

In spite of isolated cases of doubt about the reliability of things 'Made in Germany', German goods still have an excellent reputation abroad, but it can no longer be maintained that a German worker has an inborn superiority over his foreign counterpart in stamina, punctuality and precision. Dubious though the waning German enthusiasm for work may be in many cases, it has had a definitely favourable effect on foreign opinion about Germany. A German lazybones can count on being liked better than a work-mad German robot. The flood of millions of German tourists during the summer months has effectively destroyed the cliché of the Germans as obsessed with work. A British financial newspaper noted it as extremely comforting for Great Britain and her economic prospects that in 1960 and 1961 more man-hours of work were lost through people watching football on television in Germany than anywhere else.

"At what period was the worker better treated: in the Third Reich or in the Federal Republic?" was one of the questions which the Allensbach Institute put to the German public in 1955 and 1957. The first time 40 per cent decided on the Third Reich and only 15 per cent on the Federal Republic. Two years later the result looked different: only 30 per cent thought that things had been better for the worker under Hitler than at the present time, 25 per cent now voted for the present. Meanwhile the so-called economic miracle had made notable progress, in many jobs the hours of work had been reduced and wages increased.

Nowhere else in the world—including the Soviet Union—is the industrial worker wooed so assiduously today as in Germany, generally for the best of reasons but in a disturbing degree and by everybody concerned: by the state, by the employer, by the trades unions, by the consumers and by the consumer goods industries. Nothing like this solicitude is shown to civil servants and white-collar workers and to the liberal professions not at all. One has only to think of the generally inadequate salaries of young scientists and aspirants to the higher civil service, even of policemen and other state employees, to realise that as in the past there must still be many Germans who do a job for its own sake and little else.

3

THE BIRTH OF THE THIRD REICH

The 30th January 1933 was not just a day like any other. Nor, however, was it generally felt at the time to be the radical turning-point which in retrospect it seems to have been. The view that 'good' Germans should have realised at once on the very day of the so-called seizure of power that Germany was entering a reign of evil is an invention of later years.

Of course there was no lack of warnings about Hitler; but they were neither so numerous nor so clear as they were subsequently claimed to be. Evidence of this is provided by three books written by prominent eye-witnesses: H. R. Knickerbocker, Friedrich Sieburg and Theodor Heuss, who share the distinction of having written serious works on German affairs around the year 1930.

Knickerbocker was already well known as a journalist in America when he was assigned to a Germany torn between the Nazis and the Communists to find out whether the three thousand million dollars of American private investment in Germany were in danger. By their very nature neither Sieburg nor Heuss would have ever considered voting for Hitler at an election. Their books are typical of the complacency with which intelligent people of the early thirties regarded Germany's future prospects, despite all the warning shocks which they must have received. These three men are witnesses to the fallacy of the view, held with the smugness of hindsight after Germany's capitulation, that no person with a sound moral sense should have been deceived by Hitler for a moment.

The results of Knickerbocker's investigation (in *Can Europe Recover?*) were reassuring for the Americans. Hitler, he concluded, would not lay hands on the three thousand million dollars. He saw the economic depression as the chief breeding-ground of extremist parties. The votes polled for the Communists and Nazis increased in direct ratio with the unemployment figures. According to Knickerbocker, by 1932 around fifteen million Germans were living on unemployment relief of fifty-one marks per head per month. The nadir of despair had been reached.

To excuse the rise of Hitler by saying that the Germans had no choice other than the Nazis or the Communists is nowadays derided as a piece of dishonest rationalisation. But Knickerbocker, an eye-witness of those events, had exactly that impression. In the civil war between the Redshirts and the Brownshirts in 1931 two hundred people were killed and fifteen thousand wounded. Comical though it may have been, the cry of 'Heil Hitler!' sounded preferable to 'Heil Moscow!' in the ears of the worried German burgher. Even the Jews were reassured by Knickerbocker. They had been rele-gated, he said, to a place a long way behind the Communists on the Nazi black-list. The American reporter subscribed in general to the widely-held view that the Nazis had grown out of their unpleasant phase of vulgar rowdyism and were beginning to grow more moderate.

Friedrich Sieburg's book *Let There Be Germany* was written a few months before Hitler moved into the Reichs Chancellery. Sieburg, for years a foreign correspondent of the *Frankfurter Zeitung*, was far from being a Nazi. For certain of Hitler's supporters his book bristled with derogatory expressions such as "bull-necks" and "hired thugs", whilst he had nothing but scorn for Nazi racial theories. He found equally little to admire in the "von Papen Era" with its "pathetic carnival" of uniforms, titles and scandals. Sieburg saw von Papen's chancellorship as a meaningless interlude. Behind it, however, he detected "something like the creation of new values, native German values" and a "burning desire for a new faith". Just as Thomas Mann in World War I had postulated something which he called "spiritual militarism" in Germany so, according to Sieburg, the Germans of the Thirties desired "military spirit for its own sake". At any rate to this observer, the future of Germany in 1932 appeared to be "not without greatness". Sieburg refused to deny the fundamental goodness of the Germans and when he looked into the future he considered a recrudescence of German imperialism to be as impossible as a "complete degradation of the human race".

The third witness to the climate of opinion which preceded Hitler's assumption of power, Theodor Heuss, later to be first President of the Federal Republic of Germany, held political views akin to those of Sieburg. In the biography of Hitler which Heuss first published in 1931 and which, until Hitler became chancellor, went into many editions, there is as little accurate insight into what was to come as in the books by Knickerbocker and Sieburg. Heuss made not the slightest attempt to conceal his distaste for Nazi methods: he poured scorn on those who desecrated Jewish cemeteries and branded Nazi racial policies as "childish" or "the brutality of embittered inferiors". In Hitler as a man and a politician, however, Heuss detected a number of remarkable characteristics. He called him "a dynamic figure, very much of the present day". His energy was admirable and no one could "withhold admiration from the man" for the tenacity with which he survived the failure of the Munich putsch. Heuss was even prepared to accept the logic of Hitler's attempts "to paralyse parliament", on the grounds that "all's fair in politics"; nor had Heuss, who had always thought in terms of 'Greater Germany', any patience with the objection that Hitler, an Austrian, should keep his nose out of German politics. Like Knickerbocker, Heuss believed that he detected signs of moderation in Hitler: "He rants much less. He has stopped breathing fire at the Jews and can make a speech nowadays lasting for hours without mentioning the word 'Jew'." No presentiment of the horrors to come appeared to disturb Heuss' mandarin calm—proof of how even a German of great intellectual gifts was not necessarily capable of grasping the extent of the disaster implied in Hitler's rise to power. There were simply no criteria by which to judge it. What had happened in Germany was unprecedented and contrary to all probability.

The three authors, uneven though their reliability as witnesses of political events of the early thirties may be, did at least share with the German electorate the feeling that something new was due to happen in Germany. It was the Weimar mood, the feeling that the Republic was at the end of its political tether, which made the rise of the man from Braunau seem virtually inevitable. Even the majority of Germans who disliked his raucous and vulgar behaviour were not disinclined to 'give the man a chance'. The situation was, after all, so desperate that no one was in the mood to refuse any offer of salvation which seemed even remotely plausible.

Besides the political Sadducees, who even in the most violent struggles drew their middle-class skirts firmly aside, there were of course a number of uncompromising adversaries of Hitler. One of these, recognised after 1945 as one of Germany's unheeded prophets, was Ernst Niekisch, once labelled a "National Bolshevist" and author of a book published in 1932 entitled *Hitler—Germany's Doom*. Anyone who on the threshold of the Nazi regime published a book with a title like that has a certain claim to have seen what was coming. In reality Niekisch's book did little but confirm Knickerbocker's assessment of the alternative as being a choice between the Nazis and the Communists. Knickerbocker considered the Nazis the more bearable of the two; Niekisch advocated a "National Communist" Germany allied with the Soviet Union. He differed not a fraction from the Nazis in his contempt for the Weimar Republic. If Niekisch is to be accepted as having been a reliable prophet, his alternative to Nazism must also be accepted: a bolshevik Germany.

We should never, of course, forget that Hitler and his party at elections never gained as much as even fifty per cent of the popular vote. In March 1933, under the most favourable circumstances, he managed to achieve forty-four per cent. Therefore not even every second German was in favour of Hitler as chancellor. On the other hand only Hitler's party represented a united block—the non-Nazi parties were hopelessly splintered and could not even agree on the retention of the Weimar constitution. Even under Brüning the Reichstag proved to be an unworkable institution. Brüning was ousted from office without parliament being consulted and his successor von Papen was nominated by Hindenburg with an equal disregard of the Reichstag. Hindenburg was a kind of 'rehearsal' for Hitler: by electing the old Field Marshal a majority of the German people was already expressing a longing for a 'strong man'. Countries like Russia and Italy were already being ruled by dictatorships, to which the world had grown more or less accustomed. Resistance to an autocracy was finally undermined in Germany by the need to cope with the appalling economic and social emergency, which seemed to call for a subordination of all individual rights to the common good. Many reassured themselves by looking at Italy. Had not Mussolini, amid general approval, made Italian trains at last run on time? In those days dictatorships were seriously judged in terms such as these.

The true image of the Nazi period is inevitably distorted if we allow judgment of the early years of Hitler's rule to be coloured by a knowledge of his subsequent acts of horror. Of the fourteen million Germans who voted for Hitler in July 1932, most of them did so out of a mixture of fear and hope and not from any urge for nationalistic warmongering. Post-war critics of the Nazi past tend to dismiss it as a feeble excuse whenever the unemployment of 1930–33 is adduced as a major factor in the Nazis' accession to power: in their opinion this kind of plea is a dishonest evasion of the full degree of Germany's guilt—and yet A. J. P. Taylor, self-appointed scourge of the German conscience, is prepared calmly to state in his *The Origins of the Second World War* that unemployment was indeed "the main reason why Hitler gained power".

The 'Führer' promised the Germans work and public order at a time when a beggar rang the front-door bell practically every quarter of an hour and the street fighting between Brownshirts and Redshirts was spattering the city pavements with blood. In times of such turmoil there are few who waste much thought on the origin, education or intelligence of a politician who clearly has a great deal to offer. The mass misery of Germany and a parliamentary system lacking in the necessary self-preservative mechanisms—these made the advent of the Third Reich possible. The German people, with their particular characteristics, their abilities and their faults did the rest.

It may be that the Germans are more prone than others to evade responsibility for their own failures and limitations. Demagogues aware of this weakness exploited it to the utmost during the Weimar Republic by assuring the electorate that the wretched state of affairs was entirely due to a small band of political criminals. In Hitler's political vocabulary the Versailles Powers, the Jews, the Freemasons and the Bolsheviks figured in an oddly-assorted alliance as the arch-enemies of Germany. Hitler's recipe was simple: he ignored the fact that Germany had lost the war; the remedy for all ills was to kick out the present gang and give him power. The ruthless suppression of uncomfortable facts made a special appeal to the middle class, in particular to the large numbers of small traders. They were only too gladly persuaded by Hitler that the closure of shops and dwindling profit margins were not the fault of the world economic crisis or of their own inefficiency but of scoundrelly, left-wing politicians and grasping Jews. Instead of the German people being urged to buckle down and work hard, they were invited to ignore the real cause of their misfortunes. Dr. Kurt Schumacher, then a Social Democratic deputy in the Reichstag, declared in 1932 that the methods of the Nazis constituted a permanent "appeal to the beast in all of us".

Naturally Hitler's chief villain was the Treaty of Versailles. Its rigorous terms gave right-wing extremists a ready-made argument that the treaty was aimed at the cold-blooded reduction of Germany to miserable penury. The Treaty of Versailles did not, it is true, show much political foresight on the part of those who framed it. The Wilsonian gospel of peace was soon proved, to the Germans at least, to be a false prophecy; this quickly bred a form of political cynicism which was to prove fatal to the Weimar Republic. The sceptics, who from the start had dismissed Wilson's resounding Fourteen Points as a piece of anti-German trickery, seemed to have been right. The Allies at Versailles did not even try to win over the Germans by shaming them through being more generous, more peaceable and more reasonable than the defeated imperial Reich, which they had always accused (not without justification) of militarism, brutality and rapacity. Germany was, in consequence, forced to regard the victory of the Allies as a purely military triumph which had nothing to do with any kind of moral superiority. The severance of East Prussia by means of the Polish Corridor bore all the signs, to quote only one example, of the wilful creation of a potential cause of future war. Hitler had only to hang up a map of post-Versailles Europe at any election meeting to whip up a fever of nationalist resentment.

Nowadays the Treaty of Versailles might even be regarded as a comparatively mild settlement. French historians even consider that more severe terms should have been imposed in order to have truly humbled Germany. Hitler, of all people, had not the slightest right to wax indignant over the rigours of Versailles: his own later behaviour to defeated countries was infinitely more unreasonable. Nevertheless the notion that a wiser peace treaty might have spared the world a Hitler is not without substance. The farsighted Swiss historian Carl Jacob Burckhardt expressed himself along these lines in a letter written to Hofmannsthal on 12th November, 1925: "The Germans, who have long since ceased to be a great power—if they ever were one—and who have been profoundly disillusioned by the result of the war are being goaded by petty and mistrustful treatment, until all their tendency to exaggerated posturing, to violence and destruction will break loose again. Yet it would be so easy to strengthen the present more moderate governments of this country by a generous and co-operative attitude. Instead, they are continually being placed in a compromising position, until, for one after the other, an impossible internal political situation is created, leaving nothing but blind anger and demagogy to profit from German lack of judgment and political ineptitude. . . ."

The contention that dark forces were conspiring to keep Germany in subjection was dangerous as it encouraged the German people to condone a certain ruthlessness in the methods of the new man at the helm. The severity of the Treaty of Versailles and the Bolshevik menace seemed to be evils of such magnitude that the German man in the street eased his conscience with proverbial clichés such as 'you can't make omelettes without breaking eggs' or 'hard cases need strong medicine' when the first cries from maltreated opponents of Hitler began to be heard from the prisons. Even conscientious university professors comforted themselves with historical parallels. Augustus Caesar, they recalled, had been obliged to shed blood before he could usher in the Golden Age. How little blood, on the other hand, was shed during Hitler's seizure of power on 30th January, 1933—compared, for instance, with the terrible slaughter of the American Civil War which had preceded American national unity. At first the criminal reality of the Third Reich remained concealed behind such impressive achievements as the elimination of unemployment. The first concentration camps were shown off to visitors with the cynical remark that they were merely a copy of methods tried and tested by the British in the Boer War. They were, it was further explained, merely a type of re-education centre in which Communists and other dubious elements could adapt themselves to the new regime in peace and quiet! Until the outbreak of war, reports from foreign ambassadors continually stated that snap inspections of concentration camps showed that conditions in them—regrettable though they might be—were reasonable, that no inmates were starving and that conditions of health and sanitation appeared to be satisfactory.

In Germany, a country which traditionally regarded work as the main thing in life, mass unemployment induced something like panic. Fear for their very existence, which Hitler played on to gain power, seized not only the unemployed but millions of others who saw themselves as the next ones to be sucked into the vortex. Twice in ten years the middle classes (due to devalued war loans and the inflation of 1923) had lost their money. Above all they wanted protection against a third total loss. Even in the ranks of the intelligentsia the economic crisis of the early thirties had the effect of gradually blunting their political faculties and power of judgment.

If we are to believe Jung the masses are like 'blind animals' and behave less and less rationally the closer they approach a state of despair. Hitler offered the Germans the prospect of work, bread, peace and national greatness. His skill lay in his ability to camouflage his evil intentions with good. Six million unemployed, and the fear that this figure might swell to seven, ten or twelve million, were the decisive factors in his rise to power. By shouting, by hatred, terror and the spreading of disaffection he used the general economic distress for his own ends. Without massive unemployment he would never have become more than just one of the countless founders of new parties who proliferated at the time. Who, after all, payed him any attention in the years when things in Germany were going even moderately well? His wild gesticulation and rabid speeches evoked little more than derision. Between 1925 and 1928 the National Socialist Party, largely unknown in most of Germany, never even managed to attract as much as a million votes. It was represented in the Reichstag by a mere twelve deputies out of five hundred. Not until the distress became extreme did the masses turn to the man who promised them improvement wherever things were bad—and the result was just as Burckhardt had foreseen in 1923: "If it ever reaches the point where the mob, driven by naked fear, should hand over power to one man, he will surely abuse it. . . ."

Nevertheless, one should not make the mistake of regarding Hitler in the early days as nothing but an incompetent knave. Too many sensible people trusted him for such an oversimplification to have been true. The Germans do themselves an unjustified disservice by maintaining that he was an obvious lunatic or criminal whom anybody could have seen through at first glance. More recent and unprejudiced studies of the phenomenon of Hitler have come to the conclusion that there was after all something remarkable about him. In 1958 Professor Golo Mann wrote in his *German History* that if Hitler had only shown "the least moderation, 1933 would have been the start of a new and legitimate era in German history and he would be ruling to this day". This surprising statement differs considerably from the summary way in which Hitler was dismissed by Golo Mann's famous father, Thomas Mann. Golo Mann's evaluation comes closer to the result of a public opinion poll in which the Allensbach Institute put the question: "Would you say that Hitler, had he not waged war, would have been one of the greatest German statesmen?" Forty-two per cent of those questioned in 1956 answered "Yes".

Even Arnold Toynbee, in his book *Hitler's Europe*, considered that with the cards Hitler held in 1938 after Munich and in 1940 after his victory over France he could by acting with appropriate care and moderation have carried his policies through to a successful conclusion. Only later, as Golo Mann wrote in another passage, did "the diabolical powers within him, of which he was himself unaware, fully break through". Here, in contrast to the conventional view of Hitler as wholly devilish, the writer has recognised the existence of some kind of force which contained elements of both good and evil. The Hitler usually shown in carefully-cut retrospective film studies of his career—a man perpetually ranting and raving—provides no answer to the question so often put by the younger generation: how could so many people have believed in him or been taken in by him?

On 23rd March 1933 Hitler laid a draft Enabling Act before the Reichstag which was to have given him "four years of time" to rule without parliamentary intervention. It was passed by 441 Ayes to 94 Noes. The 94 votes were cast by courageous Social Democrats. Their spokesman, Wels, made a noble speech. Those who voted for the Act included the former Reichs Chancellor Brüning; the well-known politician of the Centre Party, Dr. Ludwig Kaas; Dr. Reinhold Maier, later to be *Land* prime minister of Baden-Württemberg; and Theodor Heuss. Men such as these assented to the Enabling Act for the most varied reasons. The Centre Party held the view that the time had come for a demagogue such as Hitler to be given a sobering dose of real responsibility. Hopes that he might perhaps drag the German cart out of the mud were mixed with the wish to see him make an immediate and hopeless failure of the job and be forced to resign. The Republic, as the wiseacres said afterwards, committed suicide in broad daylight. The realisation that it was dead, however, did not set in until somewhat later. Those Social Democrats who voted for him had been won over by Hitler in a conciliatory speech on 17th May 1933. Hitler's success in camouflaging his intentions was complete. When in May 1933 Alfred Hugenberg, the crude German Nationalist leader and Reichs Minister of Economic Affairs, demanded a free hand for Germany in the Ukraine, Hitler hypocritically protested his peaceful intentions and dismissed him. He played the part of the prudent German statesman whose aims, from military parity to a settlement of the eastern frontiers, were no more than those which every German party had been demanding for years.

Hitler's gift for concealing his true character was reluctantly admired even by such a ruthless critic of the Germans as William L. Shirer. In his book *The Rise and Fall of the Third Reich* Shirer begins by maintaining the view, generally held in Allied circles after 1945, that Hitler was the inevitable product of German history and the German character. In view of this summary judgment it comes as a considerable surprise to read of his confession, in later passages, that even he was deceived and thoroughly fooled by Hitler on a number of occasions. Having rather lamely asserted that only Germans could have been taken in by Hitler, Shirer then admits without much regard for logic how easily he himself fell victim to Nazi deception. And Shirer was, be it noted, an extremely well-informed radio correspondent with access to all non-German sources of news, most of which were never available to the average German under the Nazi regime. Shirer admits that no one who has not spent years under a dictatorship can conceive how difficult it is to avoid the effects of ceaseless propaganda. It was amazing, he said, how little he and other journalists or diplomats had really looked behind the scenes of the Third Reich.

In numerous passages Shirer, supported by entries in his diary, refers to the power of Hitler's oratory. The speech made on 21st May 1935 with which he introduced conscription was incontestably a "brilliant performance". The speech of 28th April 1939, in which Hitler sarcastically rejected Roosevelt's plea that thirty-one named countries be given non-aggression guarantees, struck Shirer as "the most brilliant he had ever made". The speaker held forth to such effect that he (Shirer) even failed to notice that the name of Poland was missing from the list of countries who had hastened to assure Hitler that, contrary to Roosevelt's suspicions, they felt in no way threatened by Germany. Shirer was even impressed by Hitler's last peace offer to Poland, broadcast rather hastily over the German radio on 31st August 1939, which seemed to him to indicate a significant moderation of the German attitude towards Poland.

Reading Shirer's book one can still detect, twenty years after his experiences in Berlin, evidence that he was as susceptible as anyone to the errors and illusions of the Nazi regime: his attempts to deny this are consequently all the more noticeable. American correspondents who have spent a long time in Moscow behave in a similar way. Once back home they describe their relationship with their recent hosts in a certain spirit of exorcism—as if they wanted to convince themselves and others that their temporary seduction by alien ways had left no traces on *them*. Shirer's book contains its fair share of contradictory attitudes: at one point he blames the Germans for not opposing Hitler with much greater vigour, whilst in another passage he demonstrates the impossibility of resistance in a police state. He even admits that as a rule under a dictatorship ordinary people have no idea what is going on behind the permanently locked doors, that they therefore simply lack the necessary information and standards of comparison to appreciate the evil in its full extent in order to combat it.

Odd as it may seem in view of the general tendency of his book, Shirer is undoubtedly one of the principal foreign witnesses to the blinding and confusing effect which Hitler exerted on the Germans. This relentlessly anti-German American has unwittingly provided proof that to err (politically) is human and is not a specifically German vice.

It should be no surprise if a glance into the past produces a number of figures who once, too, made their bow in the direction of Hitler. According to a document quoted by Shirer and which has never been repudiated, Pastor Niemöller helped to give the Weimar Republic one of its many death-blows, by equating it with "fourteen years of darkness". On 24th April 1933 the poet Gottfried Benn spoke of the grand new state which "will dissolve the sterile marxist opposition between workers and employers". The Rector of Freiburg University, Professor Martin Heidegger, spoke warmly on 27th May 1933 of the "glory and greatness of this revolutionary change"; there was no call, he said, to regret the passing of Germany's much-famed academic freedom: it had never been genuine. Later Gottfried Benn was to distinguish himself again when, in his funeral oration for Stefan George, he compared the spirit of the departed poet with the "steady tramp of battalions of marching Brownshirts". The historian Erich Marcks, in his declining years, saw Hitler as "a greater Bismarck".

As will be shown in a later chapter, the protestant Bishop Dibelius justified the first anti-Jewish measures of the new government. At Whitsun 1933 the Catholic bishops published a pastoral letter which greeted, in the jargon current at the time, "the strengthening of popular spirit" and the removal of "the fetters of Versailles". Two weeks after the spontaneous dissolution of the Catholic Centre Party (accompanied by a message of congratulation to Hitler), the Pope concluded a Concordat with the Nazi government on 23rd July 1933. Agreement with the Pope meant, as Napoleon put it, that "one ruled the conscience of hundreds of millions" and Hitler, until then hampered by general mistrust, regarded the signature of the Concordat as a great political and moral victory. The Vatican, an institution respected throughout the world, had accorded him the seal of international respectability. Whatever may have been the Pope's reasons for coming to terms with Hitler's government, it certainly was not a step likely to provoke Catholic resistance to the Nazis.

Right until the outbreak of war Hitler had been able to count on the approval and indeed the admiration of leading figures abroad. Whenever old supporters turned their backs on him in disappointment or horror there were plenty more waiting to shake his hand in the chancellery or to be allowed to pay a call at Berchtesgaden. Judging from the coming and going of distinguished visitors, the average German can hardly have been expected to conclude that they were all queuing up to meet the arch-criminal of the century.

Even the British government helped Hitler on his way for a time: regarding him as a 'bulwark against bolshevism' the British coolly made use of him for their own ends—as long as he observed the rules of the game and did not exceed the level of strength which the British considered proper for Germany. The Anglo-German Naval Treaty of 18th June 1935 was another blow at the Versailles settlement, but it was more potent still in lending international prestige to Hitler and as such had an effect similar to the conclusion of the Concordat two years earlier.

The line-up of prominent figures who visited Hitler began in 1936 with the British historian Arnold Toynbee, who in World War I had specialised in exposing German atrocities. He now let himself be convinced of Hitler's peaceful intentions. Lloyd George, a particularly impressive guest at Berchtesgaden with his mane of white hair, had an extended talk with Hitler, jokingly took his leave with a Hitler salute and in the *Daily Express* of 17th September 1936 he called the Führer the "George Washington of Germany" and the "greatest German of the century". As one of the authors of the Treaty of Versailles his words carried special weight. After the abdication even the Duke of Windsor did not fail, together with his wife, to pay a call at Berchtesgaden. Even after the outbreak of war Hitler still continued to hope that his silent admirers in Britain might be of use to him.

A few months after the re-militarisation of the Rhineland the Olympic Games began in Berlin. Sport, it is said, unites the nations. It can also, as was shown in Berlin, lull them to sleep. Thanks to that glorious olympic summer the world, longing for a change from international tension, either chose to forget who its hosts were or was dazzled by the skilfully stage-managed façade. The brilliant athletic achievements demonstrated the new-found confidence of German youth. Even the most obstinate sceptics had to admit that this image of German strength showed up favourably against the last dim years of the Weimar Republic. Foreign visitors came away believing that anybody who could see nothing but evil in the new Germany must be a professional grumbler. It was behind this glittering exterior that the horrors were being carried out which nobody really cared to know about. What were the book-burning, the smashed Jewish shops and the Nuremberg racial laws compared with the gigantic theatrical illusion which Hitler had begun in Potsdam and was now extending to the international arena! Nine more years of terror and atrocity were to go by before officials of those same Western powers who had done nothing about the contravention of the treaty in March 1936 and had applauded Hitler's Germany at the Olympic Games were to issue questionnaires to all the little nobodies in Germany, in which they were forced to answer the question: why didn't you see through the criminal nature of Hitler's regime?

Two years later the 'historic moment' of the Austrian *Anschluss* proved to have overwhelmed not only the majority of Germans and Austrians but even the Cardinal Archbishop of Vienna, Theodor Innitzer. Beneath a typewritten letter dated 18th March 1938 addressed to Gauleiter Bürckel, Innitzer added in his own hand "Heil.Hitler!" In the same spirit the Austrian bishops professed their approval of the incorporation of Austria into Germany and praised the National Socialist movement, which they declared to have done "great things" for the poorer classes and for the combating of Bolshevism. Cardinal Innitzer's moment of disenchantment came when hordes of youths incited to violence stormed his palace on 8th October 1938.

There were times when even Winston Churchill, if he did not exactly admire the German dictator, could not help according him a certain historical greatness. During an earlier visit to Italy, Churchill had already said of Mussolini that in his work of imposing a fascist form of order he had "done all mankind a great service". In a letter to *The Times* of 7th November 1938 Churchill did indeed complain of Hitler's inhuman treatment of his opponents. There then followed the sentence: "I have always said that I hoped if Great Britain were beaten in war we should find a Hitler who would lead us back to our rightful place among the nations." Clearly, of course, Churchill's wording does no more than express a certain respect for the undoubted accretion of power which Hitler had—even though by the most questionable methods—achieved for the German Reich.

Perhaps the last document which confirmed Hitler's genius for impressing people was the telegram sent to Hitler in June 1940 by the exiled Kaiser Wilhelm II, congratulating him on his "God-given victory" over France. Since Hitler saw the victory as due entirely to himself, he treated the Kaiser's effusion with suitable disregard.

4

THE TRAGEDY OF THE JEWS

The persecution of the Jews and their systematic annihilation form the crux of the question as to whether the Germans are, compared with other nations, fundamentally evil and corrupt. The list of their sins, already long enough even when one allows for prejudice and half-truth, suddenly assumes frightening proportions.

"We knew about it," said Federal President Heuss on 30th November 1952 at the dedication of the Belsen memorial. The question is: how many Germans knew about it? How many Germans were directly or indirectly involved in the great crime? Estimates vary greatly. Later (June 1961) Heuss added a qualifying statement: "Our imagination, bred in a civilised and Christian tradition, was incapable of grasping the dimensions of this cold, agonising act of destruction." Of the activities and the techniques of massacre used by the Eichmanns he added: "hardly any Germans" had or could have had any knowledge.

On 15th March 1962 the Minister of Justice of Baden-Württemberg, Dr. Hausmann, estimated the number of executives and specialists in the Nazi extermination apparatus at ten thousand, of which a thousand remained to be prosecuted. Since May 1945 approximately five thousand Germans have been convicted of war crimes by the occupying Powers, whilst a further 5,372 Nazi criminals were subsequently arraigned before German courts. Added together these figures make up the ten thousand referred to by Dr. Hausmann. This, however, only includes the policy-makers and the higher executive officials, but not all the men who made up the firing squads and gas chamber crews.

The extent of the guilty has been the subject of widely divergent assessment. Disputes over the numbers involved have arisen not only between Germans and foreigners, between the over-estimators and the under-estimators, but even within one family: between Thomas

Mann and his son, the historian Golo Mann. The father put the figure of those directly guilty at "hundreds of thousands", mostly belonging to a "so-called German élite", who were said to have "committed these acts of horror with the morbid fervour of initiates of a perverted doctrine". In his *History of Germany* the son did not agree with his father's estimate. He considered that the culminating evil, the gas chambers in the camps in Poland and Austria, were only known "to a limited number of officials in charge of the extermination programme". The Allies, generally much better informed than either the German people or the German army, are said to have known next to nothing about these camps. Certainly there were considerably more German witnesses to the shooting of Jews and Communist officials in Russia.

Far exceeding both Thomas and Golo Mann, Hausner, the prosecuting counsel at Eichmann's trial declared that the "overwhelming majority" of the German people had looked on at the extermination of the Jews with untroubled consciences. If one is to believe the Englishman Gerald Reitlinger in his book *The Final Solution*, the chimneys of the Auschwitz crematoria must have been something of a German tourist attraction. He claims that passengers, Baedeker in hand, would crowd to the train windows to watch the chimneys smoking. Erich Kuby, in his unceasing efforts to document German guilt and complicity, even stated that, "There was a stench of burning flesh for twenty kilometres around."

Faced with views like these, at best of dubious foundation, anyone trying to make a more precise assessment of the number of active participants, accomplices, initiates, witnesses or totally ignorant, must begin by making a distinction between the persecution of the Jews which took place between 1933 and 1941 and their extermination from 1942 onwards. In his scrupulously fair *History* Golo Mann noted that in 1933 the Germans were no more strongly anti-semitic than other European nations. Hitler found as his starting-point a form of middle-class anti-semitism based on a feeling that Jewish influence in Germany was excessive. Otto Dibelius, the Lutheran General Superintendent as he then was, expressed himself publicly to this effect over the Berlin short-wave transmitter on 5th April 1933. He asked the Americans to show understanding for the Nazi boycott of Jewish shops. On 7th February 1960 Dibelius, now a bishop, admitted that he had then himself been an anti-semite, unaware of what was to come. He had considered the percentage of

Jews in business, in the press, in films, in banking and in the medical and legal professions to be too high.

After the defeat of 1945 Friedrich Meinecke, the Grand Old Man of German historiography and bitter opponent of Hitler, apportioned part of the blame for the contagion of anti-semitism to the Jews themselves: "Among those who [after 1918] snatched all too quickly and too greedily at the cup of power which had passed into their hands were many Jews." During the Weimar Republic, when some of them had ostentatiously flaunted their wealth and power, the Jews had simply been devoid of any sense of the danger which threatened them amidst a people in the grip of hardship and envy. Not the least of the irritants felt by the anti-semites was the exaggerated behaviour of these Jews who typified all that was obnoxious in the nouveau riche. Of course, this is no shred of an excuse for what followed—only a contributory factor. It is not the victims but the murderers who are guilty!

For centuries the Germans have been used to trusting in the law and are inclined to believe that what the law directs is what is right. The same attitude was taken towards the Nuremberg Laws promulgated on 15th September 1935. To unsuspecting people words such as "host nation" and "guest nation", as used in the text of these laws, could have seemed like concepts defining a relationship of hospitality, such as any educated German might remember from Tacitus' *Germania* as being one of the praiseworthy customs of their nation. Anyone who considers this viewpoint to be impossibly naïve will, nevertheless, find it hard to contend that at the time, the Nuremberg Laws clearly pointed directly to the gas chambers of Auschwitz. In the year 1935 the programme of the Nazi government did not include mass murder. If it had, the Berlin Olympic Games could hardly have been held a year later in such a mood of international enthusiasm. The half-jewish Theodor Lewald was at liberty to carry out his functions as Chairman of the Olympic Committee. The visitors from all over the world were intended to gain the impression that the Jews led a tolerable life in Germany and that the worst was apparently over for them.

Hitler moved fairly carefully. Until 1938 he was still seeking for understanding of his anti-semitic policy. He clothed his actions in legality. Many German Jews—which may explain their tenacity in remaining—were long convinced that a total denial of all legal rights was impossible in a country like Germany. Others clung to the hope

—as we know from Dr. Nahum Goldmann, president of the World Jewish Congress—that Hitler would soon disappear like a bad dream.

To a certain extent the Poles competed with Hitler over who should first be rid of their Jews. An unspeakable traffic in human lives was carried on at the German-Polish frontier. German and Polish authorities tried to push Jews over to one another. In Hoggan's opinion the Poles far exceeded the Germans in cynicism and inhumanity over this miserable barter. Hitler was much amused at the enthusiasm with which the Polish government, at an international conference at Evian in July 1938 held to discuss ways and means of emigration, proposed a mass despatch of all Jews to Madagascar. Even before the war the Polish Jews, as Arnold Toynbee maintained in *Hitler's Europe*, had been "brutally deprived of their rights". The moral justification and description of the Western Powers' entry into the war on the side of Poland as "the defence of civilisation against barbarism" was to some extent weakened by this factor.

Hitler's tactics of deception were at first genuinely successful both at home and abroad. In 1934 C. G. Jung, later a strong opponent of Hitler, said that his Jewish teacher Sigmund Freud had failed to comprehend the Germanic soul and he enquired rhetorically whether the "gigantic phenomenon of National Socialism" would not shake his "Jewish categories of thought" to their foundations.

To judge from Peter de Mendelssohn's book *Berlin, City of Newspapers*, even the Ullsteins, the great Jewish publishing family, believed that with a little skill a modus vivendi with Hitler was to be found. The *Vossische Zeitung*, the Ullsteins' internationally respected political daily, was prepared, according to a statement made on 31st October 1933 "to serve the new state according to our fashion". When Jewish editors were forcibly dismissed on 1st January 1934 (declaring with some anger that their publishers had dismissed them "to save their own skins"), the Ullsteins themselves managed to stay. On 7th June 1934 even the Ullsteins had to bow to force majeure and were made to sell out at a loss.

Realisation of what was in store only came gradually; Jewish friends, wrote Willy Helpach in 1954 in his book *The German Character*, were still talking gratefully in 1935 of how the 'Jewish Cultural Association' of Berlin was flourishing and of the excellence of its theatre. Frank Buchman, founder of Moral Re-Armament and an advocate of racial harmony, was able in 1936 to thank heaven "for a man like Adolf Hitler", without the least apparent reservations about the anti-semitic policy of the Third Reich (*Der Spiegel*, 16th August 1961).

The Austrian bishop Hudal (who in 1960 was an official in the Vatican) could unconcernedly state in 1937, in the book *Foundations of National Socialism*, that the Jews must accept the fact that they "could no longer enjoy equal rights or esteem within the German nation". (*Der Spiegel*, 21st June 1961). An equal lack of awareness of the horrors to come marked the attitude of Dr. Rothmund, head of the Swiss Aliens' Office, when in September 1938, to stem the flood of Jews coming from Germany, he approved the stamping of the letter "J" in the passports of German Jews. This was the first use of that discriminating mark which was one day to brand the Jews like cattle on their way to the extermination camps.

In January 1939 Dr. Hjalmar Schacht appeared as the German government's commissioner to supervise Jewish emigration. He calmed the anxious: the government's concern was for a reasonably humane settlement of the problem. After the first years had passed without much increase in emigration, it began to be made more and more difficult. Movement was made harder by the confiscation of Jewish property, added to which were the attitudes of coolness or refusal of other countries towards Jewish immigration. The peripatetic Jewish emigrant, refused a landing everywhere in the world, was seen as proof of Hitler's contention that sooner or later every country would come to realise the Jewish peril and take the appropriate measures. 1939, the last peacetime year, when extensive emigration would still have been possible, passed without a saviour appearing for the Jews.

Even in democracies it is not easy to stick to the principles which one believes to be right. In the recent race clashes in the U.S.A. and South Africa, caused because the coloured people had lost patience with being inferior citizens, many a white sympathiser felt the full meaning of the powerlessness of the individual in the mass age. Naturally in dictatorship the feeling of impotence is much stronger and more justified. Apart from a small group of profiteers, who were only too glad to take over competing Jewish firms, and therefore made personal gain from the situation, the vast, unorganised bulk of the German people adopted an attitude of passivity. Only someone absolutely sure of his own courage and capacity for self-sacrifice can assert in retrospect that every decent person should, if necessary at the risk of his own life, have taken action against the persecution of his Jewish fellow-citizens.

The degree of confusion and deception which preceded the physical destruction of the Jews, was made appallingly clear in his own case by the author Jochen Klepper. The composer of religious poetry and author of *The Father*, a novel about Prussia, he was married to a Jewess; in 1942 they met their end together in a suicide pact. His diaries reveal that this man, persecuted with wife and child until the mid-war years, admired rather than abhorred National Socialism. He saw it as a means of salvation from communism—"that which, offered to the disillusioned unemployed, saved us from revolution in the streets". In the Reichs League of Authors Klepper signed a document declaring his allegiance to the new state. This was, as he confided to his diary, "no mere phrase".

Nazism seemed to Klepper a thoroughly Prussian phenomenon. In his view a state could not always afford compassion. The impressions which he gained during the Russian campaign were overwhelmingly positive. He described the efforts of German officers to treat the population as justly as possible. During his life Klepper's position was less that of an opponent of the Third Reich than of someone who felt rejected by it.

His efforts to enable his wife and daughter to emigrate brought him up against the ice-cold personality of Eichmann. When all doors seemed barred, there remained only death. Without his family responsibility Klepper would have been an admirer of Hitler, at least for as long as the naked terror had remained hidden from him. The inhuman dictatorship did not even spare those who wanted to believe in it.

Hitler was constantly holding referenda—though never on really decisive questions such as war or the treatment of the Jews. To interpret the nearly 100 per cent who voted "Yes" for Hitler as the indirect approval by the German people of the gas chambers is to imply that referenda under a dictatorship are to be taken seriously. Their real worth can be gauged from those 99 per cent polls for the Communist Parties of the Eastern bloc. The great burning of synagogues which took place in 1938 proved to Hitler that he could never bring the whole German people to approve of pogroms and destruction of the Jews after the manner of Tsarist Russia. Even well within the Nazi Party itself the sight of the fires and of plundered Jewish shops produced perplexity, if not horror.

Goebbel's assertion, that the so-called "Kristall-Nacht"[1] had been a spontaneous and irresistible outburst of national wrath at the murder in Paris of the German diplomat vom Rath by a Jew named Grünspan, was a clumsy lie. It was an organised piece of arson, carried out significantly in the hours of darkness. When Jews were finally forced to wear the Star of David, Hitler, who still needed popular approval, must have realised that the limit that the German people would publicly accept had been reached. Reports of the sympathy shown to these disenfranchised unfortunates must have hardened his resolve to carry out his further plans only in strict secrecy and with the aid of a small group of fanatics.

On 21st September 1941 Reinhard Heydrich, Chief of the Gestapo, issued the directive that all future measures against the Jews were to be "kept strictly secret". Not even Wilhelm Kube, the Reich's Commissioner in Minsk, a notorious centre of the terror, seems to have been informed of Hitler's criminal action. This man, who normally obeyed orders unquestioningly, protested furiously on 20th July 1943 against the treatment of the Jews in the occupied areas of the Soviet Union: they were unworthy of a German and if Germany's reputation were ruined throughout the world they had only themselves to blame. (Wucher, *There were many Eichmanns*.)

The perfectly functioning system of camouflage and deception even drew Jews into its service. In Berlin in 1933 there arose the Jewish National Union, which welcomed the ban on the entry of East European or so-called 'pedlar Jews' and which acknowledged the new government of the Reich. Once a split had thus been created between domiciled and immigrant Jews, the destroyers now thought up a system by means of which the seizure and persecution of their wretched victims as far as the very gas chamber could be put into Jewish hands.

For a time the Warsaw Jewish Council employed five thousand people. Under German orders it administered the colossal ghetto simultaneously as a relief organization and a police force, which earned it the hatred of its less favoured fellow-Jews. After the war this hatred took the form of a blanket accusation that the Jewish Councils had been the base accomplices of tyranny. Corrupted by fear and preferential treatment, the Jewish auxiliary police in Warsaw are known to have revealed the hiding-places of children. (Reitlinger, *The Final Solution*.) Hunger and fear drove more and more Jewish

[1] Literally 'the night of broken glass', the night of 9th–10th November, 1938.

auxiliaries to collaborate with the German police, just as there was never a lack of German informers in Soviet prisoner of war camps.

On 18th September 1942 the Board of the Jewish Community in Berlin informed the Jews of the date set for their "migration". Not more than fifty kilograms of luggage, the instruction ran, might be taken. In order to make the deception complete, the Jewish organization itself had to provide the vehicles needed for deportation. Many Jews may have suspected where their journey was taking them, but the majority clung to vague hopes that they were only being removed to labour camps and that their fellow-Jews could hardly be capable of maltreating them.

In the extermination camps the deception of the victims was continued. Thus the first gas chambers were made to look like ambulances and the railway stations at the death camps, complete with buffet and waiting-room, were made to look normal and harmless. The camp at Theresienstadt was specially fitted out to calm the fears of over-conscientious foreigners: as late as 1944 the Danish Red Cross declared themselves satisfied with the conditions in this model camp. Even the gas chambers for mass destruction were disguised. If any questions were asked they could be described as crematoria for those who died a natural death. The difficulty of discovering the exact figure of those murdered is bound up with the deliberate mixing of those who had died natural deaths with those who had died violent deaths.

Whether of the six million a few hundred thousand died 'normally', whether they perished of hunger, froze to death or died of a heart attack is irrelevant. Physically and morally this was the greatest assault on human life of all time. The Jews have a right to expect that no mere arithmetical manipulation will ever be employed to cast doubt on their suffering.

The Germans, after the peacetime years of acquiescence in the gradually increased persecution of the Jews, were helpless in the face of the covertly executed final stage of extirpation. Fear for their own lives had completely dulled their conscience. Even though Germans in 1940 did make a public protest and forced Hitler to suspend his plan for killing off the mentally unfit, no such protest was ever made against the destruction of the Jews. In Reitlinger's opinion the taking of 'non-German' life simply left the Germans indifferent. In reality many Germans themselves fell victim to the wave of murder, but by 1942 the vastly efficient suppression of information and the urgent demands of war and wartime security had thrown an impenetrable wall round the gas ovens.

In general, by the final years of the war, the value of human life had fallen to zero. Death no longer had any connection with personal guilt or innocence. The gas chambers worked as mercilessly as the bomber squadrons—to say nothing of the atomic bomb. The destruction of German cities together with the death of countless women and children formed part of the military programme of an adversary who had rapidly extended his hatred of Hitler to the whole German people. At that time many Germans imagined Winston Churchill, cigar in mouth and brandy glass in hand, walking up and down in front of an enormous map of Germany, staring with unmistakable satisfaction through a magnifying glass at each newly-bombed German city. This scene was actually portrayed in a play written in 1961 by the Frenchman Emmanuel d'Astier called *Les Grands* and recalls the savage and militarily almost pointless destruction of Dresden.

The so-called master race was itself little more than a spineless herd, driven hither and thither. Hitler despised people in general and the Jews in particular. By shortly before the final collapse of the Reich he had no more sympathy for the Germans than for the Jews. In a commentary on his 'scorched earth' order of 19th March 1945 he said: "The German people has proved itself the weaker and the future belongs exclusively to the stronger nation from the East. Whoever survives the struggle is in any case inferior, since the good will have perished."

To a Jew such explanations must seem no more than the feeblest of excuses. Nevertheless a German has no alternative but to try to explain—*not* to excuse—the incomprehensible. Among all the tons of files which were examined at the Nuremberg Palace of Justice or the Eichmann trial, not a single document has been found testifying to the general connivance of the German people or to any form of widespread approval to Hitler's policy of annihilation. Where German guilt really lies is not in the mass-murders themselves but in giving Hitler carte blanche in his early years. In the war-crimes trials at Nuremberg even the S.A. was acquitted of knowledge of the criminal acts of policy of the Third Reich and the court refrained from declaring it a criminal organization. The average German had no knowledge of the mass murder of the Jews and could not have approved of it—which, however, is not synonymous with innocence. To accuse a whole people of crimes, the scale of which the overwhelming majority only knew about retrospectively, is at the very least harsh, since murder presupposes intention, will and action.

A person wishing to define more precisely the numerical strength of the actual German murderers, their assistants, witnesses and accessories must, besides the ten thousand actual murderers referred to above, take into account between ten and twenty thousand stooges who formed the second rank of the death-squads and as mere subordinates felt themselves absolved of personal guilt. Nonetheless the number of those who knew what was happening—above all during the Russian campaign—must have run into hundreds of thousands. From hearsay to eye-witness there were many degrees of knowledge and complicity. Often the same criminals appeared on a great number of different scenes—at Hadamar when mental patients were being killed, in Polish concentration camps, at the deportation of Jews or as overseers at the gas chambers. Specialists were trained in mass murder in order that the circle of initiates should stay as small as possible.

Hitler did not lack fanatics to do this work for him, men to whom crimes of this type were made to appear as a patriotic service. They felt themselves to be devoted retainers of their Führer, who must know himself where their talents could be employed most effectively. The murder machine was coupled to an administrative apparatus which selected the victims according to certain criteria and sent them on their way, ostensibly to labour camps. To this end honest officials rubber-stamped the forms, drew up timetables and organized transportation. Each time the unfortunate Jews disappeared from an individual's field of vision his conscience was relieved until the next trainload was due. Sinister rumours alone were not enough to make an official give up his job. The soldiers of the execution squads often felt like members of a platoon detailed off to shoot a deserting comrade. The order was appalling but inescapable and here too the well-known element of automatism in the war machine played its part. Human baseness has always had—not only in Germany—a thousand forms of expression.

Today, as ever, the mass murder of the Jews strikes the Germans as something incomprehensible. The world expects them to feel some kind of personal guilt. But this is not easy for those who are unable to feel any direct link between themselves and the perpetrators. The number of victims is so huge that it simply exceeds the power of comprehension. The appalling methods of annihilation hardly allow one to believe that they were actually contrived and put into action by human beings; one involuntarily rejects the idea, not from cowardice or cold-bloodedness but from inability to connect the apparatus of destruction with normal reality.

Max Picard, who certainly cannot be accused of wanting to relieve the Germans of their unspeakable moral burden, was writing in as early as 1946, in his *Hitler in Ourselves*, that when faced with the horror of the concentration camps it was impossible to speak in terms of individual or collective guilt. In view of this monstrous crime this juridical or at best moralistic distinction became inadequate. "Not the individual and not the people as a whole, only mankind and the evil in mankind which has been concentrated to produce these atrocities, only the collective guilt of mankind measures up to the extent of this crime. Juridical and moral concepts cannot explain it—only metaphysics may do so."

Even though the Germans may not have shown enough horror and remorse to suit their foreign critics, they have on the other hand ignored the siren voices of those who have tried to juggle with figures to show that the extermination of millions of Jews was an exaggeration. There has been no lack of such attempts. Hans Grimm, the elderly author of the novel *Nation Without Space*, claimed in all seriousness that Hitler knew nothing about the massacre of the Jews—it had all been done behind his back. Grimm was also the first to cast serious doubt on the figure of six million Jewish victims; he considered it technically impossible to gas such a colossal number of people in such a relatively short time.

On 2nd May 1961 the Deputy Foreign Minister of Egypt stated that the growth in the world Jewish population from eleven million in 1939 to sixteen million in 1948 was normal and that the murdered six million was nothing but an Israeli legend, created to lend an extraordinary moral justification to the existence of the state of Israel. Even a former French concentration camp inmate, Paul Rassinier, expressed his doubts. In his book *The Lie of Odysseus* he accused leading Communists among the detainees of being responsible for the gigantic crime. The S.S.-appointed camp leaders, themselves prisoners, are said to have exercised a veritable reign of terror and to have used the withholding of food parcels, withdrawal of rations and whipping as means of driving to death any inmates they thought objectionable. For these, the real murderers of the concentration camps, the gas chambers were a fortunate solution which enabled them to cover the tracks of their own crimes.

The Germans have paid no attention to these more or less irresponsible attempts at exoneration. Nor were they much relieved when in 1960 Arnold Toynbee gave it as his opinion that Israel's treatment of the Palestinian Arab refugees was as scandalous as Hitler's extermination of the Jews.

That there is evil in the world outside Germany is self-evident. The deaths of so many German refugees, the atomic destruction of two great Japanese cities and the massacre of more than ten thousand Polish officers in Katyn Forest need no comment. Half a million people died in Germany as a result of saturation-bombing which only in exceptional instances had any military value. Perhaps one day the world will find the moral strength to recall all these victims, in one single act of mourning for the failure of our humanity. We are still far from capable of purely impartial compassion. Only after the start of the Cold War did an American commission publish a report on 12th February 1953 which showed the Soviets to be responsible for the murder of the Polish officers. In view of the newly-concluded alliance between the U.S.A. and Germany it was held expedient to exonerate the Germans at least for the responsibility of Katyn. Guilt was shown, not for the first time, to be a function of the political alignment of the day. The Soviets allowed September 1961, according to them the twentieth anniversary of the massacre, to pass without a word of commemoration. No dictatorship can be expected to make an open confession of guilt, but at least the Poles had persuaded *their* allies not to continue spreading their propaganda lies about the affair.

Long before Hitler, Stalin made use of absolute secrecy to cover up his crimes. The show trials of the '30s only allowed the public to glimpse a fraction of the actual number of victims. The machinery of death ground silently on in secret camps.

History knows no parallel to the methodical, clandestine mass liquidation which took place between 1940 and 1945. In the past massacres were usually performed in public. If mention is made here of political mass-murders that have been carried out in other countries, it is not being done as a cheap way of easing the German conscience. The very secrecy of the murder of the Jews heightens, in fact, the brutality rather than the humanity of the perpetrators but proves that public opinion was far more sensitive to open atrocities than in previous centuries.

The terrorists of the French Revolution committed murder in a 'good cause', which in their view had no reason to fear the light of day. The candidate for death, according to the philosophy of the day, was standing in the way of a better future for the French people; therefore he must be eliminated. Those who worked the guillotine could count on the approbation of their progressive-minded fellow citizens, since, as revolutionary terminology put it, only 'enemies of the people' were executed. Even so, victims were also despatched in secret and the proceedings of the mercilessly punitive courts were concealed from the public. Hitler's feeling that he was doing something which he could not admit to the German people was a sentiment unknown to the political executioners of previous centuries.

The tumbrils of 1789–1792 were not camouflaged as they were in the Third Reich—in Paris they had rumbled in broad daylight down the busy Rue St. Honoré. The blade of the guillotine whistled down before the eyes of the tricoteuses. Fouché, the Minister of Police, carried out his mass executions in the market square of Lyon with cannon. Stefan Zweig has described the scene, writing from eye-witness reports:

"The first salvo did not despatch all the victims; some had only an arm or a leg blown off, others merely had their entrails torn out, a few were even by chance untouched. But whilst the blood was still spurting in broad streams into the pits, at a second command the cavalry now charged with sabre and pistol at the still-living victims, slashing and shooting into the midst of the twitching, groaning, screaming, helpless herd of people until the last death-rattle was silenced. As reward for the butchery the executioners were allowed to pull the clothes and shoes from sixty still warm bodies, before they were heaped, naked and mutilated, into the mass grave."

The execution was followed by the inevitable proclamation: "Thus perish all the enemies of freedom."

For a public exhibition of horror, the historic balcony scene of Cambrai in 1794 provides an example which even between 1940 and

1945 would have been unthinkable. The guillotine performed in front of the house of Lebon, a revolutionary, who used regularly to invite his friends to take coffee and watch the spectacle. Mme Lebon, described as a good-natured person, contributed to the entertainment of the spectators by grotesquely imitating the proceedings on the scaffold. At the critical moment she would act out the decapitation by holding a knife to her own neck. The knowledge that only enemies of the people were dying—including a wretched old man of 94—provided the spectators, if we are to believe contemporary reports, with a feeling of satisfaction. A hundred and fifty years later not even Hitler, with his perfect propaganda machine, was able to provide his followers with this primitive sop to their consciences.

Twenty years before Hitler's seizure of power there was perpetrated an act of genocide whose main difference from Hitler's savagery was the fact that it was carried out in public: the massacre of the Armenians on the order of the Sultan of Turkey. The two crimes are, however, similar in motivation. Just as Hitler, the Sultan believed that the victims were a threat to the state. The Islamic monarch regarded the Christian Armenians within the Turkish body politic as permanent spies for Russia. In his innermost circle Hitler justified his attack on the Jews with the assertion that they were a priori in league with the hostile pluto-democracies.

1895 and 1896 had already witnessed the massacre of 50,000 Armenians. In a still extant document issued in February 1915 by the Turkish Minister of the Interior the order was literally given to "exterminate" the Armenians. Children under five were, according to an act of grace of 15th September 1915, to be spared. To the shame of those who massacred the Jews there is no sign of even such minimal humanity as this in the Third Reich. Hitler drove the Jews into the gas chambers. The Sultan preferred to force-march his victims through the desert. According to a police report, of 19,000 Armenians who set off only eleven reached the ostensible destination.

After World War I official investigation revealed the number of Armenians murdered as over a million. However, Allied war propaganda did not address their cries of horror at the Turks: even the Sultan was hardly pilloried. The whole fury of the attack was directed at the Germans as the allies of Turkey and they were made responsible for the Armenian atrocities. Germans must have noticed how no one has ever thought of blaming the French, Turkish or Russian peoples for the massacres carried out in France, Turkey or the Soviet Union in the same widespread way that Hitler's murders are generally said to have been perpetrated 'in the name of Germany'. This formulation avoids actual reference to German collective guilt but means fundamentally the same thing. The reference to 'the name of Germany' still implies a link between all Germans or all Germany and the crimes of the Nazi regime. Inevitably the rising generation, for whom Hitler and his henchmen are no more than a frightening memory, will reject this coupling of the German name with him and the crimes he committed.

If a final, just, yet unsparing attribution of guilt is to be made, it is essential not to be misled by indignation into oversimplifying the issue, into blaming the Germans for every wrong ever done to the Jews and for being the originators of anti-semitism. In this instance too the historical facts must be established and recognised. The truth is that in every epoch since the birth of Christ there have been anti-Jewish pogroms: in Byzantium, in Rome, in Spain, France, England, Germany and Russia, in varying degrees in practically every European country. That terrible expression 'the final solution of the Jewish problem' has a deeper historical significance than is generally realised. The mass murder of the Jews in the Third Reich was in fact the culmination of an indescribable tragedy in which every nation, at least for a time, has played the rôle of Jew-baiter and thereby brought guilt on itself, even though to a far lesser extent than the events of the last act. The facts have consequently often been forgotten; but in the incorruptible annals of history every crime against the Jewish people is recorded.

Anybody who believes, however, that a backward glance at the suffering of the Jews could exonerate the Germans is in error. The Germans have too frequently been involved at source in anti-semitism, since the early Middle Ages when a feeling of unease towards the Jewish immigrants began to be noticeable. Compulsory marks of distinction for these aliens, a red or yellow cross, later the pointed Jewish hat which is to be seen on many contemporary paintings, were introduced simultaneously in various parts of the Holy Roman Empire in the 12th century. The ghettos and Jewish streets, which were shut off at night or on Christian holidays by order of the magistrates, date from this period and remained almost unchanged until the last century.

In his autobiography *Dichtung und Wahrheit* Goethe describes his excursions as an inquisitive boy into the Frankfurt 'Jewish town'.

He first noticed the "narrowness of the streets, the dirt, the crowds, the accent of an unpleasant speech" as he passed the gate into the Jewish quarter. "As I did so the old tales of Jewish cruelty to Christian children, which we had seen pictured so gruesomely in Gottfried's 'Chronicles', came oppressively to my young mind. And that the modern age thought no better of them was visible from the large mural painting mocking and ridiculing the Jews which was still to be seen on one of the arches of the gateway, obviously directed against them: for it had not been put there by private whim but at public instance. Nevertheless they remained the chosen People of God and were a living reminder, whatever might have occurred in the meantime, of the most ancient times. Besides which they were people like us, active and obliging; nor could one withhold one's admiration from the tenacity with which they kept their particular customs."

This observation sums up, with all its reservations and admissions, the attitudes towards the Jews which the German middle class have held for centuries. The rôle as the chosen and their legendary cruelty, their worldly preoccupation with business and their religiosity, their alien social pattern and their approachability—all these the gentile middle class found hard to reconcile. If they formed their opinion about the Jews in accordance with the example set by officialdom, it must generally have been negative. Even books hardly ever found anything to say in approbation of the Jews, just as the clergy had equally little that was edifying to say about them.

But the complex attitude of the Christians to the Jews was not in itself a cause for outbreaks of hatred. These were originally due to three factors, at first in isolated cases then generally throughout western and central Europe: the crusades, the epidemics of plague and the vilification of the Jews produced by their commercial skill. Due to the ban on Christians practising usury, the lucrative profession of money-lender was for long the preserve of the Jews. Whether they demanded extortionate rates of interest or not, it is inescapable that whoever borrows money has no love for his creditor and starts to hate him when pressed for payment. It was an easy matter to persuade debtors that their economic misfortunes were the fault of the Jews and from there it was only a step to blame the Jews for the frightful pestilences which until well into the sixteenth century returned at almost regular intervals and claimed thousands of human lives. These alien diseases were naturally associated in the popular mind with an alien people. The crusader armies who marched off to conquer the Jews' homeland for Christendom felt bound to draw the sword in their own country to rout the local Jews as the advance guard of the enemy, notwithstanding their complete defencelessness. They stormed the ghettos, supported by mobs incited to hatred of the alleged murderers of Christ.

Astonishingly enough it was the princes of the church, the original instigators of the crusades, who chiefly opposed the persecution of the Jews and took—in Cologne and Speyer for example—courageous measures to protect threatened Jews by concealing them in secret hiding places or even in their own castles. The Emperor Friedrich Barbarossa, as Charlemagne had done before him, ordained severe penalties for persecuting Jews but he had no reliable executive force at his disposal which might have curbed the fury of the mob. Since Pope Innocent III promulgated the laws on the Jews at the Lateran Council in 1215, there has been no crime of which the Jews were not suspected—ritual murder, desecration of the Host, well-poisoning, exploitation of the poor, demagogic machinations . . . with an un-exampled power of passive endurance, on which they were for so long forced to rely, the Jews sustained all the accusations and vile penalties which delivered whole Jewish communities—in Basel, Strasbourg and three hundred and fifty other German towns—to death by incineration.

There were some rulers who offered sanctuary to the Jews, though hardly out of compassion and chiefly in order to profit from their commercial and financial acumen. These privileged Jewish courtiers in turn aroused the envy of the other courtiers and of the clergy, who incited the mob to new pogroms. Defilement of synagogues and acts of vengeance against individual Jews occurred daily and as a rule went unpunished.

In order to stem the growth of Jewry a limit was put on the number of residence permits, Jewish inhabitants were burdened with heavy imposts and poll taxes, they were excluded from guilds and municipal privileges and there was even—especially in the great Imperial cities—a quota placed on their marriages. Only the eldest son, the "*familiant*", could buy permission to marry and then only when the death of a Jewish paterfamilias produced a vacancy. One product of this system was Karl Marx, whose grandfather had been a rabbi and had borne the name of Marx Levi. His son, Herschel Levi, a lawyer in Trier, was deprived of the right to exercise his profession as a result of the anti-Jewish laws of 1816. As he had already expressed deistic leanings, he saw no moral objection to adopting the Protestant faith. This rootless position in between Judaism, Deism and Protestantism partly explains Karl Marx' hostility towards everything concerned with religion, in particular with Judaism. It is not true that he attacked only the capitalists among his fellow Jews; even Ferdinand Lasalle, the founder of the Social Democratic movement in Germany, repelled him because his works according to Marx "smelt of garlic". Marx found the Jewish problem so intellectually disturbing that in an essay on the Jewish question written in 1844 he flatly denied that it existed: it had been, he asserted, invented as a camouflage for other and more urgent problems, it presented no particular difficulties but was rather a product of the general social chaos which so badly needed to be set right. This was of course a piece of wishful thinking and as far removed from reality as Lessing's ideal of racial tolerance so sublimely expressed in the parable of the ring in *Nathan the Wise*.

When this work was written, in 1780, the Enlightenment had greatly enhanced the prestige of German Jews, particularly in cultural life. This period, in which Moses Mendelssohn founded the great reputation of German-Jewish literature and the salons of intellectual Jewesses in Berlin and Vienna set the tone of an epoch, was perhaps the happiest age for the Jews in Germany. It did not last long and led to consequences that were tragic and absurd: the long-waited emancipation and the repeal of the discriminatory laws against Jews immediately produced a counter-reaction which was to give itself the deliberately misleading name of 'anti-semitism'. The coiner of this expression, who apparently intended it to apply to the whole semitic race—including the Arabs—but in fact directed it entirely against the Jews, was a journalist named Wilhelm Marr who in 1873 published a pamphlet entitled *The Victory of Jewry over the German Peoples regarded from the non-confessional standpoint. Vae victis*. In it he defended the Jews against all attacks on them made from religious motives and against all slanders against their character. Describing their abilities and their numerical strength Marr conjured up the threat, supposedly based on biblical and historical evidence, of a coming domination of the world by the Jews against which the Occident and especially "Jew-ridden" Germany must defend itself. Marr produced the slogan "We or they!" which was readily made use of in subsequent years whenever there was an economic crisis or when pan-German nationalists from all levels of society needed an emotive rallying-cry.

The origin of this anti-Jewish campaign was to be found 60 years before Marr. In a certain sense it began with one of Napoleon I's none-too-numerous humane gestures. He extended the equality of status which the Jews had enjoyed in France since 1792 to all the countries which he had conquered, including Prussia. Thus after the successful Wars of Liberation against French suzerainty a patriotic German regarded it as shameful that a measure such as Jewish emancipation which had been imposed on him by his arch-enemies the French should be retained or re-introduced as part of the Stein-Hardenberg reforms. The patriotic gymnastic societies (*Turnvereine*), the student leagues and other nationalistic organisations were allowed to exclude Jews from their membership without breaking the law. '*Artfremdheit*'[1] became the fashionable word. In order to avoid the stigma of intolerance the anti-semites declared themselves ready to grant the Jews equality of status as soon as they should discard their 'Jewish characteristics'. (As early as 1793 Fichte had ironically proposed a special form of 'extermination of the Jews' which was about as practical: all the Jews should be decapitated in one night, their Jewishness cleansed and their heads immediately replaced.)

In their new zeal for assimilation, which was spurred on by the emancipation guaranteed by the 1849 constitutions and at least officially affirmed by all the German states, many Jews attempted the impossible task of 'denationalising' their characteristics. They discarded their Jewish names and took new ones from flora and fauna, they took an active part in the life of their new churches, acted more German than the Germans and by so doing aroused the particular scorn of their adversaries.

At the most the Jews succeeded in breaking the spell of Jewishness only in their own imagination: to most of their gentile fellow-countrymen it was as strong as ever. Throughout mid-19th-century Europe writers, historians, biologists and theologians were tirelessly occupied in proving that the Jews were an unabated danger. Not infrequently the arguments used were so crassly contradictory and the mutual hostility of the various anti-semitic theoreticians was so violent that the whole problem was reduced to absurdity, but at

---

[1] A noun coined to describe the pseudo-Darwinian concept of 'alienation from the species'.

least they agreed that the Jews were 'a misfortune'. Mediaeval attitudes were resurrected. In a number of Rhineland towns and in other provinces terrible outrages were committed in the wild belief that the Jews were acquiring Christian blood for ritual purposes. Count Gobineau preached the disastrous theory of the superiority of the white and Aryan race. Paul de Lagarde called the Jews "bearers of corruption". Houston Stewart Chamberlain, the germanophile English pseudo-philosopher claimed anatomical and biological proof that Christ had not been a Jew but an Aryan who happened to live among Hebrews. This corresponded exactly with the widely-proclaimed views of his father-in-law Richard Wagner, who was one of the bitterest anti-semites of his time and who denied that the Jews possessed any artistic or musical talent.

All these views, even though scattered sparsely throughout the corpus of their various authors' works, were zealously collated by Hitler and his anti-semitic propagandists and reproduced as the authentic voices of world-famed figures of unimpeachable authority. The personal factors and prejudices which were responsible for producing most of these totally misleading judgments were of no importance whatsoever to the men who had decided on the ultimate extermination of the Jews. Professional jealousy, fury at Jewish journalists and critics whose malicious wit is famous to this day, their infuriating talent for earning money by financial manipulation and finally the ever-recurring '*Artfremdheit*' were the principal causes of an insurmountable antipathy. Nor was it diminished by the fact that it was not shared by the most respected personages of Imperial Germany: the three emperors and Bismarck.

"From Bismarck's political salad days, when as a country squire he was a member of the United Provincial Diet in Prussia, a number of anti-Jewish remarks can be cited which he uttered when the emancipation bills were being tabled. But as a statesman he showed no anti-semitic prejudice. In his immediate circle were a number of colleagues of Jewish origin . . . and his economic adviser was the Jewish banker Bleichröder, who was ennobled. Kaiser Friedrich II and later Kaiser Wilhelm II were regarded as 'philosemites'. They elevated many Jews to the nobility, including those who had not been baptised, such as the Rothschilds who were raised to the rank of *Freiherr*[1] without being required to abjure the Mosaic faith . . . Wilhelm II was a personal friend of Albert Ballin, the Jewish man-

[1] The junior rank of hereditary nobility.

aging director of the great Hamburg shipping line of HAPAG."
(Friedrich Glum, *The Rise and Fall of National Socialism*.)

Bismarck refused to be moved from his pro-Jewish and—on this
point at least—strictly constitutional attitude either by the dubious
form of Christian Socialism preached by Stoecker, the court chaplain, or by the Centre Party and their press mouthpiece, the *Kreuz-
zeitung*. Bismarck completely disregarded a petition with 250,000
signatures which demanded the prohibition or at least the reduction
of Jewish immigration, "since there are 45,000 living in Berlin alone,
as many as there are in the whole of France or the whole of England",
accompanied by the exclusion of all Jews from the civil service,
restricted Jewish access to the courts and the removal of Jewish
teachers from high schools and universities. One of the spokesmen
of this proposal was Bernhard Förster, the husband of Nietzsche's
sister, and in complete contrast to his brother-in-law a rabid anti-
semite. He planned a kind of anti-semitic colony in South America
where he could breed a new race of pure German manhood.

Hitler was forced to accept the fact that two of his idols, Bismarck
and Nietzsche, differed radically from him in their attitudes to the
Jews. Unfortunately this gave him no cause for serious thought. The
philosopher of decadence and of the superman anticipated "that this
very mixture with Jews would have a great educative effect on European man" (Glum) and he is the author of the remark: "How good
to see a Jew among Germans". If anti-semitism tended to bring
conservatives and socialists together, pro-semitism was equally
effective in producing a rapprochement between members of opposing
political camps. Wilhelm Liebknecht, who at first had shared the
dislike of the founding fathers of socialism, particularly the French
and English, for the capitalistic outlook and the "narrow nationalism
of the Hebrews", began after a stay in England to prefer Judaism to
Christianity and proposed to substitute the word 'Germans' for
'Anglo-Saxons' in Disraeli's statement that the Anglo-Saxons and
the Jews were the two races most suited to practise world domination.
He believed that in future 'Judaeo-Germanism' was more likely to
be libertarian than so-called 'Christo-Germanism'.

This remarkable piece of wishful thinking may well have motivated
many Jews and Social Democrats when at the outbreak of war in 1914
they acquiesced in the Kaiser describing them as "only Germans".
Political anti-semitism was as good as overcome and now the last
barrier to Jewish equality was removed: they were allowed to be

commissioned in the Armed Forces. The only member of the Reichstag who volunteered for war service was a Jew, who was killed in action. Albert Ballin, who remained at the Kaiser's side until the end, committed suicide from despair at Germany's defeat. By now a revival of anti-semitism seemed impossible.

In Austria there was a marked increase of official anti-Jewish feeling at the turn of the century. Karl Lüger, Mayor of Vienna, and Georg von Schönerer, leader of the German nationalist movement, were its two protagonists. Typically, von Schönerer's admiration for Bismarck stopped short of sharing his great exemplar's views on the Jewish question. He preferred to believe in the same tendentious literature produced by international anti-semitism which Hitler was to refer to in a later era. In wartime Austria it was passed round from hand to hand and achieved a considerable influence in certain circles made up of racial theorists and the lunatic fringe of anti-semitism.

People have tried to prove that Hitler got his ideas from garbled versions of the works of men such as the apostate Cistercian and charlatan Jörg Lans von Liebenfels and from the occultist Guido von List. It is possible that the influence of various anti-semitic groups in Munich and the writings of such controversial philosophers as Alfred Schuter and Ludwig Klages may have served to convince him of the alleged 'Molochistic' element in Judaism, but fundamentally Hitler's plan for a radical extermination of the Jewish race was neither German nor Austrian: it was the conception and the action of a madman. Even the most savage Jew-baiter before him had never dreamed of a comparably sadistic system of annihilation; all the pogroms of the Middle Ages and of modern times had been more or less spontaneous outbursts of the mob or eruptions of violence by despots who were prone to direct such sporadic blows now at one, now at another group of their subjects. Preconceived antipathy to Jews and the readiness to give it drastic expression are a world-wide evil which—as we have seen—attacks even those Jews who want to cease being Jews. Anti-semitism as practised by Hitler, however, has no parallel in the history of Germany or of any other country.

Even disregarding the question of every individual German's share of guilt for the massacre of the Jews in the 1940's, the sad fact remains that there is not a single example of a German having made an effective public stand in defence of the persecuted—such as that made by King Christian X of Denmark. On hearing that the German occupation authorities intended to force Danish Jews to wear a yellow star as a mark of identity, the king announced that from the day such an ordinance was put into effect he and his court would also wear the Star of David.

In secret the mass murder was carried out; equal secrecy covered the aid and comfort given by ordinary Germans to the victims. It has been held up as a reproach that the German resistance movement against Hitler did not primarily arise from horror at the inhuman treatment of the Jews. The resistance to Hitler dates from the earliest days after his seizure of power when the horrors which were to be visited on the Jews in later years were unforeseeable. And even when they were under way only a fraction of those who opposed Hitler knew of the nature and extent of the atrocities. Nevertheless an honourable and equal place for the German Jews was a major point in the programme of the resistance for a new and better Germany. After 1945 a remarkable number of cases—in view of the mortal danger involved—were made public of German opponents of Hitler who had hidden Jews and saved them from death, to which the grateful Jews themselves testified.

In April 1962 the German businessman Oscar Schindler was solemnly welcomed to Tel Aviv. During the war he had managed a number of German factories in occupied Eastern Europe and had fought, at the risk of his own life, to ensure that several thousand Jews instead of being deported and liquidated should be allowed to stay and work in his factories. During his visit to Israel, where he was greeted by numerous men and women with tears in their eyes as their saviour, Schindler was among the first to have the honour of planting a tree in the newly laid-out "Avenue of the Righteous Gentiles", an avenue created to honour all Gentiles who defended Jews during the Nazi persecution.

In the West Germany of today there is no virtue in merely not being an anti-semite. The real question which every German should ask himself is roughly as follows: Given the conditions of the early '30's, how would I have behaved towards the Jews? Anyone wanting to give an honest answer must examine his conscience as to whether, in those years of desperate unemployment, he would have had the moral courage to resist the violent anti-Jewish smear campaigns propagated by the Nazi leaders and to stand up for his Jewish fellow-citizens in spite of all the consequences. The tears shed for Anne Frank were posthumous tears.

One frequently hears the despairing question: "What else can we do to wipe out the stain?" There are businessmen in the Federal Republir who do not dare to turn down a proposition made by a Jew, either from a sense of piety, from a genuine desire to make reparation or simply from fear that otherwise they may acquire the reputation of being anti-semitic. One publisher confessed that he had a guilty conscience every time he was obliged to refuse a book from a Jewish literary agent. German writers carefully avoid putting Jewish characters into their novels who are anything less than perfect. Otherwise the critics would accuse the author of anti-semitic tendencies and this, professionally speaking, would be the equivalent of a sentence of death. An example: in his film *Black Gravel*, Helmut Käutner the director allowed an unpleasant Jewish bar-keeper to appear. He proves to have been an inmate of a concentration camp. Immediately complaints poured in from all sides, against which the director tried in vain to defend himself. There would have been no objection to an unpleasant American, Frenchman or German, but to portray a nasty Jew was to violate a taboo.

This panic fear of taking an objective attitude to Jews is resented most of all by intelligent Jews. They do not want special treatment, they do not want to be a 'problem' over which everyone is forced to take up one position or another. The unpleasant—and often, frankly, false—pro-semitism of present-day Germans not only retards the assimilation of Jews into the society of the Federal Republic but actually evokes a form of latent anti-semitism which makes itself heard in such exasperated remarks as "Haven't we been humiliated enough?" or "They're no angels either!"

In a speech made in Düsseldorf in 1960 Golo Mann expressed his views on this kind of 'neo'-anti-semitism bred of nervousness, thoughtlessness and habit. "We are all more or less anti-semites and yet none of us wanted this terrible crime to happen. None of us is entirely free from the infuriating and anti-rational habit of judging those who belong to a distinct . . . group, not according to their personal natures, their characters or their achievements but simply by asking whether they are Jews, and if they are our immediate reaction is negative." Since this was true of practically all Germans, they all had the duty "to keep a firmer check on their anti-semitic feelings now than they did before the Jewish catastrophe. This is above all a question of will-power and self-discipline . . ."

When this self-discipline breaks down, as in the case of Herr Zind, a high school teacher from Offenburg who exclaimed in a convivial moment that not enough Jews had been gassed, it is probably more a case for the psychiatrist than the public prosecutor. The same is true of those thugs who around the turn of the year 1959–60 smeared swastikas and Nazi slogans over synagogues and Jewish memorials. But the rest of the world allowed itself to be convinced all too easily that this marginal phenomenon proved the continued existence of Nazism in Germany. The Federal Republic experienced the first major crisis of confidence in its short history. From the United States to the Soviet Union spread the doubt as to whether the Germans could ever be induced to behave reasonably and decently. The Soviet Union seized the opportunity to make a great show, in governessy tones, about being the champion of freedom and human dignity and Chancellor Adenauer found no sympathy even among his best friends abroad when he drily observed that the daubing of swastikas was probably the work of badly-behaved teenagers.

It later transpired, after an official investigation of all 'Nazi provocations', that Adenauer's sober diagnosis was right. In every country there is a certain percentage of rascals who get a kick out of giving their fellow-citizens a shock. As soon as we succeed in depriving such people of the feeling that there is something heroic about their nocturnal daubs, the first step has been taken towards putting a stop to their activities.

The trial held in Cologne on 7th February 1960 of the people who defiled a synagogue established that the accused, who had painted swastikas on the walls, had acted out of pure mischief and that there was not a shred of evidence for the theory of 'men behind the scenes', according to which an anti-Jewish organisation was spreading its contagion. Nevertheless the two accused, Strunk and Schönen, succeeded with their stupid pranks in setting half the world's opinion against Germany. The number of photographers and cameramen who rushed from all over the globe to cover this trial bore no relation to the obviously low mental and moral calibre of the accused. Still, it is better to stamp on the smallest beginnings, even if they are little more than practical jokes, than one day to wake up and find oneself engulfed again in an avalanche of guilt.

Anything forbidden has an attraction and thus swastika-daubing quickly spread over half Europe and even as far as the U.S.A. It even appeared in Communist countries, although it was never mentioned officially in order to preserve the impression that the West was the sole abode of incorrigible neo-Nazi elements.

Anyone who still refuses to believe that henceforth Jews cannot finally live peacefully in Germany must at least admit that nowadays an anti-semitic movement is completely devoid of any remotely convincing arguments. They could not even succeed in effectively revising the mindless rubbish that was talked about the inferiority of the Jewish race. The existence of the state of Israel has finally and effectively put paid to this notion. There Jewish farmers, workers and soldiers have proved the stupidity of the picture of a Jew as a purely parasitic creature.

Before the persecution, Germany had a Jewish population of eight hundred thousand; now there are no more than about forty thousand. Other survivors find it impossible to live their lives in Germany again. Ben-Gurion, for years prime minister of Israel, made many visits to the Federal Republic and convinced himself of the determination of the Germans, within the limits possible, to make reparation for the past. Israel, said Ben-Gurion in 1964, should forgive Germany because "Germany today is a different country, if only because it can never again become the Power it once was". During his period of office the prime minister approved some small tokens of reconciliation such as sending the famous Ramat-Gan chamber orchestra to West Germany, although the tour had to be cancelled when it was already arranged due to the intervention of other Israeli politicians. Such incidents may make a rapprochement between the two countries more difficult, but in the end it is every individual Jew who must decide for himself when the time has come for a normal relationship with the Germans. Even Jews who have an open-minded and sympathetic attitude towards the Federal Republic believe that a general reconciliation will only be possible in the next generation.

It has not escaped those who have given serious thought to the causes of German unpopularity that there is a certain resemblance between the German and the Jewish destinies. It is not mentioned here as a cheap attempt to reduce the German debit balance of guilt. The similarity does exist, even if it is contested by one side or the other and it has been noticed for centuries. "We Germans," wrote Carl Zuckmayer, "share with the Jews a certain unpopularity in the world which always distorts other peoples' view of us."

Goethe saw the common ground between Germans and Jews in slightly different terms. He considered both Jews and Germans incapable of surrendering their innate individualism in order to create a harmonious political structure. The individual German, he thought, could achieve more on his own than in the strait-jacket of the state. In contradiction of Chancellor von Müller, Goethe declared on 14th December 1808 that Germany was nothing but that each individual German was worth a great deal, yet the Germans imagined exactly the opposite. Then came the much-quoted sentence: the Germans should be "transplanted and scattered throughout the world . . . in order fully to develop the solid worth which lies in every one of them for the good of all nations".

Goethe recognised that both Jews and Germans had tremendous stamina. Germans, he thought, never give up, "no less than the Jews", because they are such individualists. Goethe still believed as a matter of course in German individualism. "Even without a country," said Goethe when further pursuing his comparison in a later passage, the Germans remained "undiscouraged and strongly united"—both Germans and Jews might be "oppressed but not exterminated". He could never have known that it would be his own people who would undertake an attempt at exterminating the Jews and yet he was right: the attempt failed.

Heine saw the similarity between Germans and Jews as having its origins as far back as the period of the Germanic tribes. In his study of Shakespeare's Jessica (*The Merchant of Venice*) in 1838 he postulated an "inner affinity" between Jews and Teutons. Both were the bitterest enemies of the Romans. In his opinion Palestine could be regarded as the Germany of the East and Germany itself had many of the characteristics of the soil which had nurtured the prophets of the Old Testament. Following in Heine's footsteps Hendrik van Dam, the Secretary General of the Central Jewish Council in Germany made the discovery in 1960 that in the world of the Cold War anti-semitism and anti-germanism generally went hand in hand—in Communist countries, for example.

Both Jews and Germans have long harboured a sense of being an elect. The German language, according to Schiller, will one day "rule the world". In one of his hymns Hölderlin invoked "Germany the Chosen". Foreign writers such as Charles Dickens and Maurice Maeterlinck confirmed this German claim and spoke respectively of "a chosen people" and "the moral conscience of the world". To the Jews the consciousness of being a chosen race has been innate since the earliest days of their historical existence.

It was for long the fate of both Germans and Jews to be held responsible for all the imaginable evil in the world. In both cases—and only here does the parallel begin to have its significance—it has been assumed that the victim of persecution has in a certain measure shared in the guilt, so that his fate—in view of our human imperfection how could it be otherwise—never appears entirely undeserved.

What Goethe once said of the Germans, that they were "so admirable as individuals, so wretched in the mass", has often been said of the Jews. Even during their reign of terror German anti-semites distinguished between the individual and the mass. Hitler said scornfully that every German had "his" Jew whom he wanted to see safe from persecution at all cost. The resemblance goes further. One's existence as a Jew or a German cannot, however hard and often one may try, be cast off like a cloak or changed. German-ness is "as inescapable . . . as hard to shake off", wrote Freidrich Sieburg, "as Jewishness". Outward appearance contributes to this. It is particularly hard for Jews as well as for Germans to 'shed their skin', due to their proneness to marked physical characteristics such as noses, mouths, gait and the colour of eyes and hair. They are easy to recognise, they are conspicuous and consequently they create the impression of being numerous, so numerous in fact that they are like a plague. In the immediate post-war years anyone speaking German in London immediately attracted unfavourable attention. Because of their appearance Jews have long had to submit to the 'music-hall' treatment in many countries.

Similar too is the way in which Jews and Germans react to hos-tility and criticism. If they feel themselves strong, they can be arrogant; if in the minority they incline to react with servility. They oscillate between the two attitudes without finding a just mean. There are very few countries in the world where they are welcome. Even where they are deemed indispensable for their skills, the feeling that they are also a nuisance is never far away. In times of persecu-tion and misfortune both Jews and Germans have learned from long experience that other peoples are not over-inclined to show them pity.

One must beware of overstraining the comparison; but Heine's allusion to the Jewish-German affinity seems to have been confirmed by the state of Israel. With its disciplined army, its unswerving perseverance in the face of a hostile environment and its programme of spartan frugality the young Jewish state has developed virtues which were also long regarded as among the most admirable of the German qualities.

For generations the Jews have patiently borne hostility in almost every country in the world. It is now up to the Germans to practise patient forbearance. Wise Jews, even in times of their greatest affliction, when the injustice of their tormentors was most marked, never failed to examine themselves to discover how far they were responsible for their own misfortune. A similar self-examination is now the inescapable lot of the Germans.

5

THE GERMAN RESISTANCE

The courage, the sacrifices and the failure of the men who plotted against Hitler can only properly be assessed and appreciated by those who know what it means to live under a dictatorship which deploys every means of coercion and deceit. They are in no way conventional story-book heroes and the view of them, put about after the defeat of Germany, as men who were so decent as to have been incapable of ever believing in Hitler was simply false. The stereotype of 1945, according to which a good German should have seen through Hitler and hated him from the beginning, made it easy for those who belittled the German resistance to point to the complicity of individual conspirators in the errors of the Third Reich and to cast doubt on the whole German resistance.

The victims of the 20th July 1944 included not a few members of the Nazi Party, who must at first have felt attracted by Hitler and his movement. The would-be assassin himself, Count Stauffenberg, who planted the bomb in Hitler's Headquarters on the 20th July 1944, regarded his act as an expiation of a long-standing personal and national guilt. For a short while he too had succumbed to Hitler's blandishments: it is on record that on the 30th January 1933 the then Lieutenant Stauffenberg led a torchlight procession whose object was to celebrate the new (Nazi) government of the Reich. Count Stauffenberg, whose ancestors included Gneisenau and Yorck, was sobered by Hitler's criminally irresponsible warmongering and forced to join those who opposed him He was appalled by the idea that twenty years after the 1914–1918 war a madman was exacting yet another immeasurable toll of blood from the German people.

Stauffenberg died with the words: "Long live our sacred fatherland." His death expiates the sins of omission of which he and others may have been guilty. Beyond all petty dispute and calculation Stauffenberg felt the rebellion against Hitler to be a cleansing of Germany's reputation.

Nor was the Mayor of Leipzig, Dr. Karl Goerdeler, one of the best minds of the resistance, a declared enemy of Hitler from 1933 onward; even after Röhm's bloody revolt—which according to one of the over-simplified notions of what constituted a 'decent German' was the final opportunity for turning away from Hitler—he continued in office as Reichs Commissioner for Price Control. In a memorandum which Goerdeler drafted for Hitler in 1935 it was assumed that a war against Poland was inevitable; Goerdeler was presumably one of those Germans who doubted the wisdom of Hitler's Non-Aggression Pact with Poland signed on 26th June 1934. By 30th May 1941 Goerdeler's plan for peace included the retention of the German-Polish frontier as attained in the war. For this reason Communist historians have simply relegated him to the ranks of German imperialists and refuse to make any distinction between him and Hitler; consequently no streets can be named after Goerdeler in the Soviet Zone.

It is to the credit of Goerdeler's widow that she left unaltered a passage in praise of Hitler which, in accordance with the custom of the time, her husband had worked into a speech made on his retirement as Mayor of Leipzig on 21st March 1937. Goerdeler did not fully realise the danger of Hitler until after the outbreak of war, however repellent he may have found some of the previous measures taken by the regime (not the least those directed against the Jews). Even during the war he still considered that he might be able to bring Hitler to reason if he were only allowed to talk to him alone. This is an example of the notion, held even by a German of intelligence and good will, that Hitler had somehow got into bad company and could be put back on the right road by sensible advice—a variant of the less sophisticated attitude of 'If only the Führer knew that this was going on.'

In foreign policy Hitler and the resistance were by no means diametrically opposed; their differences concerned methods rather than aims. They did not share Hitler's megalomania, which eventually developed into a project for expansion as far as the Urals, but a revision of the Treaty of Versailles was in their programme as well as his. The English historian A. J. P. Taylor has observed ironically that the German rebels had wished to eliminate Hitler whilst retaining his conquests; that resistance only began to show itself when there was a danger of Hitler losing the war. This verdict is unjust. On the other hand there were not many Germans who considered the reincorporation of Danzig, the abolition of the Polish corridor or the Austrian *Anschluss* to have been wrong or immoral.

It is a remarkable fact that hardly a single foreign observer finds anything unnatural in the apparently complete lack of a resistance movement in the Soviet Union, whereas the same people have often dismissed as totally inadequate the German attempts at resistance, costing as they did thousands of lives. Everybody assumes the universal silence and conformism in the Soviet state to be inevitable; yet the difficulty for the Germans of avoiding Hitler's clutches is never conceded.

"Many men of the most impeccable views," wrote the American journalist Lochner after several years spent in Germany, "found themselves in the years after 1933 placed in a chamber of horrors which they had entered voluntarily, even with enthusiasm." In the transitional period, as the horror of Hitler's dictatorship filtered through, many Germans were torn between revulsion and admiration, a state of mind which is far more typical of those living under despotism than are either unconditional resistance or unconditional acceptance.

In those days the struggle between good and evil took place within men themselves. Those who still admired the achievement of national unity felt uneasy at the first measures against the Jews; those impressed by the elimination of unemployment were faced with the agonising fact of the persecution of the Christian churches. This is the only explanation of that ambiguity which, to the confusion of foreign historians, was exhibited by many members of the resistance. At first they were partly for Hitler and partly against him, which explains the dubious air surrounding such figures as the Prussian Minister of Finance Johannes Popitz, Dr. Schacht and Admiral Canaris.

With the greatest personal courage Canaris helped many Jews and other victims of persecution to flee; the ill-treatment of a human being, so friends report, could move him to tears; the mere sight of Hitler could frequently reduce him to impotent rage. Yet there are other sides to the character of the Third Reich's chief of counter-intelligence: Canaris was an expert, fascinated by the exercise of his dangerous profession. For years he rendered Hitler great service and his work frequently inspired him to make dubious decisions. To judge from the book *The Tragedy of the German Counter-Intelligence* he seems to have been one of those Germans who, when asked, approved the compulsory wearing by Jews of the Star of David. Canaris knew that inevitably the persecuted Jews were potential saboteurs and spies; in his professional capacity he therefore felt it essential to give them a distinguishing mark, whilst cursing the system which forced him to stoop to such methods. Ultimately, torn between professional ethics and the resistance, he chose the latter and his life ended on the gallows.

Another contradictory figure was Erwin von Witzleben, who approved of the suppression of Röhm's revolt as a cleansing purge and himself perished as a consequence of the 20th July. An equally ambiguous impression is given by Freiherr von Fritsch, who on 30th July 1935 ordered Franz Seldte, president of the *Stahlhelm* (militant ex-serviceman's organisation) to disband his organisation as one suspected of opposition to National Socialism and who was later, as a silent opponent of Hitler, to be ignominiously relieved of his office as Commander-in-Chief of the army. There was one Dr. Schacht, Reichs Minister of Economics, holder of the golden Party badge who wrote to Hitler on 12th November 1932 expressing his wish to see the Weimar system destroy itself and who a few months later started collecting funds for the Third Reich—yet Dr. Schacht was sent to a concentration camp for his resistance to Hitler's hectic re-armament.

At first the promises of National Socialism impressed even Colonel-General Beck, who was forced to commit suicide on 20th July 1944 as one of the leaders of the plot against Hitler. In the spring of 1930 the then Colonel Beck, at a court martial in Ulm, had ranged himself on the side of three Reichswehr officers who had attempted to form Nazi cells in his regiment. Beck approved of re-armament in the first years after Hitler's seizure of power and his nomination as Chief of the Army General Staff was due in no small measure to his attitude at Ulm. The honesty and courage of his subsequent rebellion are all the more estimable since he only joined Hitler's adversaries after a searching scrutiny.

In an office intended by its very nature to prepare for war, at least on the sand-table, Beck passionately opposed all plans for a war. He cried shame on any German officer who did not dissuade Hitler from making war. In his lecture notes for the years 1937 and 1938 Beck boldly rejected war, not only on grounds of expediency, because in his opinion Germany could not win it, but like Count Stauffenberg he was fundamentally opposed to another passage of arms. There is hardly another example in history of a man who by virtue of his office was less fitted to pronounce an unqualified warning against war and yet who did so with unvarying consistency.

It was only after taking part in an extermination operation in the Soviet Union that S.S. Gruppenführer Nebe joined the ranks of Hitler's opponents and there met his death. Finally, as an example of the crisis of conscience that a dictatorship can impose on those who live under it, there is Field Marshal von Kluge: in 1943 he was half won over to a removal of Hitler by force. After the 20th July 1944 he dissociated himself from the abortive rebellion. Shortly before his arrest and suicide Kluge took his leave in a letter of 18th August 1944 which bears shattering witness to the confusion and pressures of that time: "I leave you, my Führer, I who stood closer to you than you may have realised . . ."

Hopeless as it must have seemed on close examination, the selfless action taken by Hans and Sophie Scholl, brother and sister, has from the first, and rightly so, attracted the sympathy and admiration of young people in particular. Anti-Hitler pamphlets were a futile weapon at the time; that they were nevertheless distributed by this pair does not diminish the heroism of their gesture.

As another shining example of resistance there is Count von Galen, Bishop of Münster, who on 6th September 1936 preached against the "crude slavery" of the Gestapo with shorthand-writers sitting in the church. For the bishop to brand as murderers those who destroyed 'useless lives' in sanatoria and mental hospitals was only the beginning of a career of ceaseless and intensified resistance to the Nazi tyranny.

Thomas Mann from his fixed political standpoint was of course incapable of understanding a phenomenon such as the Bishop of Münster. Because Count Galen had at first warned against regarding the advancing Americans, British or Russians as anything but enemies, he was reprimanded by Thomas Mann (who naturally saw the Allies entirely as liberators) for being an "incorrigible priest". The count's words of encouragement addressed to troops leaving for the Russian campaign were also taken amiss. To have expected him to have greeted the advancing Allied armies with joy, simply because he was an opponent of Hitler, was to misunderstand him. Thomas Mann's censure was proof of how hard it was for the Germans to justify their past, not only to the victorious powers but to themselves. In the very hour of affliction a sense of national dignity made it impossible for this prince of the church to align himself on the side of the victors with the agility of many who fell over themselves with zeal to compensate for the past. For men of his stamp, to have been an opponent of Hitler did not mean rejoicing over Germany's defeat.

Those who judge the anti-Hitler conspirators by too harsh standards should not in justice overlook the fact that they were supported neither by their own people nor by anyone abroad. The very loneliness of their struggle increases their stature the more. Hitler's urge to destruction was opposed from outside by a destructive urge of equal intensity. At the end of the first world war President Wilson did at least propose an alleviation of Germany's fate provided that the Germans repudiated Wilhelm II. For those who fought against Hitler there was no such promise. The Allies' demand for unconditional surrender made reality of Goebbels' equation that "Führer and People are one". With biting sarcasm William Shirer declared that it was not that the conspirators missed the bus: "They never even reached the bus-stop."

Previous to Shirer the British historian Wheeler-Bennett had already dealt scornfully with the resistance of the German generals. In his book *The Nemesis of Power* Wheeler-Bennett adduced as proof that the officers' revolt was not a serious affair the fact that the chief defendant, Field Marshal von Witzleben, tried to give the Hitler salute when in the dock before the People's Court. This historian cannot be said to show much comprehension of what the Gestapo terror meant in terms of human agony. Shirer and Wheeler-Bennett made fun of the fact that the German generals only began to take an active part in the struggle against Hitler when it began to look as though he would lose the war. The accusation that the internal resistance was practically dormant as long as Hitler was winning victories is unjust, since in the years when national enthusiasm ran high they were simply unable to muster enough supporters to subvert the widespread apparatus of Hitler's state.

Traces of the lack of comprehension and cynicism with which in the war years the Allies treated the German resistance are still detectable today. By the evening of 20th July 1944 most American newspapers had adopted Hitler's angry description of the instigators of the revolt as a "clique of ambitious officers". It was a convenient formula. It was easily distorted to imply that the rebels had merely sought to cheat the Allies of their victory. The *New York Times*, in a leader written at the time, considered that the bomb which was made to explode in Hitler's headquarters was "an instrument typical of criminals". On 1st August 1944 the *New York Herald Tribune* scoffed: "Let the generals kill the corporal or vice-versa—both would suit us." This sentence epitomised the view that there simply are no good Germans, but in the early years the concentration camps were filled exclusively with Germans. As the Jesuit, Father Delp, was led to the gallows he said with a smile to the prison chaplain: "In a few minutes I shall know more than you." Germany produced such martyrs in great number.

People risked their lives to hide Jews. Thousands of the persecuted and oppressed were saved by their fellow-countrymen. Flamboyant personalities such as Reichs Bishop Müller were laid low through their unrelenting internal opposition. Again and again Hitler felt the icy rejection of his warlike adventures. Many a German general despairingly sought death on the battlefield; every person who turned against Hitler exposed not only himself but his family to danger by doing so.

It is to the credit of the Bundeswehr that it has done its utmost to reconcile decent men from both sides of the controversy over the resistance, although a silent conflict between the holders of extremist views had to be settled before the 20th July 1944 could be unequivocally rooted in the consciousness of both new and old soldiers through the naming of the barracks after victims of the Third Reich. The contrast between those soldiers who had obeyed Hitler up to the very end of the war and those others who had wanted to remove Hitler might have caused discord in barracks. There were officers of the new army who were concerned that an attitude of unreserved approval of the conspirators might undermine military discipline. For years the advocates of both parties were engaged in debating the ethics of a defiance of orders. It was argued at great length that it cannot be left to the discretion of every individual soldier to decide when he might step out of the ranks and refuse to obey a command.

As awareness grew of the murderous aspects of National Socialism, the fewer became the doubts as to the justification of the resistance movement of 20th July 1944, even though in a formal sense it involved breach of an oath of allegiance and disobedience. Whoever rose up against the criminal progress of the Third Reich was entitled to honourable consideration in the name of a higher justice, whether in a legalistic sense his behaviour were impeccable or not.

With his keen eyes for intrinsic merit Winston Churchill had already, in the midst of the war, expressed his respect for Field Marshall Rommel as a commander—even before he swung over to the side of Hitler's opponents.

The way in which the late Field Marshal Rommel has been honoured in the barracks of the new German Army is proof of what care has been taken at the same time to spare the feelings of that section of the German people which believed in Hitler up to no matter what point in time. Until his moment of insight Rommel was one of those who put faith and hope in the Third Reich. For a while he was, even though unwillingly, the Nazis' star general. His resistance against Hitler's final military lunacy, for which he paid with his life, is a symbol of the shocked awakening of the Germans out of a period of incredible misguidance. A personality such as Rommel's is best suited to reconcile the principles of both well-intentioned obedience and well-intentioned refusal to obey and to put a stop to the arid dispute between the so-called oath-keepers and oath-breakers.

After the 20th July 1944 nearly ten thousand people were involved in the investigations and persecutions. By the end of the war five thousand conspirators had been executed, including seven hundred officers. There were also about ten thousand Germans who, after May 1945, were called to account by Allied or German courts as Nazi criminals. It seems more than coincidence that the active opponents of Hitler should have numerically balanced out the actual criminals of National Socialism. The equilibrium of good and evil, of reason and unreason reveals the supreme crisis of conscience into which men are plunged under every form of tyranny.

6

VICTORS AND VANQUISHED

The violent phenomenon of Nazism and the years of war and occupation from 1939 to 1954 have inevitably affected all views once held of Germany. The nature and the acts of the Third Reich form part of the outside world's image of Germany, although there is a notable difference in the way the eastern and western blocs have reacted to Germany's immediate past: in the West a willingness to forgive and forget the memories of Nazism contrasts with the Communists tireless efforts to continue exploiting them.

As early as the first months of the war the question was being asked in enemy countries, whether the villainous Hitler was a typically German product or whether he was to be regarded as the kind of dreadful accident which can befall every country at one time or another in its history. Curiously enough it was Stalin who was the first to affirm that a clear dividing line should be drawn between Hitler and the German people. In contrast to Roosevelt, who equated Hitler and his clique with the whole German people, Stalin declared on 23rd February 1942 that history taught us that "Hitlers come and go, but the German people, the German state remains". The Communists who entered Berlin in the wake of the Red Army took care to paste this very reasonable sentence on every hoarding; later it became clear that only those Germans who were willing to switch at once from 'Heil Hitler' to 'Heil Moscow' could expect forgiveness.

In the West the process took the opposite course. Roosevelt considered Hitler and the Germans in one category. As a student in Heidelberg he had found the Germans dreary, philistine and provincial and by the time that Hitler was in power he made no further effort to distinguish between good and bad Germans. Only at elections did he assure German-American voters that he greatly prized the German virtues. In his 'soup-kitchen letter' of 26th

August 1944 Roosevelt amused himself at the prospect of the beaten German supermen queuing three times daily for their soup ration.

By the end of the war Churchill, on the other hand, was taking up a different attitude from Roosevelt and no longer thought that the removal of Hitler would simply represent the triumph of good over evil. Churchill was disturbed by the concentration of power which the Communists had managed to build up on the very doorstep of the British Isles. For Churchill Greater Germany had grown intolerably large—but now the dismemberment of Germany was going too far. West Germany at least must be kept as a dam against bolshevism. For this reason Churchill was soon prepared to assure the Germans that they would not be forced to bear Hitler branded on their foreheads forever as an indelible mark of Cain: Hitler was a disaster less for Germany than for the whole human race.

The more western politicians made use of Stalin's formula that there was a difference between Hitler and the German people, the more the Soviets, irritated by the successful creation of the Federal Republic under their very noses, were reluctantly forced to hark back to Roosevelt's equation of Hitler and Germany as one. The roles had been exchanged. From pure political expediency one side was now prepared to concede to the Germans a certain moral standing which the other side was obliged to deny. The ease with which national attitudes are manipulated for political purposes could hardly be more clearly illustrated.

But even in the West, however much the Germans may be valued as allies, a great many people have still not forgotten about Hitler. There still exists a broad spectrum of common reservations about the Germans which is shared by East and West. In the view of others the Soviet Union still enjoys the enormous moral advantage of having fought on more or less the right side during the war. When the battle of Stalingrad was raging, Americans, British and Frenchmen were praying for the Soviets to win. The knowledge that in the ultimate life-and-death struggle the Russians were on their side has impressed itself deeply into the consciousness of the West. Thanks to the war, the image of the enemy is still that of the Germans, even though there has since been a radical change of alignment.

This state of mind, with its obvious contrast to the present pattern of alliances, can emerge in unexpected ways. It only needs a pretext —such as the arrest of the Yugoslav Vracaric by the Munich police on 2nd November 1961. Vracaric had been on the German "Wanted" list since 1941, when in Agram he and two other civilians had attacked three Luftwaffe men from behind, and two of whom had died. Immediately the old wartime solidarity formed up against the German action. The Germans were once more the enemy. There was not a newspaper of any importance which was prepared to condemn Vracaric's action, although in international law it ranked unquestionably as murder. The elimination of German soldiers, whether achieved regularly or illegally was in every case an act of heroism. This attitude, the criterion which had grown up in World War II, had retained its validity in spite of all the intervening shifts of circumstance.

The other side of the story, of course, is the stupidity of the German police in arresting the Yugoslav at all. Under the treaties signed with the victorious powers a trial of Vracaric was impossible, making his arrest in any case pointless. A country such as West Germany, which must itself hope for the past to be forgotten and forgiven, should never have allowed Vracaric to be arrested. Nevertheless, the most remarkable aspect of the whole affair was the immediate reawakening of wartime memories which united East and West across the Iron Curtain in a unanimous protest against the attitude of the German police.

There are other and more important aspects of the unbroken wartime accord between East and West. Both are firmly determined that Germany shall never again be allowed to make the decision between war and peace. German sovereignty today is restricted by certain rules of the road which allow one-way driving only. The mistrust of the victor powers of both East and West is reflected in the alliances which have been concluded with both halves of divided Germany, by which both sides exercise a check on any German initiative. No one on either side has the slightest intention of allowing a reappearance of the German Reich in its old 'glory' and menace.

Chief among the feelings of unease which determine people's attitude to the Germans in times of crisis is still the idea of the German peril. The fear of being dragged by Germany into a new war is equally alive and creates a form of agreement between East and West which has survived their post-war discord.

When on 17th June 1953 a rebellion broke out in the Soviet Zone, Washington displayed hardly less anxiety than Moscow. The West only began to applaud the East German freedom fighters when it became clear that Soviet armoured forces had the rebellion well under control. American newspapers anxiously posed the question as to whether Germany was not about to plunge the world into war for the third time in the century.

Secretary of State Dulles, so detested by the East as the original 'brinkman' and the man who was going to "roll back" communism in eastern Europe, made a speech on Easter Monday 1957 in which he modified his earlier slogans about liberation—which were apparently not meant to have been taken seriously in any case. The United States, he said, was not contemplating the incitement of "massive rebellion" behind the Iron Curtain. For dissatisfied Germans in the Soviet Zone Dulles' exposition of his position clearly meant that the United States were not prepared to risk a clash with the Soviet Union on the East Germans' behalf.

Under these circumstances it does not need much imagination to realise the degree of embarrassment caused to the western Powers by German demands for the restoration of the 1937 frontiers. The Soviet Union has declared any claim for a revision of the Oder-Neisse Line to be a casus belli. The West, in attempting to woo their new German allies, have taken refuge in the relatively harmless doctrine of 'postponement', according to which the frontier question will be settled in due course when the moment has arrived for the conclusion of a peace treaty. Only General de Gaulle has coolly invited the Federal Republic to reconcile itself to the status quo. If American and British statesmen express themselves rather more discreetly this does not mean that they too do not regard Germany's territorial losses as a kind of punishment which the Germans must accept. Any difference between East and West in their attitude to German revisionism is in fact—at least at the moment of writing—only detectable with a magnifying glass.

The feat which German foreign policy is required to accomplish is to stop the hostile pressures from East and West from meeting in a clash across Germany. The outside world is afraid of a war being sparked off over Germany: the German equivalent of this fear is that the victors of 1945 might, in order to remove a potential war-risk, unite again and re-impose a four-power control of Germany. Whether this occurs depends on the success of the Soviet Union in convincing the western Powers, by tireless harping on the memories of Nazism, of the undiminished German peril and in proving that a system of direct supervision of the Germans, as practised in the Soviet Zone, has definite advantages.

The differing influences which the Germans exert on the victor Powers' current policy towards Germany bears a certain resemblance to the varying impressions which the Germans left behind after their spell as an occupying power from 1939 to 1945. Confusion at once arises because the thesis that a country which has once experienced German occupation can only regard the Germans with detestation has proved, despite everything, to be inaccurate. In the June 1962 number of *Life* magazine a Greek woman declared in a letter to the editor that no country which had ever groaned beneath the German jackboot would ever lift a finger in defence of West Berlin. If this Greek woman's assertion is correct, there ought to be much greater sympathy for the Germans in Great Britain and much less in France than there actually is. After the historians' congress held in July 1962 in Warsaw, Vladimir Dedijer, the (since disgraced) biographer of Tito came away with the impression that the Poles, who experienced the German occupation regime in positively hellish form, seemed to hate the Germans least of all the once-occupied countries—"because they have realised that hate alone leads nowhere". In France the comparatively tolerable German occupation favoured the healing of old wounds, once the first reaction of hatred had spent itself.

When in September 1939 the German army attacked Poland, it entered regions which had already experienced German occupation twenty five years previously and once again the appearance of German troops brought with it a rapid deterioration in living conditions. Memories of the years of suffering between 1914 and 1918 were mingled with the disastrous events of the present. Bombs, deportation, ruined houses, hunger and oppression seemed to be the inevitable accompaniment to the sight of German troops. In both wars German attempts to make attack and occupation appear to be the result of other peoples' war guilt failed completely.

Since hatred is an old and trusty weapon of war, 1939 saw the Allies harking straight back to the old atrocity stories of World War I, at least to those which had not been totally discredited. Imperial Germany had tried without noticeable effect to defend itself against accusations that German soldiers had hacked off the hands of Belgian children or converted corpses into soap. Hitler concluded from this that lies could not be fought with denials but only with bigger lies. In its turn the German propaganda apparatus, under the direction of Joseph Goebbels, deluged the rest of the world with stories of the bestial misdeeds committed by the enemy. Goebbels had no compunction, when the war was only a few months old, in making the British prime minister responsible for sinking an American ship carrying women and children, which in reality had been struck (in error) by a German torpedo.

In World War I much of the bestial behaviour attributed to the Germans was pure invention. Allied propaganda portrayed the Germans as brutes who had to be destroyed by a concerted effort for the good of mankind. The German as barbarian was the recurrent theme of a number of books by Arnold Toynbee, for instance *The German Terror*, which began appearing in massive editions in 1917. The shelling of hospitals, abuse of the Red Cross flag, mutilation of prisoners, raping of women and the incineration of children and old people were all, according to Toynbee, everyday aspects of the German method of waging war.

In its positively touching concern to refute even the most wildly improbable of the foreign atrocity stories, the German High Command, in the middle of World War I, invited the Norwegian author Björn Björnson to make an extensive journey throughout the German-occupied territories. He described his experiences in a book entitled *The German Character*. Many of his observations remained equally valid in World War II. Björnson had no intention of letting himself be misused for propaganda purposes; his book is by no means an unqualified paean of praise for wartime Germany. He found that the German still suffered from an absurdly exaggerated respect for ranks and titles and that the combination of an arrogant officer class and the parade-ground bark of non-commissioned officers was as unsavoury as ever. The perpetually schoolmasterly tone of the Germans got on his nerves everywhere—none of the countries under German occupation were spared it. He approved, however, of the frank and courageous way that junior officers expressed themselves, which was greatly preferable to the cowardly, servile tone used by most civilians.

It is somewhat embarrassing for a German of today to read in this book by a Norwegian how in World War I the Jews in Russia greeted the German troops as friends and saviours. Jewish traders felt perfectly safe when they hung up a sign in their shop-windows reading in German "Jewish Shop". Whenever the Russians recaptured a village from the Germans they hanged the Jews, if Björnson is to be believed, as punishment for collaboration with the Germans.

Generally speaking this Norwegian writer pronounced favourably on the behaviour of German troops in the occupied territories. They were not deliberately destructive. There was however one characteristic, which was also noticeable in World War I and which led to serious trouble: the chilling German passion for order. The German, whom Björnson described as fanatically orderly, hated irregular partisan warfare. The German was no guerrilla and wanted to wage war according to fixed rules. Fighting without uniform and without standard weapons drove him to fury. A similar attitude was observable among German troops in World War II.

Everywhere, Björnson found, the Germans strove to bring conditions of order to the countries they occupied. Often it was merely a case of the orderly distribution of scarcity. In Belgium German doctors were able to reduce the infant mortality rate. In the factories German officials with their measuring-rods could be seen checking that each Belgian worker had his statutory area of working-space. The same degree of German efficiency, however, was used in shipping Belgian workers off to Germany. Björnson concluded that there was no doubt that the Germans were in the main well-meaning: they simply had to realise that no country welcomes intruders.

Immediately after the defeat of 1918 numerous Germans sought an explanation for the boundless hatred which imperial Germany had succeeded in arousing throughout the world. In his book *Mass-Madness* Kurt Baschwitz came to the conclusion that the hatred of Germany engendered during World War I was only explicable as a kind of spiritual disease similar to that which accompanied the witch-hunts of the Middle Ages. Any attempt at exoneration was therefore hopeless and no rational means were of any effect in dispelling the "anti-German miasma". Baschwitz had sufficient insight to see that envy of Germany's more advanced economic and social structure was often an important cause of anti-German feeling.

How small is the link between reason and sympathy was demonstrated by Baschwitz with examples of the double standard used by world public opinion when judging similar events. In World War I the French carried out executions for collaboration with the enemy. The neutral press considered in this case that the French were justified in taking such drastic action. When the Germans executed Miss Edith Cavell in Brussels for abuse of the Red Cross, this measure was violently condemned by the neutral press. Baschwitz mentions a further example of the inconsistency of national sentiment. In World

War I the Germans were comparatively popular in Ireland—but only as a corollary of Irish hatred of England. The same, indirect, triangular friend-foe relationship was also to be found in World War II.

Even though it gradually became clear after 1918 that the Germans had neither hacked the hands off Belgian children nor converted dead soldiers into soap, it was still widely believed as a result of the accumulated resentments of two world wars and two German occupations that the Germans had almost without exception behaved like monsters in the countries which they had occupied for the second time in two generations. No attempt has yet been made from the German side to impose a more balanced view of this sombre picture, which still overshadows other countries' relations with Germany.

The occupying power tends to regard its presence in a foreign country as unobjectionable, often even as a piece of good fortune for the people concerned. Even General de Gaulle has harboured this illusion of the victor: in his *Memoirs* he describes how German office-holders greeted the entry of the French occupation forces with enthusiasm. Many German politicians mentioned by de Gaulle in this connection actually had considerable trouble later in reducing to 'decent' proportions the extreme pro-French enthusiasm—amounting at times to separatism—ascribed to them by de Gaulle.

Those soldiers who enjoyed their time in occupied countries are all too prone to come to the false conclusion that the local population were equally happy. After the war many German soldiers trustingly revisited their wartime French and Belgian billets and were disappointed when their enthusiasm for a reunion was not generally shared!

Even though a period of occupation by its very nature is hardly likely to leave behind pleasant impressions, it is nevertheless wrong to assume that the German soldiers attacked these countries in a spirit of brimming hatred. In reality Hitler succeeded in setting the German war machine on the march with surprisingly little hatred in the minds of the troops. Hitler, after all, came to power with the help of a number of propitiatory and thoroughly un-nationalistic slogans. A front-line veteran of World War I such as he, he repeated on many occasions, who had been almost blinded in a gas attack, should surely be the first to appreciate the blessings of peace. Not even the German attack on the Soviet Union was made in a spirit of hatred. There was not in any case time to generate a spirit of animosity because right up to the eve of hostilities the Hitler-Stalin pact was still in force. The mood of 'Gott strafe England', which originally had diffused itself almost without official encouragement, refused to re-appear in World War II in spite of the efforts of Nazi propaganda.

It is altogether a mistake to assume that Hitler had a definite plan for the subjugation and exploitation of the occupied countries of western Europe. In the West he hoped for a while to win sympathy. The orders which he issued for the protection of cultural monuments and civilians made people believe that he wanted to appear as a lenient conqueror. Western Europe was fortunate enough—if that is the correct term—in having the war break over it with the speed of a sudden thunderstorm. Brutality, of the kind which is almost unavoidable in long drawn-out fighting, was nowhere evident—there was hardly time. The armistice did not destroy the physical substance of the conquered countries and the casualties on both sides were relatively low. Collaboration between the occupying forces and the population seemed possible, for a time at any rate.

In the east, on the other hand, Hitler considered that the violent clash of two opposing ideologies would exclude any form of *rapprochement* or collaboration. His extravagant plans for territorial annexation were based on a policy of colonisation and enslavement and contained no provision for collaboration or even fraternisation. Even in the East, however, Hitler's occupation policy cannot simply be reduced to a common denominator of planned subjugation. His considerations were at first of a purely military character. He had made a careful study of Napoleon's disastrous winter campaign outside Moscow and his first concern therefore was to bring the war to a conclusion. But a victory in the East, since he was convinced that the enemy would fight with extreme fanaticism, could only be achieved by the use of an absolutely merciless kind of warfare. Hitler intended to settle the details of occupation policy after he had won his battle. He overlooked the fact that the unleashing of violent warfare in itself created a situation which inevitably imposed a pattern of relationship between the invaders and the local population.

When victory could not be achieved quickly enough, Hitler had recourse to a series of contradictory improvisations. He gave carte blanche to a Party tyrant such as Erich Koch, Reichs Commissioner for the Ukraine, to rule with unbridled harshness. Simultaneously Alfred Rosenberg, Reichs Minister for Occupied Eastern Europe, was trying to win the loyalty of the populations of eastern Europe. In many Ukrainian villages the inhabitants had greeted the advancing German troops with bread and salt, a gesture whose significance should not be over-estimated, but which nevertheless indicated that some sort of collaboration might be possible. Rosenberg wanted to disband the collective farms and satisfy the peasants with a distribution of land. The experts opposed this with the view that a disruption of the collective farms was impractical in wartime—there would be too great a drop in yield. Whilst Rosenberg was organising village entertainments to amuse the Ukrainians, other Party functionaries were dragging their last cow out of the byre.

Throughout the years of the occupation of eastern Europe Hitler himself pursued a zigzag course. When the winter took the German army by surprise without any proper equipment, they lacked not only ear-muffs and skis but also a plan for dealing with the occupied countries in times of hardship. All the arrogant talk about the sub-human Russians was silenced by the blows dealt by the gravely underestimated enemy. It was obvious to the peoples of eastern Europe that only stark necessity now forced the Germans to adopt an official policy of concessions. Slav volunteers, called *Hiwis*[1] for short, soon became a permanent feature of every German unit in Russia.

Goering's notorious remark of 4th October 1942, that if anyone in Europe was to go hungry then it would not be the Germans, was repeatedly quoted by enemy propaganda to increase anti-German feeling in the occupied countries, but it quite needlessly obscured the efforts of the German nutritional experts to secure at least subsistence rations for the occupied countries. Incidentally the full version of Goering's statement ran as follows: The peoples of the German-occupied countries "shall not, as far as we can avoid it, go hungry. But if the supply position is endangered through enemy action, everyone must know that wherever else people may go hungry, it shall not be in Germany". On this point recent research—as in Toynbee's *Hitler's Europe*, for instance—is worthy of note. It has shown that not even in eastern Europe could it be said that the Germans followed a policy of deliberate under-nourishment of the local populations. According to Toynbee Allied officials were amazed when they examined the state of health of the population after the German armies had withdrawn. It was better than could have been

[1] *Hiwi* =a contracted form of the word *Hilfsfreiwilliger*, meaning 'auxiliary volunteer'.

presumed from the indignation expressed in other countries at the German policy of starvation. Many a German farmer sent to eastern Europe had seen to it that the unfortunate population was spared the worst.

Simultaneously, of course, there was ruthless exploitation. Relations worsened as the war dragged on and Germany needed more and more foreign workers for her arms industry. At first volunteers came forward. A victorious Germany exerted a certain attraction and offered better living conditions than were to be found in the neighbouring countries. Later the unceasing bombing attacks removed any attraction that Germany might have had for foreign workers. Reichs Commissioner Fritz Sauckel, who had to get labour to Germany at all costs, soon developed a system of conscription, fraud and coercion which turned into something indistinguishable from slavery. Influenced by memories of this press-gang system people have forgotten that in general the Germans, considering all the difficulties produced by wartime conditions, did their best to ensure tolerable living and working conditions for foreign workers. The prosperous Federal Republic of today has in the meantime discovered how hard it is to accommodate a few hundred thousand foreign labourers satisfactorily. To treat them all fairly would undoubtedly have strained the resources of other countries under similar conditions.

When the German soldier marched to war he carried in his knapsack *The Ten Commandments of Warfare*. In turn they bade him spare the man who surrendered, respect the Red Cross, treat wounded humanely, respect churches and monuments and only to exact reprisals on express order. On the western front these rules were largely observed. On the eastern front a more pitiless form of war was waged from the beginning. The true picture of the German occupation from 1939 to 1945 has been obscured by the understandable need of the liberated countries to secure themselves a good place in the queue for reparations. Details which would have brightened the general picture of the occupation years were suppressed. "German guilt," said the French expert on German studies, Count Robert d'Harcourt, "is the Allies' moral bastion." Whole nations pressed forward to receive financial restitution for their heroism and suffering and because terrible things had happened under the Germans, their claims were interpreted liberally. No one wanted to say a good word for the Germans, for fear of being accused of collaboration. Thus was recorded an image of the occupation of unrelieved drabness and shocking cruelty which, although not deliberately falsified, is certainly one-sided.

Three examples of the German occupation—the Soviet Union, Poland and France—illustrate how the Germans behaved as an occupying power. In Poland Hitler showed how he proposed to subjugate the whole of eastern Europe. No other occupied country experienced such brutal treatment. Murder became an official instrument of policy. The Governor-General of Poland, Hans Frank, one of the most repulsive products of National Socialism, was interviewed on his appointment by the *Völkischer Beobachter* and had this to say about it: "If I were to put up a poster for every seven Poles shot, the forests of Poland would not be sufficient to supply the paper for those posters". In a government session of 16th December 1941 devoted to the Jewish question he declared: "The Jews are a menace and they eat too much. We have approximately 2.5 million of them in the Government-General and their near relatives probably bring the figure up to 3.5 million. We can't shoot 3.5 million and we can't poison them but we will take action that will end in their extermination, action connected with a major operation which is being planned in the Reich. Poland must be as free of Jews as Germany is."

To the Germans who were outraged by the Morgenthau Plan the Allies could with justice pose the question whether, six years before, they had protested against the brutal treatment of the Poles and the Jews. Every eighth Pole lost his life as a consequence of the war and the occupation. Hitler personally ordered the entire Polish population to be earmarked as "the slaves of the Greater German Empire". They were to be reduced to the level of menials. The extermination of the Polish intelligentsia was planned in detail and a third of them actually killed.

The tragedy of the Polish Jews passed all imagining. Already maltreated by the pre-war Polish republic, when the Germans invaded they went through hell. It is impossible to feel anything but horror and shame when reading the report of S.S. Major-General Stroop, written with the coldness of a junior book-keeper, on the liquidation of the rebellious Warsaw ghetto. With overwhelmingly superior forces, 56,065 Jews were "seized and confirmed killed". To this figure, Stroop went on, should be added "those Jews who were killed by explosion, fire, etc., but who could not be numerically accounted for". For sheer bureaucratic smugness this report is one of the most revolting documents produced by the de-humanised military mind.

As is known, the Soviet Union also took part in the overthrow of Poland. She waited until Germany had occupied half of Poland and then secured her share of the booty. The Red Army's advance into eastern Poland was ostensibly caused by the White Russian and Ukrainian minorities asking for Soviet protection against the advancing Wehrmacht. When the Germans objected, Moscow suppressed this curious statement with its dubious implications for the durability of the Hitler-Stalin pact. In Moscow on 28th September 1939 the foreign ministers Molotov and von Ribbentrop signed a pompous declaration of peaceful aims which made the French and the British responsible for the continuation of the war.

Stalin's calculation that he could divert Hitler's war machine westwards seemed at first to be correct. The Soviet Union gained a breathing-space which was violently broken off by the German attack on 22nd June 1941. Hitler justified this step with the assertion that Stalin had been merely biding his time to pounce on a war-weakened Germany. There is no proof of this intention, although Soviet troops were conspicuously massed around the borders of the German sphere of influence. Here again, as in all cases of disputed war-guilt, since there is no prospect of an objective assessment one can do no more than ask: Who fired the first shot? The answer was Germany.

This war between two Powers, which expanded into an ideological war, contained the inherent danger that like all wars of faith it would lead to atrocities. The Soviet leadership justified their merciless tactics by declaring that every means was justified in repelling an aggressor who had violated a treaty. A further reason was Stalin's need to avoid at all costs any form of concord between the German army and the Russian population. Only by generating an intense hatred of the Wehrmacht could the hard-pressed Red Army hope to win.

At that time the most rabidly distorted view of the Germans was propagated by the author Ilya Ehrenburg. In his memoirs *Men, Years and Life*, published in 1963 by the Moscow literary magazine *Novy Mir* Ehrenburg depicted the advance of German troops into Russia. He reported a kolkhoz peasant woman as saying that resistance to these motor-borne, brilliantly uniformed, chocolate-eating German soldiers was pointless. Ehrenburg tried to combat this widespread attitude of resignation by writing pamphlets. He wanted to demolish the respect which the Red Army men felt for Germany as they admired the evidence of *kultura* in the form of German watches, cigarette lighters, books and cameras. Hate should take its place.

"Our hatred," writes Ehrenburg, "grew all the greater because they look like human beings, they laugh, they stroke a dog or a horse . . . they are . . . disguised as human beings." It was absurd to talk of the "other" Germany, of a Germany of workers and peasants—to Ehrenburg all Germans were alike. "Lanky and ugly, with square, brutish skulls, with eyes that seemed like murky glass, they goose-stepped onward, these beer-swilling, chicken-guzzling, duelling supermen . . . these Prussians, Saxons and Bavarians."

In Ehrenburg's book *The War*, published in Moscow in 1944, the Germans are "clockwork automata". Ehrenburg substantiated the order to kill them on sight by citing atrocity reports based not only on the horrors of the time but on texts borrowed from World War I. The "boiled human heads" put in an appearance again. According to Ehrenburg the Germans tortured girls and in Vitebsk they "buried old women alive". On 14th June 1940, when watching the German troops enter Paris he claimed to have seen "the blood of crushed children" still sticking to the tank tracks. He regarded German sentimentality as a lie: "They kill Russian children and then send sweets to their own children."

In 1944 German propaganda even improved on Ehrenburg's outbursts. They attributed to him the proposal that soldiers of the Red Army should capture blonde German women and drink their blood. Ehrenburg was unquestionably one of those responsible for inciting a degree of hatred unique in any theatre of World War II. (One should not forget, of course, that at the same time the German propaganda machine was busily exploiting the theory of the Soviet peoples as an 'inferior race'.)

It was the task of the Soviet partisans, by means of assassination and sabotage, continually to exacerbate the tension between the population and the occupation forces. A German army forced to carry out a constant series of acts of retribution and reprisal would inevitably win back to Stalin's side even those who had been disillusioned with bolshevism and were toying with the idea of collaborating with the Germans. Chaos became the ally of the Soviets. The fact that Stalin stirred up hate in the German rear to assist the Red

Army cannot of course absolve the German Wehrmacht for the savagery of some of their methods.

When dealing with a country such as the Soviet Union it is probably hopeless to expect any form of agreement over mutual attribution of guilt. Chancellor Adenauer was made aware of this when he visited Moscow in 1955 to seek a just settlement of outstanding differences. In reply to the Soviets' unsparingly frank publication of the balance sheet of German crimes, he said on 10th September 1955: "It is true that much wrong was done. But it is also true that the Russian armies then—as a counter-blow, I grant you—advanced into Germany and that in Germany many terrible acts were also committed." The Soviets rejected this German counter-claim. Khrushchev simply denied that Red Army troops had ever committed crimes on German soil. He stuck to the line taken at the Nuremberg trials, according to which not a word might be said about any criminal acts which might have been perpetrated against the Germans.

The Soviet Union is the only Power which has built its policy towards Germany on the refusal to forget Hitler's crimes. Not a month goes by without the Nazi period being recalled to the Germans of the Federal Republic—for in Soviet terminology they are the only dangerous Germans.

For the Soviets it was a great disappointment that by spring 1945 the forces of victorious Communism only reached as far as the line of the rivers Elbe, Werra and Fulda, since according to a long-held Soviet theory the conquest of Germany would have guaranteed the triumph of Communism throughout the world. The Soviet leaders stare at the free half of Germany with that same mixture of hope and fear as that with which they had regarded Germany in the year 1920. At that time they considered that a shift to their side by Germany would have tipped the balance of world power in their favour. Since, however, they have failed to make Communism attractive enough to draw West Germany into their sphere in the wake of East Germany, the free and western-orientated bastion which is the Federal Republic must be brought down by other means. It does not need much imagination to understand why the Federal Republic of Germany, founded with American aid, is such an embarrassment to the Russians. The appeal for reunification necessarily calls the legitimacy of the Soviet Zone Communist state into question. Free elections and self-determination as demanded by Bonn would in practice result in the dissolution of the ramshackle German Democratic Republic.

For Moscow the West German state, flourishing by comparison with East Germany, is a permanent denial of their propaganda speeches about Communist progress. Because the Soviet leaders are aware of the difference between the indigence of East Germany and the 'golden' West, they propagate an exclusively favourable image of the Eastern Zone state: according to Moscow the G.D.R. is the very home of freedom, justice and social welfare.

To discredit the Federal Republic there are well-stocked archives which the Communists seized when they captured Berlin. They contain incriminating material which is supposed to prove the dubious character of West Germany's governing class. The Soviet Union continues to pursue a solo version of the Nuremberg trials. Documents are constantly being published which prove that the Federal Republic is simply an uninterrupted sequel to the Third Reich. The denunciation of leading figures is very carefully timed: first they allow someone such as for instance the West German Judge Fränkel[1] to climb the ladder of his astonishing career in peace, until he reaches the rank of Attorney-General. Then they attack him, with the well-aimed publication of details of death sentences for which he was responsible in the Nazi period—and lay him low. The wicked West German is simply a necessity for Soviet foreign policy. On 31st August 1961 Khrushchev stated during the German general election that a vote for Adenauer was a vote for a new Hitler and that the Federal Chancellor had inscribed on his banners the same slogans "with which Hitler came to power and unleashed World War II". As early as 6th April 1960 Bonn had been obliged to defend itself against the use of such provocative and misleading comparisons. *Izvestiya* even went so far as to maintain that on a visit to America Chancellor Adenauer had personally drawn swastikas in a visitors' book.

The Eichmann trial revealed the criteria by which the Soviet government judged the German people. The Communists soon lost interest in the trial, because contrary to expectations men in high office in the Federal Republic were mentioned only marginally or

---

[1] According to statements from East German sources it transpired that in 1942 and 1943, in a number of trivial cases such as petty larceny committed by conscripted foreign workers, Fränkel as a judge of appeal in Leipzig had not exercised his right to reduce punishment but had confirmed the severe sentences meted out by special Summary Courts, which were often tantamount to sentence of death.

not at all. Nor was the Soviet Union very anxious to entertain any claims for better treatment for the Russian Jews, who have not had the best treatment in late years. When evidence was given of mass murders of Jews in Russia, the Soviet press took a very reserved line. Perhaps they did not want to offend Nasser, who saw in the Eichmann trial an international enhancement of the status of Israel and made the Egyptian press write off the whole story in a few lines. Moscow is clearly not interested in uncovering the past unless there is political capital to be made out of it in the present.

For a long time western politicians have been trying to discover whether the Soviet leadership—aside from considerations of day-to-day expediency—is really afraid of the West German state and its twelve divisions. On 24th November 1961 Khrushchev compared the Bundeswehr with a lap-dog barking at the Soviet elephant. In his book *Conversations with Stalin* the former Jugoslav party leader Milovan Djilas reported that Stalin had once predicted to him that a beaten Germany would quickly recover and would be on her feet again in twelve or fifteen years. Djilas described how, as Stalin said this, he rolled up his sleeves, took up a boxing stance and imitating a German he cried: "We shall recover in fifteen or twenty years, and then we'll have another go at it."

Eden wrote in his memoirs that during the Geneva summit conference in the summer of 1955, Bulganin and Krushchev were at pains to recall how many of their own relatives had been killed in the war, to prove how lively was the Russians' memory of the German attack which had penetrated as far as Stalingrad before being halted. Eden was impressed. Hé tried to explain to his Soviet vis-à-vis that the alliances which the West were concluding with the Federal Republic were intended precisely to neutralise the dangerous aspects of the German military machine. This argument did not convince Bulganin and Khrushchev. They thought that if German militarism had to be kept in check then it was better not to allow the Germans to have another army at all.

In Geneva Bulganin and Khrushchev pointed to the tragic balance-sheet of the Soviet-German struggle: 70,000 Russian villages were destroyed by enemy action. It was therefore no wonder that the Russian people should demand that their government keep a watchful eye on the Germans. This, on the face of it, is entirely unreasonable, since the Soviet Union is a world power, which according to the eminently credible assertions of her leaders is capable at any moment of turning tiny West Germany into a nuclear graveyard. Whether under these circumstances they themselves believe their own cries of warning about the 'warlike and aggressive' Germans seems doubtful. Only its connection with the American war potential gives the Bundeswehr a certain military significance, in which case the danger is an American and not a German danger; but the Soviets are determined not to admit that their thesis of the ever-present danger of an independent German attack on Russia is meaningless as long as the American government retains control of its nuclear weapons.

Adenauer frequently tried to satisfy what he called the Soviet Union's "subjective need for security". He emphasised the purely defensive character of the West German army, but the 'German peril' nevertheless remains a Soviet article of faith which nothing will shake. On 21st June 1962, the anniversary of Hitler's attack on Russia, *Izvestiya* wrote that even though only a little remained of the old arrogant Germany of the Kaiser and of Hitler, the fondness for dangerous military adventure remained an "ineradicable characteristic" of the German soldier.

Now and again the Soviet government makes an effort to improve the strained relations between Moscow and Bonn by references to history. The line then used is that Germans and Russians have always got on well together when they lived in friendship. Even Hitler, in a telegram to Stalin in 1939, referred to German-Russian friendship as something which "for centuries past has benefited both nations". Thereupon von Ribbentrop flew to Moscow, where he was greeted by the same foreign minister, Molotov, who was to greet Adenauer sixteen years later. On 7th June 1955 Adenauer had been invited to Moscow with the words: "In the years in which friendly relations have existed between our peoples both nations have benefited from it." There was a notable resemblance in the wording of the text of 1939 and 1955, but the power relationship was very different.

On 10th September 1955 Moscow's Bolshoi Theatre witnessed the famous balcony scene which produced a brief improvement in German-Soviet relations. The programme included the ballet *Romeo and Juliet*. As the heads of the Capulet and Montague families embraced each other, Adenauer imitated the action on the stage and demonstratively, to the applause of the public, laid his two hands on the hands of Bulganin. This moment of 'uplift' could not conceal the fact, however, that under today's conditions there is little prospect of permanence in German-Soviet friendship.

Nevertheless Soviet history books still keep alive the memory of numerous auspicious moments of Russo-German relations in the past. The Soviet historians work on the principle of praising all those Germans who aimed their alliances in the right direction, i.e. eastward. The favourable references begin with the Convention of Tauroggen, where on 30th December 1812 the Prussian general Count Yorck left the Napoleonic forces and initiated Prussia's move into the Russian camp. Bismarck, too, is favourably treated, thanks to the opinion expressed in his memoirs that the non-renewal of the Reinsurance Treaty with Russia was a disaster. During the Bismarck era the Germans were enthusiastic about all things Russian, Bismarck himself having often praised the Russian people during his years in St. Petersburg. He also recalled how the Tsar once asked him, not without embarrassment, for two Pomeranian grenadiers as masseurs: he felt quite safe, he said, with two of his Russian subjects when face to face with them but he would prefer not to have them behind his back.

This is in itself one explanation for the employment of so many German advisers at the Tsar's court. At times, because they seemed so reliable, they may even be said to have represented the real government. The fury of the mob, which built itself up against the Tsar, was inevitably transferred to his German advisers, who had in any case caused much bad blood because they were preferred over Russians. After 1871 in any case, Germany's pro-Russian sympathies were reciprocated only with reserve.

In Dostoyevsky's novels the Germans are always portrayed as shaven-headed pedants. Everything about them is horribly tidy, even their love-making. German professors frequently talk learned rubbish, German doctors are shown as little better than quacks. This period saw the origin of the Russian saying about the Germans, that they had invented monkeys—a mixture of ridicule and admiration which is still to be found in the present-day Soviet image of Germany. For a long time the nickname for the Germans was 'sausage-maker' —a word whose sound is far removed from the hatred which can be concentrated into a monosyllabic expletive such as 'Boche'. German music, poetry, science and philosophy aroused great respect among the Russians. For centuries German was the first foreign language to be learned, just as the Romanov dynasty itself was largely German by blood.

According to the rule of praising Germans who served Russia well, even General Ludendorff rates a favourable mention in Soviet history books as the man who in 1917 allowed Lenin to make the journey from Switzerland to Russia in a sealed railway coach, where he took the expected measures to ensure that Russia left the war. Such memories may have weighed with Stalin more than thirty years later when he allowed 'his' Germany to have a small army whose uniforms much more closely resembled the old German uniform than did the Americanised garb of the Bundeswehr.

German-Soviet relations were overshadowed at their very start by a mysterious assassination. On 6th July 1918 Count Mirbach, first German ambassador to the Soviet Union, was seated with a number of officers at the breakfast table when two Russians were announced. Hardly had they sat down when one of them drew a revolver and fired three shots in rapid succession, which all missed. Count Mirbach had almost reached the door and safety when a final bullet struck him mortally in the back of the head. Apparently the assassin had chosen this means of bringing Russia back into the war. The pool of blood left behind a stain on the parquet which could not be removed and for years this formed a subject of conversation for dancing couples as they waltzed round the floor at embassy parties. The assassin, however, was released after a short while.

The culminating event in Soviet recollection is the Treaty of Rapallo signed on Easter Monday, 1922. On the thirty-fifth anniversary of Rapallo the Soviet embassy in Bonn recalled how by means of that treaty Germany had "been enabled to avoid a total subjugation by the victorious Powers, who had bound the German people in chains by the Treaty of Versailles".

The Germans might have found such recollections more appropriate had not a shift in power occurred in the meantime which showed up even the preamble of the Treaty of Rapallo, with its reference to the "complete equality of both powers" as hopelessly out of date. At the time of the signature of the treaty Germany and Russia were two equally strong, or more correctly, equally weak countries. Rapallo saved Germany from making reparations payments to Russia whilst the latter was able to prevent the creation of an anti-Soviet west European bloc. The common experience of defeat was a further cohesive factor.

Historical reminiscence can be a two-edged weapon in Soviet hands. In the same month of April 1957, in which the Soviet embassy in Bonn was trying to flatter German nationalists by reference to the "oppressive" Treaty of Versailles, French-language broadcasts from Moscow were emitting warnings against a resurgence of German nationalism. And at the same time that a Soviet aide-memoire of 27th December 1961 was praising the "gifted German people", presenting the Soviet Union and the Federal Republic as the "greatest states in Europe" and unmasking West German rearmament as part of a diabolical western plan to weaken the economy of the Federal Republic, other sources of Soviet propaganda were beaming warnings at Washington, London and Paris to the effect that Germany's incorrigible bellicosity would once again plunge the world into misery. This playing on two pianos, with one hand knowing perfectly well what the other hand is doing, does not make for confidence in the sincerity of Soviet foreign policy.

If during the Tsarist period official German-Russian relations were better than the popular mood, it is probable that today the reverse is true and that beneath the surface of a pretty cool official relationship the people themselves have retained a certain appreciation of the Germans. Visitors from the Federal Republic are generally well received in the Soviet Union. Young people, to the distress of their elders, seem to have forgotten the war and its horrors and the immediate hatred of the Germans has correspondingly receded. As in Dostoyevsky's time, however, the old scorn of German didacticism is at once aroused whenever a German starts playing the model pupil or delivering a heavy-handed lecture—to which East German party officials are specially prone.

Responsibility for the disastrous history of the thirties and forties is largely ascribed to Germany. In recent years, with the oppression of the people of East Germany and the refusal to allow the reunification of Germany, it is the Soviets who must bear the main responsibility. In Germany a great reservoir of good will has been built up which will welcome the day when the major obstacles to German-Russian friendship are removed. To live in peace with the Soviet Union—there can hardly be a more sincerely-held wish than this among the Germans. It is coupled with the hope that one day the Soviet leadership will realise how little their present treatment of Germany redounds to their credit.

One of the greatest disappointments of Soviet foreign policy is their failure to make France maintain a common policy of keeping Germany weak and under control. During his visit to France in

March 1960 Khrushchev was at pains to revive the traditional Franco-Russian friendship based on a joint encirclement of their hereditary enemy, Germany. Hardly had he landed in Paris than he recalled the blood shed by French and Russians in their common cause against Hitlerite Germany. After a visit to the tomb of the Unknown Soldier Khrushchev repaired to the memorial to the French resistance fighters, many of them Communists, who had been shot by the German police. Every step taken by the distinguished guest had its political significance.

France took a different path. Memories of war and occupation are by no means dead, but they no longer dominate French foreign policy as they did in previous years when the plan for a European army could still be voted down in the National Assembly with references to German concentration camps. The reference to the common suffering of French and Russians during the war seemed to General de Gaulle particularly uncalled-for at a moment when the Soviets, in addition to their already rich post-war booty, were also striving to engulf West Berlin. He considered the Germans, with their reduced frontiers, no longer dangerous. On the contrary—without the Germans as allies he would have felt pretty isolated in the face of the Soviets' superior power. The General therefore invited the Soviet premier to see the present-day *Boches* less in the defeated Germans than in the sinister Chinese. In his view it is they who will one day challenge the Soviet Union to a life-and-death struggle, but Khrushchev was not then much inclined to agree with that viewpoint.

When during his French tour he repeatedly referred to the crimes of Hitler, he was politely reminded that the German panzer armies which had overrun France in 1940 were generously supplied with Soviet petrol. Nor could the French, once they had been induced to make loaded references to recent history, refrain from mentioning that Hitler's victories had been greeted by congratulatory telegrams from Moscow on a scale far in excess of the requirements of diplomatic politeness.

In contrast to eastern Europe the German invasion and the initial stages of the occupation of France had been carried out in the conciliatory spirit of Marshal Blücher's Order of the Day of 7th July 1815, which was recalled in German army newspapers in 1940: "I expect the army not to dishonour itself by arrogance but to behave even as victors with humanity and modesty."

The occupation of Paris began with an unfortunate incident: a German truce negotiator, who had reported in accordance with a Franco-German agreement to the Parisian suburb of St. Denis, was shot in error by the French. After some hesitation the Germans decided against reprisals. It should also be pointed out that, however grim the Nazi behaviour may have been in the interior, the Germans left Paris with as little violence as they had taken it. Instead of obeying his orders and fighting for every street and every bridge General von Choltiz, the last German town commandant, handed over Paris more or less untouched. By preserving this incomparable city at least one bridge to a future of better Franco-German relations was preserved.

When the German troops marched into Paris in June 1940 they found the city virtually empty. French propaganda to improve the fighting ardour of their army had broadcast horrifying stories of the behaviour of German troops in northern France. By comparison the actual behaviour of the Germans seemed to the French extremely moderate. There was little sign of the swaggering victor. Purchases were conscientiously paid for with money of whose worth and validity the buyers, at any rate, were convinced. The cafés on the Champs Elysées brought the chairs out into the June sunshine and soon Germans and French were seated side by side embarrassed, indifferent or in conversation. In view of the great help given by the German army to refugees returning to Paris, the placard drawn by Matejke with the wording "Frenchmen! Trust the German soldier" and showing a French child on the arm of a German soldier could claim to offer at least some grain of truth.

After the armistice at Compiègne, at which the ceremony of capitulation which had taken place twenty-one years before on the same spot was re-enacted with the rôles reversed, the Italian foreign minister Count Ciano wrote in his diary that he had admired the German dictator for the "moderation and good sense" which he exhibited towards defeated France. For a few months it seemed that Heine's remark, made in Paris, that German behaviour was like German beer, neither seemed capable of ever being improved, was about to be refuted, so winningly did the Germans behave. Bareheaded they paid their respects at the tomb of the Unknown Soldier. The French, at first amazed at the efficiency with which the German military machine functioned, gradually regained their self-confidence. The German soldiers even produced a slightly comical effect when they began appearing everywhere with their cameras and behaving as if they had been brought to the French capital by a travel agency rather than by war.

The occupation was made up of many contradictions. Whilst German police rounded up screaming Jewish children to deport them eastwards, officials of the German Fine Arts Commission busied themselves with protecting French monuments and pictures. Hardened recruiting officers for foreign labour, whilst ceaselessly mouthing phrases about saving Europe from bolshevism, were loath to leave their comfortable billet once they reached Paris. Generals fell prey to the fascinating intellectual worlds of Sartre and de Montherlant. Misery and magnanimity were inextricably interwoven.

Marshal Pétain, eighty-four years old, then offered himself as saviour in the hour of need. By a parliamentary majority he was elected Head of State. It was generally hoped that as an old soldier he would be able to restrain Hitler. After making allowance for a certain amount of natural vanity, to which old age is notoriously susceptible, historians today are prepared to confirm that Pétain did function as a shield between the French and the Germans, notwithstanding the denial of this rôle which was subsequently pronounced at his trial. He was arraigned in July 1945 and condemned to death, although the sentence was commuted in view of his advanced age. The accused declared to his judges that during the four years of the occupation he had defended the French people just as once he had done so at Verdun.

The comparison with Verdun was an exaggeration, although taken in conjunction with General de Gaulle's decision to carry on the fight from London, Pétain's attitude unquestionably made sense. Whilst he did his best to mollify the occupation regime, de Gaulle with equal justification ranged himself alongside the eventual victors and thereby secured for the French a place by their side. At the time, of course, things did not seem so clear-cut and simple. On 22nd October 1940 Marshal Pétain, to whom a guard of honour of a German batallion presented arms, met Hitler in the little town of Montoire to agree on a policy of Franco-German co-operation. In French it was called collaboration and the opponents of the policy wrote it as in German with a "K". At the same moment de Gaulle was proclaiming from London that hostilities were to be continued against Germany. France, he said, had lost a battle but not the war. The fact remains that thanks to Pétain France was able to remain physically largely intact. She was spared the thorough-going regime of tyranny of the kind to which Poland was subjected. Germany aimed at winning French compliance by promising her that if she did what the Germans required she would not have to bear the costs of the war, besides which she was assured of the undiminished retention of her colonial empire. Secretly it was agreed that a defeated Great Britain would be made to pay most of the 'bill' for the war.

In the antagonism between Pétain and de Gaulle both knew that history, with its notorious weakness for preferring the winning side, would only justify the one of them who had correctly guessed the victor. Pétain and his prime minister believed, even though without enthusiasm, that Germany would win the war. In London de Gaulle put his money on the British cards and they won. This difference in prognosis, which admittedly disregarded the moral aspect of the quarrel, lies at the base of the subsequent division of France into Pétainists and Gaullists. If Hitler had won the war, which at that time seemed by no means impossible, then Pétain's policy would have been no more than a coolly-reasoned step to have taken in the service of France.

The subsequent course of the occupation can hardly be said to have been conducive to amicable Franco-German co-operation. Various circumstances contributed to a rapid worsening of the climate of relations. The optimistic French received their first body-blow when the ostensibly magnanimous victors presented them with a staggering bill for occupation costs. By the autumn of 1940 the first listless queues were forming outside food shops. The low official ration expressed in calories meant little in a country where virtually every urban family had some close connection with the inexhaustible countryside. Need and scarcity existed side by side with gluttony and debauch. Black market restaurants attracted many Frenchmen who, thanks to profiteering deals with the occupation forces, were well able to pay the inflated prices. The farmer buying himself a château with the proceeds of black market dealings was no mere cartoon figure.

The London radio skilfully directed the resentment of the hungry French at the Germans. Like locusts, as the clever simile put it, they were eating the land bare. That this was at least partly a propagandist's exaggeration was cheerfully confirmed by the C.I.G.S. Field-Marshal Lord Alanbrooke in his book *Victory in the West*. He writes that on landing in France in June 1944 he was amazed at "how little affected the country had been by the German occupation and five years of war". He had found good, tolerably weed-free soil, well-fed cattle, horses and chickens in great profusion, "and the French population did not seem in any way pleased to see us arrive as a victorious army to liberate France". According to the British field-marshal's impressions the French were "quite content as they were and we were merely bringing war and devastation to the land".

Only when the Wehrmacht withdrew did the French notice that not only the enemy's ill-will had been responsible for the adversities of the occupation. In the first two years after the occupation there was no marked improvement in the food situation. The British, who throughout the war had never ceased to assure the French by radio of their sympathy, were nonetheless obliged to act according to strictly military considerations. On 25th June 1940 the British blockade was extended to France. Bombing attacks on bridges, factories and railways, in which housing was inevitably damaged, were carried out regardless of their effect on the French civilian population.

Most Frenchmen began to doubt German generosity when in August 1940 Alsace and Lorraine were, practically speaking, annexed to Germany. "Germanisation" was obtusely applied to purely French Lorraine with such measures, calculated to irritate any reasonable person, as the changing of nameplates on streets, shops and railway stations. In all seriousness Nancy was renamed Nanzig and there was no lack of pendants to produce laborious proof of the justification of this change of name. Fraught with far graver consequences for Franco-German relations was the deportation of French workers for the German war economy. At first a few thousand volunteers reported to the recruiting offices, but when the slogan of saving Europe from bolshevism proved unable to attract any more Frenchmen to work in German factories or on German farms, Reichs Commissioner Sauckel began deploying his system of combined deception and coercion. Under threat of punishment hundreds of thousands of French workers were shipped to Germany, until by 1944 approximately a million workers and a further million prisoners from France were living there. Their experiences varied. Brutality was the exception and as a rule most of them managed tolerably well. After the war the irreconcilables did not include many who had experienced life in Germany as prisoners or workers. Just as old soldiers at Old Comrades' reunions twenty years after their service tend to forget the joylessness of barrack life, these Frenchmen were inclined to recall their pleasanter memories of Germany.

The German occupation forces in France did not practise terror for its own sake. Any occupying force would have been forced to prevent the shots in the back, the attacks on railway lines and the sabotage of military installations. The centres of resistance, which attracted all those seeking to avoid forced labour, soon came under the influence of Communist extremists, who feared neither man nor devil in the struggle against the Germans. Their courage was admirable. Fanaticism made them into a fighting force which the Germans were obliged to take very seriously. The French Communists, of course, only took on their leading rôle in the Resistance when the great fraternal Power, the Soviet Union, entered the war. While the Hitler-Stalin pact was still in force some of them had even attempted to collaborate with the Germans. During the summer months of 1940 communist publications attacked the British as the "real war-mongers", using typically Nazi phraseology and General de Gaulle was pilloried with equal violence in Soviet and German publications as the servant of British monopoly capitalism. With singular unanimity they accused him of selling the French to the British as cannon-fodder. The sudden switch of the French Communists to an anti-German position coincided with the harsher turn in the recruitment of workers for Germany. Thus began the disastrous exchange of blow and counter-blow. The consequences, which included thousands of dead on both sides, requires a serious examination of conscience—and not only on the German side. The retribution which the Resistance carried out during the final months of the war against so-called collaborators constitutes one of the darkest chapters of the war.

Over the radio from London General de Gaulle issued the fateful order that every hedge, every pathway and every barn in France must become an ambush. Björn Björnson had already described in World War I how rapidly German troops lose their self-control when they find that the enemy is not waging war according to the rules. In France the Wehrmacht prepared for a conventional war fought in a defined locality against a visible enemy. The French Resistance, firing from ambush, seemed to be contravening international law. To the German mind a military revolt by civilians against an occupation force is absolutely impermissible. At first, therefore, French partisans who concealed their weapons and wore no recognised uniform were shot under martial law. The German high command saw the use of deterrents as the only means of dealing with the Resistance. On 8th June 1944 the Commander-in-Chief, West, ordered the most severe measures "to discourage the inhabitants of the worst-affected areas from harbouring resistance groups". The partisans were to be starved out in the woods.

The tragedy of Oradour-sur-Glane has come to be remembered as a catastrophe which defies comparison even in an age hardened to cruelty. Oradour-sur-Glane, a village in central France which was destroyed by S.S. troops on 10th June 1944, has been left as a ruin "in memory of German barbarity", as a memorial tablet recalls. It is hard even today to find an explanation for this inconceivable act of cruelty.

When the invasion started in early June the "Das Reich" S.S. Panzer Division began the move to the scene of action in Normandy. Their movement was constantly hindered by francs-tireurs acting with increasing boldness. In Tulle, a town in south-western France, forty German soldiers were attacked by Resistance fighters and shot. The Germans responded by hanging twenty-nine Frenchmen, whom they seized at random in the street.

This was the mood when an advance guard of the S.S. Panzer Division met renewed resistance in a village called Oradour. Two senior officers disappeared without trace. Rumours spread that a Red Cross vehicle had been attacked and burned with its inmates. Oradour was said to be the scene of this misdeed. In that district there are three villages called Oradour; another Oradour was probably intended as the target for revenge. The village which suffered was Oradour-sur-Glane. All the men were rounded up and shot. The church, into which all the women and children had been driven, suddenly caught fire. Everybody inside it died. When the news of this appalling reprisal became known, German headquarters ordered a court of inquiry. It closed without making a finding, as the responsible officer, S.S. Lieutenant Dickmann, was killed in action shortly afterwards and the unit concerned was practically annihilated. In the report submitted by the S.S. unit the incineration of the women and children was not mentioned. A witness hazarded the assumption that the Resistance had stored ammunition in the church which had exploded when the fire broke out and completed the destruction.

The terrible incident was revived when on 12th January 1953 a French court martial in Bordeaux opened proceedings against the sixty-one members of the Waffen—S.S. who had been concerned with the crime. Forty of the accused were dead or missing. Of the remaining twenty-one seven were Germans and fourteen were Frenchmen, or to be precise Alsatians. As the authorities in Alsace had repeatedly insisted that all Alsatians who were in the S.S. had joined it under duress, influential voices demanded their immediate release.

Sentence was passed on 13th February 1953. Two of the accused, a German and an Alsatian who had voluntarily joined the S.S., were condemned to death. The rest were given terms of imprisonment of up to twelve years. Alsace reacted to the verdicts against their fellow-countrymen in which nearly all parties joined, from the Socialists to the Gaullists. Paris was shaken. To avoid a crisis in relations with Strasbourg it was decided to grant an amnesty to all Frenchmen who had been impressed into service with the Wehrmacht and had committed war crimes "under orders". Next day all the Alsatians, except the man condemned to death, were released.

The outcome of the trial destroyed the legal grounds on which the summary trial of German war criminals had hitherto been based. The then Minister of Justice in the Bonn government, Dr. Thomas Dehler, regretted the obvious inequality before the law of the two groups of accused—why had obedience to orders been held as mitigating circumstances for the Frenchmen but not for the Germans? Justice, said Dehler, seemed to stop at the Rhine.

When in May 1962 General de Gaulle visited the ruins of Oradour and was introduced to the survivors, not a word was said against Germany. Any word from a German would be superfluous. The Bordeaux trial, by implicating Frenchmen in the monstrous act, at least contributed to destroying the French sense of moral superiority. Certainly the men who gave the orders were Germans, but at the crucial moment in Oradour Frenchmen, too, had shown themselves unable or unwilling to control the bestial nature of men at war.

Meanwhile France herself has learned, in her disastrous war in Algeria, how hard it is to fight according to the conventional rules of war against an enemy who operates in the dark. There, too, inhuman acts of maltreatment occurred. Villages were burnt to the ground, prisoners tortured. The French came to realise how guerilla warfare leads to tactics of savagery. Now the rôles were reversed—Frenchmen had to defend themselves against Algerian francs-tireurs just as the Germans had been forced to act against the Maquis. No nation, wrote the Nobel prizewinner, François Mauriac, was fundamentally more cruel than any other—under stress all human nature was unpredictable.

Where lay the fundamental difference between the atrocity of Oradour and the 8th February 1958 when twenty-five French bombers and fighters destroyed the Tunisian border village of Sakiet, killing seventy-five inhabitants? Shortly before, a French reconnaissance machine had been fired on from this village and had as a result made a forced landing. Four years later, on 2nd May 1962, O.A.S. terrorists blew up a truck laden with explosives immediately outside a labour exchange in front of which unemployed Algerians were standing in a queue. A hundred and ten people died and a further hundred were severely wounded.

On 17th January 1946 François de Menthon, senior French prosecutor at Nuremberg, drew up the as yet unstained French balance-sheet after four years of German occupation: "France, who has been systematically exploited and oppressed; France, so many of whose sons were tortured and murdered in Gestapo prisons and deportation camps; France, who was forced to endure yet another frightful attempt at total demoralisation and a regression to the diabolical barbarity of Germany; this is the France which demands of you, above all in the name of the heroic martyrs of the Resistance, who are numbered amongst the greatest heroes of our history, that justice be done!"

It is a far cry from this summary judgment to General de Gaulle's surprising statement of 3rd July 1962 when he greeted Adenauer in Paris: Even during the Hitler period, he declared, there had been evidence of that will to unity of the two nations which had been mutually recognised since Charles V, Louis XIV, Napoleon and Bismarck. These brave words must have confused quite a number of people who until then had been busily explaining away the events of the recent past. De Gaulle did not of course mean to condone any crimes by his grandiose review of history; he had simply found the courage to affirm that even during the Nazi regime there had been decent Germans who had continued to dream the dream of Franco-German reconciliation.

Whilst observing all appropriate discretion, a word should be said about those Frenchmen who during the four years of the occupation co-operated with Germans in the spirit of the Montoire agreement. In the first blaze of retribution the collaborators were regarded by other Frenchmen as the scum of humanity. Among them there were unquestionably a number of worthless characters of the type that every occupation regime produces, but there is no reason to consider them as being any worse than those Germans who after May 1945, when the situation was reversed, put themselves at the disposal of the French occupation forces in order to co-operate with them in restoring life to post-war Germany. There were unscrupulous profiteers on both sides, but there were equally men of good will, indeed idealists, whose crime was blindness rather than evil intent. The judgment on collaborators was a French affair. But a German cannot remain silent if they are treated without exception as criminals.

Even before the war the French writer Robert Brasillach had dreamed of a Franco-German rapprochement. It was his misfortune to be dazzled—as happened to quite a number of Frenchmen—by the glittering facade of Nazi Germany. Other French intellectuals have been impressed by the achievements of the Soviet Union, without being accused of being the lackeys of a dictatorship. The 'sound sexual morality', the advances in technology and the stress on physical fitness which all form part of Soviet policy have long had their uncontested admirers in France. Brasillach felt himself more attracted to the type of right-wing dictatorship as represented by pre-war Germany. He saw the Germans as industrious, efficient, reliable and honest. They had furthermore, Brasillach believed, found the just mean between intellectual and physical education.

In retrospect we can all recognise the mistake which Brasillach made. His German idol had feet of clay. He paid for his mistake with his life. General de Gaulle rejected his plea for clemency to which a year or so later, when the first wave of hatred had receded, he would certainly have paid more attention. Brasillach's execution by firing-squad fills a German with shame for his own nation's failure. We learn from his diaries written in the condemned cell that he was most of all impressed by the Germans when defeat became a probability after Stalingrad and they had lost all the glamour and magnetism of victory. General de Gaulle's words in 1962, that even in the worst of times some were still dreaming of Franco-German unity, exonerate Brasillach too.

France, the country which since 1871 has been most responsible for creating the international image of Germany, has become the country which in recent years has most thoroughly revised it. The barbarian has become a good neighbour. The Soviet accusation that the Germans think of nothing but war has been rejected by the one country which, if Moscow's charge were true, would have the most to fear from Germany. The adjustment reached between France and a Germany reduced to the size of the Federal Republic rests, of course, on the fact of a weakened Germany, a state of affairs of which the French perforce approve. The French find co-existence with Germany so much the easier since their neighbour has ceased to parade in boots and spurs up and down their common frontier.

Over the centuries the Germans have gained the impression that the French, much as they prefer a strong centralised government in their own country, are happiest with a divided Germany on their flank. After the Thirty Years War the Empire dissolved, as France had wished, into 343 principalities. They were admittedly less the consequence of Richelieu's and Mazarin's policy than the inborn German urge to particularism. After the Wars of Liberation against Napoleon it was once more not the French but the German princes who barred the way to German unity. France was rather the beneficiary than the instigator of Germany's division into countless minor states. The German princes even retained the new states which Napoleon had created for his own imperial purposes.

After the Wars of Liberation nothing stood in the way of an amicable Franco-German rapprochement. In his book *Le Rhin* Victor Hugo admitted that if he were not a Frenchman he would like to be a German: he harboured an "almost childlike devotion to this noble and sacred land of thinkers", meaning—although we might not realise it today—Germany. That was before the days of petty calculation as to whether Teutons or Gauls had been more bellicose; people contented themselves with the reasonable viewpoint that both Gauls and Teutons had been no strangers to aggression and had each been responsible for starting a roughly equal number of wars.

It was not the war of 1870–71 as such which produced in the French mind such an antipathy for Germany. The real cause was the annexation of Alsace-Lorraine. It was this which in the French popular consciousness transformed the land of castles and dreamy principalities, of *Gemütlichkeit* and poetry into a nest of robbers and sauerkraut-guzzlers, barbarians and sabre-rattlers. Even so, memories of the German virtues so long praised by French poets were still strong enough to prevent the slogans about the Germans being the barbarians of the modern age lasting much longer than the few months of the war. Typical of the French mood immediately after a lost war was the book by Gabriel Monod *Allemands et Français* published in Paris in 1872. Monod had been through the war as a medical orderly. He now attempted to make a fair assessment of German behaviour during the months of war and occupation.

Monod began by citing evidence of German ruthlessness such as the burning of villages from which German troops had been sniped. The Prussians, accustomed to strict adherence to the rules of war— here the author anticipates Björnson's observations of 1916—were taken completely unawares by the outbreak of popular feeling against the invaders. Monod came to the conclusion that the francs-tireurs did more harm than good. Their military value was negligible, whilst other Frenchmen, who fell victim to German reprisals, were made to suffer. Such an admission in the not dissimilar case of World War II would have been impossible in the general hardening of attitudes caused by modern ideological warfare.

Women and children, wrote Monod, were without exception treated by German soldiers with respect and affection. German fondness for children was positively proverbial. The French Red Cross flag had always been respected. There had been identical treatment of French and German wounded in German field hospitals. Monod could not resist a jab, however, at the German army chaplains; they had bored everybody by their interminable declarations that the German victory was the judgment of God. Victory would, Monod concluded, drive the Germans to megalomania; already a ruthless get-rich-quick fever had transformed the idealised Germany of the Romantic movement.

France took her revenge for 1871 by exchanging her admiration for Germany for contempt. As in the summer of 1940 the French interpreted their defeat as the triumph of cold German precision over French refinement. A steam roller had devastated their beautiful garden. That was all. Innumerable books on the causes of the fall of France emphasised that not personal bravery but only massed artillery had brought the Germans victory.

The German intellectuals continued to admire France as much after 1871 as before. Paris remained the great centre of attraction. It was Nietzsche who coined the phrase that might had triumphed over mind, but that the reputation of the French mind was all the greater for it. It was a well-aimed piece of French revenge to laugh at the German nouveaux riches of the early years of the Reich, who had no talent for good living and had to rely on uniforms, titles, medals and pompous buildings to bolster up their self-esteem whereas their neighbours to the west had no need of them. In the years before World War I the German as a worthy example was banished from French intellectual life. German sensibility, long held up as an example in French schools, was transformed into mere posturing when the anger and pain at the loss of Alsace-Lorraine spread through French society.

Maurice Barrès, the chauvinistic author and politician, saw Imperial Germany as the very antithesis of French civilisation. In his novel *Au service de l'Allemagne* written in 1905, he describes the German high school teacher Dr. Asmus in Metz spreading German boorishness with his green felt hat, shabby overcoat, heavy boots and crude table manners. German professors in the novel revealed themselves as blockheads, mouthing opinionated banalities.

In this generally unfavourable atmosphere a few sober French businessmen did realise that the Germans were worthy of better treatment, at least as potential customers. On 23rd September 1871 an advertisement appeared in the *Berlinischen Zeitung* under the heading "Champagne" in which a champagne firm from Reims announced the setting-up of a depot in Berlin, "whereat we permit ourselves the observation that during the siege of Paris our wines enjoyed the highest commendation of the distinguished (*German*) officer corps". Such commercial candour would have been unthinkable after the two world wars.

Even after World War II it was in economic affairs that a relatively quick return was made to normal relations. Angry politicians were still waving their banners whilst new bonds were being forged across the Rhine in the European Coal and Steel Community. In his memoirs the one-time President of the National Assembly, Edouard Herriot, called the German foreign minister Stresemann a villain—he it was, claimed Herriot, who had paved the way for Germany to make her third attack on France since 1870. Such warning voices may have made sense in the past, but in the post-World War II world they were a sign that the writer had been left behind by events. However it is quite true that in the twenties German right-wing extremists were quite mistaken in dismissing as ridiculous France's complex about the security of her eastern frontier. The image conjured up by Reichswehr generals of the French armed to the teeth was little more than a calculated lie. Compared to the very real danger represented by Hitlerite Germany, France was indeed weak.

But what was true in the pre-Hitler and Hitler periods is not necessarily so today. The fundamental improvement in Franco-German relations dates from the partition of Germany and the loss of her eastern provinces. When in Strasbourg on 22nd November 1959 General de Gaulle described the reconciliation of the two nations as the greatest miracle of the post-war era, he was thinking—and as a Frenchman who can blame him—of a Germany weakened by division and loss of territory. France is prepared to extend political trust to a truncated western Germany only. Whoever is inclined to regret this should remember that once again it was not France who caused the carve-up of Germany; it is the direct result of the delusions of grandeur which drove Germany to war in 1939 under Hitler's leadership.

German territory, which under Wilhelm II corresponded approximately to the area of France, has contracted by three fifths. The Federal Republic is just half the size of France, a fact which must have a reassuring effect on the French, although they in fact bear no responsibility for the situation. The partition of Germany is maintained by the Soviet Union. France is not capable of resisting the reunification of Germany by so much as one day if the Soviets would permit it.

That the Germans appreciate friendship with France is demonstrated by the reception which they gave President de Gaulle during his state visit to the Federal Republic in September 1962. *Paris-Match* described the historic event under the heading "The conquest of Germany by Charles de Gaulle".—"It was like a spectacular produced by Cecil de Mille and directed by Leni Riefenstahl. The journalists had never seen such gigantic crowds. The sympathy and excitement were greater than on the last lap of the Tour de France. Even in France, to say nothing of Italy or the U.S.A., de Gaulle has never been hailed like this ... To find any comparison at all one would have to hark back to the liberation of Paris." Did the President remember, one wonders, as he spoke in front of the Feldherrnhalle in Munich or at Schloss Ludwigsburg and proposed a Franco-German union to his hosts, that twenty-eight years earlier he had poured scorn on the suggestion of friendship with Germany? In his book *Vers l'Armée de Métier*, published in 1934, he wrote: "The Frenchman, who has so much order in his thoughts and so little in his actions, this logician who casts doubt on everything, this creature who works in fits and starts, who loves tailcoats and public parks but dresses sloppily and throws litter on to the grass—in short, how can the Teuton appreciate, understand or trust this unreliable, contradictory nation of weathercocks who change with every breeze? And Germany disturbs us, this hotbed of vague but violent instincts, of born artists devoid of any taste, of technicians with mediaeval minds; with its hotels that look like temples and its lavatories that look like Gothic palaces; this land of oppressors who want to be loved, of slavishly obedient separatists, of lounge lizards who feel sick when they have drunk too much beer."

The humorous paper *Le Canard Enchaîné* commented on the great reconciliation in its own way. It issued a special number in which Canard was spelt Kanard—recalling the capital "K" with which collaborators had been stigmatised during the occupation.

In December 1962 the British journalist Sefton Delmer put the new-found Franco-German harmony to the test. Disguised in a loden and a tyrolean hat he travelled round France in a Volkswagen without once, in spite of all his efforts, inducing anybody to mention the horrors of the occupation. To round off the trip Delmer visited the erstwhile German extermination camp of Strudhof-Natzweiler in the Vosges. The guide, imagining that he was dealing with a German, answered Delmer's insistent questioning as to the responsibility for World War II with the astonishing reply: "It was the British. The British with their perfidious intrigues stopped us [the Germans and French] from being friends." The British journalist, hardly famous for his love of Germany, described his amazement at these experiences in an article in the *Sunday Telegraph* of 23rd December 1962.

By way of France, defeated Germany has been accepted back into the family of nations, but it is certain that the reconciliation would not have occurred at such astonishing speed without the assistance of the Americans. They provided the first impulse to banishing the ghosts of the past.

In a very few years the Americans exchanged the spirit of the Morgenthau Plan, which proposed stripping Germany of all industry and reducing it to a purely pastoral and agricultural economy, for a policy of solidarity with the Federal Republic. The changed American attitude is all the more remarkable for following on an official policy of hatred which during the war was hardly exceeded by that of any other belligerent.

The Cold War was not the only reason for the switch in American occupation policy from harshness to mildness. There were a number of economic, political and military reasons. In a few years a majority of Americans changed from crusaders against German arrogance and aggression into friends and protectors of the truncated but free West German state. Between 1950 and 1960 the Federal Republic, without gaining much popularity for it in other countries, earned the reputation of being America's 'model pupil'.

Watching the Germans busily rebuilding their towns and villages the Americans imagined they were watching the old pioneer spirit at work. The addition of German military efficiency to the Nato potential became desirable. German-American collaboration became so close that during the lifetime of Secretary of State Dulles hardly a move of any importance was made in Europe without prior consultation with Chancellor Adenauer.

The Germans repaid this affection with an imitation of the American style of living which far exceeded the phenomena of Americanisation in other countries. Unfortunately the imitation was not confined to such higher manifestations as Abraham Lincoln's constitutional doctrine or to literary models. 'The American way of life' became for many Germans the easiest way of denying and forgetting their dubious past.

American observers reported that West Germany was well on the way to becoming more American than the Americans. Simultaneously German reporters in the U.S.A. noticed that the ostentatious adoption by the post-war Germans of an alien style produced less than total approval—Americans began to seek for possible ulterior motives.

When he visited America in February 1961 the Social Democratic politician Carlo Schmid noticed that the barometer of American friendship had "fallen sharply". The swastika-daubing episodes, the Eichmann trial and the German tendency to drag their feet over aid to under-developed countries were, he reported, the main causes. Chancellor Adenauer felt himself challenged by this report from a Social Democratic source. Carlo Schmid had tried to direct American dissatisfaction against Adenauer's policies. Thereupon the patriarchal old chancellor, on his trip to America in April 1961, did his best to mobilise American sympathies for himself and against the Social Democrats. The C.D.U. declared that never before had the Federal Republic stood in such high regard in the United States. North America had become the arbiter and criterion of German politics.

The American influence also had its effect on German election campaigns. From now on aged German political faces could be seen practising the art of 'keep smiling' which had been a feature of American electioneering since the days of Theodore Roosevelt. Now even in Germany the choice of candidates for the chancellorship began to be influenced by their 'public image'—particularly as projected on the T.V. screen. The party platforms shed much of their old-style philosophical baggage.

American enthusiasm for Germany is liable to fairly regular fluctuation caused by mistrust of German motives, but against this the German-American element in the United States acts as a significant stabiliser. Even Roosevelt took it into account. According to the latest count, every sixth American is of German descent, but the numerical proportion of German stock does not imply a correspondingly strong influence in America because of all immigrants the Germans tend to slough off their national links more rapidly than those from other countries.

Many Germans left their homeland in the last century in anger and distress. It is therefore not surprising that only a few of them retained their customs and speech. The German influence on American life has been correspondingly weak. Similar to the Germans of the Federal Republic, who have chiefly copied the somewhat meretricious external features of American life, the Americans tended to absorb the more superficial aspects of the German character. Gesangverein, leberwurst, wanderlust and sauerkraut have gone into American everyday language. Many of the older generation of German-Americans, who continue to regard Germany as their homeland, complain of the exaggerated urge to assimilation exhibited by their countrymen. Fewer and fewer new members are joining the German-American associations, including even the football clubs. Statistical data shows the Germans to be one of the few immigrant groups which almost without exception discard their language in the second generation.

The first comprehensive picture of post-war Germany on a popular level was presented by a special number of *Life* magazine in May 1954. The vulgarity of its Madison Avenue-type launching at Lüchow's Restaurant was only equalled by the hackneyed nature of much of its social comment: Germany, it implied, was still the land of guzzlers and swillers, children kow-towed every morning to their teacher (the children illustrated were actually doing their morning gymnastics) and German girls still thought of nothing but finding a husband to whom they would then give their complete obedience, their married lives still circumscribed by the classic 'three K's'— *Kinder, Küche, Kirche.*

Many pressure-groups determine the American image of Germany. The influence of the numerous Polish-Americans tends to maintain a permanent mistrust of German attitudes to frontier revision. Nor can the American Jews be expected to harbour much goodwill towards the people which has caused them so much misery. These and similar views came strongly to the fore when President Kennedy took office. Suddenly the American government regarded the German contributions to defence and development aid as inadequate. Sharp words were exchanged across the Atlantic. The close and trusting relationship of the Dulles era seemed over and the new American attitude of impatience provoked the Germans to some angry retorts. "Only when we pay," declared the F.D.P. leader Dehler, on the Bavarian Radio on 8th March 1964, "and as long as we keep on paying are we regarded as respectable. If we don't, then the wheels of the opinion-making machinery will start grinding against us and it will only stop when we produce some cash again—a splendid prospect." Bonn showed signs of nervousness. Certain politicians thought that they detected a dangerous "softening" of the American attitude towards Soviet pressure on Berlin. The U.S.A. exhibited a certain impatience with the perpetually dissatisfied Germans. When the *New York Times* published a photo of an old woman weeping in front of the Berlin wall, many readers wrote wondering whether this woman had also wept when Hitler massacred the Jews, subjugated Poland and terrorised women and children with his bombs.

This mood of exasperation favoured the success of the 72-year-old Katherine Anne Porter's novel which was published in Spring 1962 and headed the best-seller list until November of that year. Its title, *Ship of Fools*, was taken from a German original, namely a pre-Reformation satire written by Sebastian Brant in the fifteenth century. Mrs. Porter's *Ship of Fools* was a German vessel sailing from the Mexican port of Vera Cruz to Bremerhaven in the summer of 1931. Even in 1931 a German passenger is made to leave the Captain's table because it turns out that he has a Jewish wife. A certain Frau Schmitt sheds tears when a dog is hurt, but agrees wholeheartedly that Jews should be dealt with "as severely as possible". The culmination of German arrogance is reached when the man who had to leave the place of honour because of his non-aryan wife consoles himself with the reflection that he can at least purify her inferior Jewish blood with his own superior German blood. The novel is another attempt to prove that Nazism, even in its most virulent form, exactly reflects the German character. As with Shirer the implicit moral is that the Germans will never change. Mrs. Porter sees the Jews as having been purely chance victims of German brutality: it could in her opinion be directed equally against any other non-Germans.

By continually recalling the horrors of the Nazi period the anti-Germans, who from 1933 to 1945 had demanded the repression and subjugation of the aggressive Reich, are trying to justify their attitude at a time when America and Germany are allies. No one who has once demanded that the beastly Germans should never again bear arms and were best deprived of their industry and reduced to a nation of indigent farmers likes to appear in retrospect as having been a fool or a monster. A great deal of American anti-Germanism springs from a need for personal justification. The most that such people will concede to the Federal Republic is that it proves that the Germans are schizophrenic and that behind the democratic exterior lurks the old German peril.

Such regression to Roosevelt's attitude, however, no longer seems capable of influencing U.S. public opinion towards adopting an exclusively anti-German stance. Taken overall, majority opinion today is favourable. The American national sport of public opinion polls revealed that in 1942 more than half those questioned thought of the Germans as brutal and aggressive. By 1961 only every tenth American questioned considered brutality a German characteristic. Seven out of ten described the Germans as orderly, hard-working and honest. Compared with wartime 1942, by 1961 only half of the earlier 31 per cent thought of arrogance as a specifically German vice. The rôle of villain, previously shown by polls as being played by the Germans, is now held by the Russians.

If the Soviet image of Germany is characterised by a firm adherence to the past, the French by having overcome the past and the American by its changeability, Great Britain's attitude to Germany tends to lie somewhere between those of the other three divided victors of the last war. It is made up of common sense, cool calculation and occasional rays of sunshine, which are nevertheless likely to be clouded by muddled thinking.

When in 1945 after the defeat of Germany the moment came to determine the level of German steel production, the yardstick of a country's standard of living, the British attitude was outstandingly generous. As Germany had produced 12 million tons of steel in 1934, the first year of Hitler's rearmament policy, the British considered that they should be allotted a figure for 1946 of 9 million tons. The French recommended 7, the Russians 4.5 and the Morgenthau-minded Americans 3.5 million tons. The order is revealing: in a comparative table made today the British would no longer head the list of Germany's well-wishers.

The British attitude to a defeated Germany was at first unusually magnanimous. Having smashed the Third Reich Churchill wanted to build up West Germany as a bulwark against the Communist East. In his Zürich speech of 19th September 1946 he amazed the French with his prophetic view of future Franco-German friendship which at that time was regarded in France as extremely premature. It is significant of the changing value placed on friendship with Germany that when the French finally accepted Churchill's vision, Great Britain withdrew into insular reserve.

Before the first feelers were put out towards the Common Market, the British government expressed their irritation and suspicion at the Franco-German rapprochement. On 31st March 1960 Prime Minister Macmillan angrily compared the European Economic Community with Napoleon's Continental System. Since, in contrast to previous centuries, the British could no longer wage war on this issue they decided instead to join the economic block which was being created on the continent. General de Gaulle prevented them from doing so. British indignation over the French veto included a suspicion as to whether the General's ally, Chancellor Adenauer, had really been playing straight when in late January 1963 he allowed his ministers Erhard and Schröder to plead so warmly in Brussels for Britain's entry into the Common Market.

British mistrust of continental power-blocs is one of the roots of the traditional British coolness and reserve, of which Imperial Germany was made aware at the turn of the century. In the year 1910 some British nationalists discovered that the German birthrate of 800,000 per annum represented a potential threat to Great Britain. The Reich was growing too powerful. British Cassandras predicted that the Kaiser would cut Britain's lifeline to India by means of the German-financed Baghdad railway. Every German coaling-station abroad was regarded as a blow at British trade. There then began the near-tragic interplay of German attempts at friendship and their rejection by Britain. The matter was complicated by the fact that at times they were genuinely keen for a rapprochement with their German rival, but at these moments the Germans were invariably smarting under their last rebuff and disinclined to take notice of a change in the British attitude.

The German hatred of England which brimmed over in World War I bore all the characteristics of rejected love. The years of striving to be recognised as gentlemen by the one nation capable of bestowing this accolade had ended in failure. Now the British were to be made to pay; German scholars such as Max Scheler and Werner Sombart compiled books which drew a savage picture of the island race. The degree of German hatred of the British can be judged from the *Hymn of Hate* composed by the hyper-patriotic German Jew, Ernst Lissauer:

> "Hate on water and hate on land,
> Hate in the head and hate by the hand.
> Hate for their people and hate for their kings
> In the hearts of seventy million rings.
> United as one to strike every blow
> At England the hated, the only foe."

German hatred was never able to attain such a peak in World War II and after the war it vanished like the air from a pricked balloon. The Germans have never ceased to regard British behaviour as exemplary. Even during the Third Reich German diplomats were urged to cultivate 'British coolness'. One of the noisiest peoples on earth decided to become an exponent of British calm, believed to be the secret of British success. Under Hitler tremendous efforts were again made to gain British friendship, but the Britons were unwilling to clasp the proferred hand as they could not feel sure that its next move might not be to seize them by the throat. They were further annoyed by the imitation of their country's name: Hitler's 'Greater Germany' was felt to be a tasteless distortion of the concept of 'Great Britain'.

On 10th October 1958 Queen Elizabeth, in her speech of welcome to Federal President Heuss, generously disregarded all the darker aspects of previous Anglo-German relations. She referred to the ever-popular memory of Prince Albert of Saxe-Coburg-Gotha, the consort of Queen Victoria. From this Anglo-German union, said the Queen, both she and her husband were directly descended. Several British newspapers took this piece of family history amiss. Had not the British royal family been obliged, in World War I, to change their name from Saxe-Coburg-Gotha to Windsor? In November 1960 Prince Philip was reminded almost accusingly of his German blood when he expressed his opinion that an obsessive fixation on the sins of the past was fruitless. Prince Philip did not allow his natural and unprejudiced attitude to the Germans to be affected. On 28th April 1961 he told the story of an American who was asked by a Russian journalist to give his views on Soviet successes in space travel and who replied: "Well, I guess your Germans were better than our Germans."

During his visit to England President Heuss still had to contend with a great deal of reserve. He himself considered the trip a success and was annoyed by those sections of the German press who said that a state visit was premature. By 1958 a certain amount of ill-will had built up between London and Bonn. The old problem of B.A.O.R. support costs was angering the British taxpayer, who felt that the Germans could pay for Britain's Rhine Army because it was defending Germany too. The German objection, that it was Great Britain that was being defended on the Rhine, was not calculated to improve the mood of the British press. *Punch* published a cartoon showing a well-fed German, seated in a luxurious inn named "Germania", throwing ten pfennigs into the cap of a British soldier collecting charity for the Rhine Army. Military problems produced other tensions; official England was indignant at the cancellation of German arms contracts which occurred around the time of Heuss' visit and the Queen's speech. British armament manufacturers were furious at the barnstorming methods by which the Americans appeared to be forcing the Germans to buy American arms. On 10th November 1958 *The Times* declared that it was no longer chance that British weapons were so little appreciated by German buyers; an anti-British attitude must be rooted in those German ministries responsible for buying British arms. How odd that arms purchases had now become a barometer of friendship in British relations with Germany, the one country which had always been accused of a dangerous over-fondness for arms. Significantly *The Times* omitted the usual article welcoming Heuss. Other London newspapers regarded the state visit as an appropriate occasion to make a résumé of German blood-guilt. One tabloid raised the figure of murdered victims to 10 million. Heuss, a conciliatory man, strove to overlook all these open and covert attacks.

The growing economic and military strength of the Federal Republic made many English people suspicious. As an exporter Great Britain suddenly found herself taking second place to Germany; nor were the comparative figures for working days lost by strikes in 1960 likely to improve the morale of British exporters: in Great Britain 3 million, in West Germany 37,723. For those inclined to mistrust, it seemed that Churchill's remark about the Germans being either at your feet or at your throat was being confirmed and that the German pendulum was now in full swing from servility to arrogance.

When de Gaulle and Adenauer met in 1962 to hold a spectacular ceremony of reconciliation, something like jealousy was aroused across the Channel. Many British people thought that the Germans could well spare more energy towards gaining the sympathy of Britain. But the Germans had already experienced the results of their efforts to woo the British; the old mistake of importunity was not going to be repeated. And soon British sources were complaining, after incidents had occurred between Rhine Army troops and German civilians, that the soldiers had too little contact with the German population. Germans had in fact simply avoided British soldiers because they assumed that this was what the troops preferred. But after 1960 this very isolation began to make the British feel uncomfortable.

British newspapers (in this case the *Daily Mail* of 11th July 1962) complained that the need for a rapprochement with Germany seemed to have been grasped more readily in France than in England. Not blood-soaked northern France, where de Gaulle and Adenauer had taken the salute at a joint Franco-German parade, but Wales had been the scene of angry demonstrations against the German ally. A German armoured unit had almost had to be smuggled into their British training quarters under cover of night, although the general reaction of the Welsh people was to treat the Germans as kindly as any other visitors. The demonstrators were hardly able to organise a procession. On 28th August 1961 the *Guardian* saw the only danger to the inhabitants in the possible success of the boys in field-grey with the local girls. The Welsh town of Pembroke had known

German P.o.Ws during the war. "They were perfect gentlemen," declared one woman in the local newspaper. Another reader said less kindly that where Hitler had failed, Adenauer had succeeded in invading Great Britain.

The phrase used by an innkeeper in Minden, Westphalia, that British troops had behaved in his pubs like "incorrigible, poisonous little dwarfs" led to heated British press comment in the summer of 1962. One cartoon showed a burly little sergeant assuring his squad that if the Germans thought of them as poisonous dwarfs, he was their Snow White. A Labour M.P. went so far as to declare that British women had been spat at by Germans in buses. A group of M.P.s convinced themselves by an on-the-spot investigation that the reports of clashes between troops and civilians had been exaggerated; it was on this occasion that the complaint was made of insufficient means to help Germans and Britains to get to know each other.

Anyone who recalls that the British feel slightly sorry for all non-Britons, because they have not been lucky enough to have been born in Britain, will find their attitude to the Germans quite normal. The 'midway' attitude to Germany which is prevalent in England has its advantages. Tests made in British schools showed that parents and teachers transmit a generally favourable image of Germany. British schoolchildren saw the Germans as hard-working, musical and hospitable. Physically they are thought of as being blond, hefty and blue-eyed—a stereotype with as much relevance to the facts as the conventional picture of the thin, tow-haired, buck-toothed Englishman.

A special supplement of the *Daily Mirror* of 9th July 1962 produced an image not unlike that which emerged from the schools questionnaire. The German emerged as above all hard-working. The only complaint made by this left-wing paper was of the German passion for titles. Otherwise the Federal Republic was revealed as more than anything else a 'little America': anyone driving last year's model of a car felt awkward and out of date.

Anti-Germans and pro-Germans continue to thunder back and forth; typical are Cassandra and Sefton Delmer. Delmer, the son of an Australian professor, born in Berlin, was covering Germany for the *Daily Express* from the beginning of the Third Reich. After the Röhm affair described in his book *Trail Sinister* (1962), he had to leave the country. During the war he ran the British propaganda radio station aimed at German troops. Today this skilful journalist still exerts a considerable influence on the British image of Germany. His articles about events in the Federal Republic, motivated by a curious kind of love-hate feeling for Germany are charged with a messianic urge to enlighten not only England but the world about Germany.

But in spite of constant cries of warning from the press the British government and people have constantly proved ready to make gestures of conciliation. No one who took part will ever forget the consecration of the newly-built Coventry Cathedral twenty-two years after the German bombing attacks. Germans too were invited to the ceremony, which was entirely imbued with a spirit of international understanding. Not a word was spoken against the German people; on that day none spoke of guilt in terms of one nation or another.

7

WHOSE HANDS WERE CLEAN?

It is a painful matter to justify oneself as a citizen of a country which has been beaten in every respect. If—unlike the proverb—the big criminals were hung, it did not mean that the little ones were allowed to get away. When the victors entered Germany in Spring 1945 armed with their questionnaires about every man's doings under Hitler, the whole German people began the flight from their own past. From one day to another people forgot the hurrahs for the Führer and for the Reich, the flags, parades, party rallies, the jubilant women and the glowing children's faces which for the twelve years of his rule had accompanied Hitler's every move. Forgotten too were the persecution of the Jews, the rumours about the concentration camps and everything else which only yesterday had formed part of an accepted, or at least tolerated order of things and which were now suddenly revealed as dishonourable and even criminal.

One can hardly blame a defeated people for attempting as far as possible to evade the clutches of the occupying Powers. The so-called 'Persil certificates', or affidavits of non-complicity in Nazi activities, which those Germans who could do so traded between themselves, were regarded as a legitimate weapon against the over-inquisitive Allied authorities. This spectacle of individual sauve-qui-peut was not edifying, but it was not unnatural. Altogether it amounted to a falsification of history from which the Germans are still the sufferers. If one added up the number of Germans who, in filling out their Allied questionnaires, admitted to having voted for Hitler in 1932 or 1933 the result was only a ridiculous fraction of the the number of votes by means of which Hitler actually came to power.

These millions of questionnaires settled like a blanket of fog over the real state of affairs in the Third Reich and distorted them. Since the new dispensation would only give jobs and other privileges to the so-called 'non-involved', the creation of a new and clean personal record became a matter of life and death. Germans who confessed to the Allied authorities that they had once believed in Hitler aroused general admiration. Others grew so rapidly accustomed to their new past that they gradually came to believe their own answers to the questionnaire and to regard them as reality.

Fortunate were the possessors of unequivocal documentation of their membership of the Resistance, although even they, if they claimed a record of continuous opposition to Hitler, were not always speaking the truth. In writing down the saving formula that he had "always been against the Nazis" the average German was obliged to repress a great deal and to 'blow up' a great deal more beyond its actual significance. Thus a random remark against Hitler was exaggerated by memory into an act of high treason. A sympathetic word about some Jewish neighbours appeared in the questionnaire as a death-defying attempt at rescue. Omitting by mistake or on purpose to hang out a swastika banner, failing to give the Hitler salute or an argument with a minor Party official became proofs of permanent opposition.

One can hardly blame the individual German for this juggling with his past if it helped him over his immediate difficulties and if he had committed no crime, but for Germany as a whole the general refusal to face the facts was disastrous. It enabled others to say that the Germans had failed to come to terms with their past and were therefore unreliable in the future because they had taken part in the greatest mass evasion of truth in their history.

Flight from the truth is not unknown in Germany; the Germans have had some practice in it. To combat "our tendency to run away from facts" Schiller recommended the exact study of history. He seemed to know the German tendency to doctor history to make it fit their requirements. The years 1815, 1848, 1871, 1918, 1933 and 1945, that is to say the end of the Wars of Liberation, the abortive German revolution, the foundation of the Reich, the end of the monarchy, Hitler's chancellorship and the German capitulation were recorded, with the military, political and economic changes which they produced, in new flags, oaths of allegiance and national anthems. German street names are a witness to the constant upheavals which have characterised German history.

During World War I Hindenburg became a favourite patron of street names. Social Democratic aldermen only discovered their enthusiasm for him in 1932 when Hindenburg became the Social

Democrats' candidate for the Presidency. In 1933 the Nazis began to approve of Hindenburg's name on streets when the aged Reichs President renounced his dislike of Hitler. After 1945 Hindenburg's name disappeared but began to reappear around 1950. A similar fate overtook Karl Marx who, after many ups and downs in his career as a namer of streets had to accept his removal from the street gazeteer of Bonn in 1962. The names of President Ebert and Foreign Minister Stresemann were removed from street name-plates during the Hitler regime as though they had never existed. Of the names of Communists such as Thälmann, which began to reappear on German streets around 1945, most did not last as much as ten years in West Germany.

These examples illustrate the German tendency to see history and its figures less as a succession of unalterable facts than as a moral institution in which every new political system respects its own special heroes and punishes the villains by rejection. This changing of nameplates, common to all dictatorships, is a proof even though a superficial one of the fickleness of the Germans as historical creatures.

The past, unless it is understood and acknowledged in all its shadings and complexity, will always continue to disturb the present. As early as summer 1945, when the Swiss theologian Karl Barth began his dispute with Eugen Gerstenmaier, later to be Speaker of the Bundestag, it became clear that the taints of the Nazi regime were to become a favourite political weapon. Gerstenmaier had, after all, emerged straight from a concentration camp. He had stood before Hitler's notorious Peoples' Court and bore the scars of Gestapo brutality. His months of suffering were not enough for the harsh Barth, who had left Germany in 1935 before the ruthless persecution of the leaders of the confessing church had begun. He considered that Gerstenmaier's claim to have resisted Hitler was largely imagination. Barth's diagnosis was based on external appearances: he pointed to Gerstenmaier's adherence to the Student S.A. and his activity on the Berlin Ecclesiastical Board. According to Barth every administrative body in the Third Reich was a Nazi institution. Anybody who expected Barth's attitude to lead him to reject all forms of dictatorship must have been the more surprised at the advice Barth later gave to the Germans in the Soviet Zone to come to terms with Communist rule. Like Thomas Mann, Karl Barth was inclined to judge Communist and Nazi dictatorships by different standards.

To remain unmolested in post-war Germany was often dependent on pure chance, to such an extent that a new species came to be identifiable, the *"Zufallsdeutsche"*.[1] A man of this kind would have declared himself on his questionnaire as an opponent of Hitler and may have thus reached high political office. One day, though, a malicious investigator discovers among some yellowing papers a signature, the text of a speech or a photograph of the person concerned wearing a dubious uniform, which at one blow involves this unsuspecting *"Zufallsdeutsche"* in the dark Nazi past. Brown stains appear on the lily white hands. How much more fortunate were those who knew that all incriminating traces of their past had been destroyed in time. They are the *"Zufallsdeutsche"* who got away with it. The element of chance is the most arbitrary and unsatisfactory factor in the question of individual guilt and atonement. In a number of cases people with a Nazi past were allowed to forget it— as long as they gave good service to one or other political party. As soon, however, as they exhibited any weakening of allegiance or signs of wanting to change sides, their Nazi activities (hitherto known about but suppressed) were dragged into the open and their further careers ruined. The past was a kind of political missile which could be pulled out of the drawer and used in case of bad behaviour; guilt became a matter of expediency.

As time went on particular organisations began to specialise in the investigation of the past—always other peoples', of course. In the Federal Republic the "League of Victims of Nazism" (*Verein der Verfolgten des Naziregimes*, abbreviated to V.V.N.) made a name for itself with its tireless pursuit of Nazis. The history of the V.V.N. is typical of the tortuous progress of such organisations. In the immediate postwar years it included distinguished personalities of all political complexions whose common fate it had been to be persecuted by Hitler. At that time East and West were still acting in concert and it was natural that the V.V.N. should reflect the unanimity of the Great Powers who after all had established a joint court of justice at Nuremberg. In those days the Communists were still regarded as unimpeachable defenders of freedom and human dignity simply because much wrong had been done to them in Hitler's concentration camps.

---

[1] A practically untranslatable expression, meaning here "the unlucky German whose past catches up with him by chance whilst others, equally or even more guilty, escape by fortunate lack of evidence about their past".

When the wartime alliance of the victorious Powers broke up, the V.V.N. began to show cracks too. It suddenly appeared that the common experience of persecution under Hitler was no guarantee of a similarity of views. The Communists had meanwhile been demonstrating in the Soviet zone just how much store they really set by freedom and human dignity. Hitler's maxim that enemies of the state should be locked up was valid in East Germany too, where the concentration camps at first bore a devilish likeness to Hitler's camps. The V.V.N., whose task it should have been to decry all barbed wire fences, applauded those which were put up in the Soviet zone. The East German branch of the V.V.N. voted for its own dissolution on the grounds that freedom in this state was now secured and therefore any special organisation in defence of liberty was superfluous.

The continuation of the V.V.N.'s work in West Germany, of course, seemed more urgently necessary than ever. Lists were circulated with the names of suspect judges or police officers, all of whom without exception lived in the Federal Republic. Whoever turned Communist, such as the ex-Wehrmacht general Vincenz Müller who became an S.E.D.[1] minister, went unharmed. The strongly left-wing V.V.N. suffered from a defect of vision which only enabled it to see Nazi criminals in the non-Communist part of Germany.

In 1961 the V.V.N. succeeded in bagging a really big piece of game; at any rate it was this organisation which took the credit for having removed the Federal Minister for Refugees, Theodor Oberländer, from office. Under Hitler, Oberländer was an active, if not always politically reliable adviser on East European policy questions. He was one of the ideologues who saw Germany's future in expansion eastward. His objections to Hitler's Russian campaign were directed less at the war as such than at the blunders of the German occupation authorities. Because of a courageous appeal for an alleviation of living conditions in occupied Russia, he was given a punitive re-assignment. Having suddenly been accused by Adenauer in the Bonn Press Club as having been "dyed deep brown", Oberländer, already buried under the rubble of his own past, now found himself accused of having taken part as a Lieutenant in the Lwow mass murders of June 1941. When the S.P.D. leader Professor

[1] S.E.D. = Sozialistische Einheitspartei Deutschlands (Socialist Unity Party), the sole political party in East Germany, created from a forced merger of the K.P.D. (Communists) and S.P.D. (Social Democrats).

Carlo Schmid was asked about Oberländer during a visit to Israel, he made no attempt to diminish ·the suspicion against his fellow member of the Bundestag. Oberländer took his revenge by reminding Carlo Schmid in March 1962 of a speech which the latter had made, in his capacity as head of the Legal Branch of the Military Governor's headquarters in Lille, to the Nazi Academy of German Law in Berlin in the summer of 1941. Carlo Schmid had spoken of the unsuitability of the Hague Convention on Land Warfare in modern total war in so far as it concerned the necessary exploitation of the economic resources of a country such as France "in the interests of final victory". Schmid claimed that the speech, which sounded like a justification of Hitler's policy of exploitation, had been written under duress. Everybody knew that under the Third Reich many people were forced to do many things; but this was the first intimation that an ex cathedra speech such as this was ever delivered under compulsion.

No clear results were achieved by this duel with stones between two men in glass houses. By February 1962 Oberländer was able to produce a document signed by Adenauer which withdrew the "deep brown" stain from him and wished him, since the Lwow accusation had been proved groundless, an active and successful future career. Obvious though the difference between Oberländer and Carlo Schmid may be, the discovery of their true past is obscured in both their cases by their 1945 questionnaires, which instead of admitting that their attitude to Nazism had been one of "both-and" (i.e. *both* acceptance *and* resistance) had instead claimed their total non-involvement—a condition which under a dictatorship is only possible in the cradle, in prison or in emigration.

People such as Kurt Ziesel, who in 1962 dug up much damning evidence against many leading personalities who had claimed to have opposed Hitler, would never have had a job to do if only the Germans concerned had not deserted the truth and had admitted the facts about their past. It should be obvious that in a dictatorship no one in a responsible position can fail to be involved however much they may later deny it.

At Nuremberg the judges at the war crimes trials had kept the accused in uniform and referred to them by their ranks in order to have some point of reference and as a rule of thumb criterion of guilt and responsibility. For simplicity's sake organisations such as the S.S. were given a blanket condemnation as criminal. In contrast to traditional jurisprudence, whoever had belonged to them was obliged to prove his own innocence. Before long this procedure failed to satisfy discerning German jurists, more subtle criteria were sought and the Nuremberg formula was dropped.

On 6th November 1954 the ailing former Reichs Foreign Minister von Neurath was released from the war criminals prison in Spandau. Spontaneously, Federal President Heuss sent his fellow Swabian a telegram in which he expressed his pleasure that "the martyrdom of these years has come to an end for you". Neurath had, after all, been Reichs Protector of Bohemia and Moravia and had been an 'honorary' *Gruppenführer* in the S.S. By Nuremberg standards he could not have been anything but guilty. For this reason *The Times* wondered on 8th November why Heuss had used the word "martyrdom", which was supposed to refer to someone who had suffered in a good cause. Heuss saw only an unhappy, even though foolish and mistaken, fellow countryman. He saw through the S.S. uniform which for him was not an automatic bar to feelings of compassion.

With some hesitation the S.P.D. also admitted the need to judge people as individuals. On 14th July 1958 the S.P.D. press service published a short statement in recognition of former members of the *Waffen S.S.* who showed evidence of political maturity: they were welcome as fellow citizens of the new state with equal rights. This had been preceded by a speech by the former S.S. Panzer General Meyer at an S.S. reunion in Lemgo. Meyer had praised the first post-war chairman of the S.P.D., Dr. Kurt Schumacher, as a "true resistance fighter". Since then the S.P.D. believes in the possibility of a transformation not only from Communist to Social Democrat but also from Nazi to democrat.

In the first edition of the Bonn parliamentary handbooks it was noticeable that those Members who could produce no evidence of time spent in a concentration camp made no mention of what their activities had been between 1933 and 1945. Whoever had occupied an official post during this period strove, with unusual modesty, to deprecate its importance. Whoever had written a book dated it in his curriculum vitae back to a slightly less compromising time. Thus the Third Reich, in contrast to its real nature, was made out to be an era of shrinking violets. The Federal Constitutional Court, in its judgment of 17th December 1953 to the effect that between Hitler's seizure of power and the capitulation the German state had really been nothing but an expression of arbitrary Party rule, involuntarily lent countenance to the general urge to shrug off those twelve years of Nazism. The hour of truth had been allowed to pass by. When with the issue of the new parliamentary handbook in March 1962 it seemed about to recur, at least as far as Members of the Bundestag and their past history was concerned, it transpired that the Germans were as liable as ever to swing with the current political breeze. This time the silence over the years of the Third Reich was at least broken on such points as war medals, war wounds and notable services in the Wehrmacht. Now a Member would add a Knight's Cross of the Iron Cross to the War Service Cross which he had been awarded for his contribution to ensuring German food supplies. Timidly German parliamentarians admitted to membership of Nazi organisations, whilst the tendency to record Communist connections was correspondingly reduced.

That a clearly indispensable senior civil servant could be absolved of responsibility for his activities in the Third Reich by his personal chief, the Federal Chancellor, is demonstrated by the much-discussed case of Globke. The Permanent Under-Secretary in the Chancellor's Office in Bonn, Dr. Hans Globke, had not in fact been a member of the Nazi Party, but his involvement in the more sinister aspects of Hitler's dictatorship far exceeded that of the average Party member. He is a text-book example of the inadequate criteria hitherto employed in evaluating the Third Reich.

Globke the civil servant spent the period of the Third Reich in a 'sensitive post' in the Reichs Ministry of the Interior. With his harmless-sounding job of Registrar of Births, Marriages and Deaths he could hardly have chosen a worse position to have occupied. Even during von Papen's chancellorship Globke was marginally involved, through his part in the ordinance which made it difficult for Jews to change their names. The 'infiltration' of East European Jews, contemptuously publicised as the rapid rise of the immigrant Polish Jew from pedlar to department-store owner, was to be checked, or at least hindered, by administrative measures against such people changing their names. The street-corner demogoguery of the Brownshirts, who noisily tried to turn East European Jewish immigration into a national disaster, had penetrated, even if in modified form, to the Ministries, in which under the chancellorship of von Papen and Schleicher a swing to the political right began to be noticeable. One can assume that Globke then considered it right and proper to prevent Jews from concealing their origins by a change of name.

Due to its function as a demographic record office, the Registry of which he was in charge then took an increasing part in the ruthless anti-Jewish policies of the Third Reich. His immediate colleagues were spared this fatal involvement, because their field of competence only included matters such as food and medical supplies and not demographic questions. Globke seems to have been convinced that the traditions of the German civil service would be maintained under the Third Reich provided the civil servants of the Republic continued to staff the Ministries. Considering it his duty, in 1935 Globke wrote the commentary to the Nuremberg Racial Laws promulgated in the same year, by virtue of which all Jews living in Germany were to be segregated like lepers from 'pure-blooded' Germans. On his own initiative he contributed an article on 15th January 1937 to the *Journal of the German Academy of Law* in which he welcomed a clear and strict interpretation of the so-called "Racial Purity" clauses under which all intercourse between Jews and Germans was made heavily punishable.

The evidence is clearly sufficient to refute the assertion of Globke's defenders that he had always been basically anti-Nazi. Only a warped mind could have produced Globke's utterance of 16th February 1961 that when he wrote his Nuremberg commentary he expected his friends in the resistance movement to realise, once the tyrant had been removed, that this revolting work had merely been written to camouflage his real views—another piece of wisdom after the event, so typical of the present German attitude to the Nazi era.

If Globke had been really convinced in 1935 that Hitler was soon due to be liquidated, he could safely have refrained from commenting on the deplorable Nuremberg Laws. Views which after 1945, when the whole horror was revealed, were seen to have been repulsive and untenable, did not necessarily seem so in 1935, the year of Globke's commentary. At that time not even the most thorough-going Hitlerite so much as thought of a radical extermination of the Jews. Conventional middle-class anti-semitism, of which Globke was obviously guilty, found relief in 1935 in the thought that the unpleasant Jewish problem had now received its final and proper legal solution. The Jews, or so it seemed then, were now segregated and since their influence in Germany had clearly grown excessive, a certain repression of them could do no harm. This was the mentality which made the Nuremberg Laws acceptable.

We need waste little time on the assertion that Globke's

commentary was really meant as a secret help to the Jews, even if Jewish witnesses can be produced to support this particular piece of white-washing. In the general flight from the past there is nothing which cannot be proved. Equally weak is the argument that Globke's commentary was a sort of secret weapon which enabled a civil servant working for the Resistance to retain his important post in the Ministry. Such claims are all too obvious post hoc rationalisations and only serve to prove how difficult it is, in a Germany which stubbornly refuses to face facts, to admit to the simple fact of a civil servant staying at his post under a dictatorship. Clearly Globke himself, impressed by all the self-justifying documents which he composed after 1945, gradually came to believe his own story that his funda-mental motive in writing the Nuremberg commentary had been sympathy for the Jews.

In his *Observations on World Politics* Jacob Burckhardt, in a moment of scepticism, once described the writing of history as a collection of inventions and distortions. If this is true in general, how much greater violence is likely to be done to the facts when a person sets down his own personal history. It would be revealing if the three versions of his curriculum vitae which a civil servant such as Globke wrote, or might have written in 1932, 1935 and 1945 could be laid side by side. We would then have a piece of German history with its typical erasures, alterations and emendations which the author re-garded (in their time) as the truth.

In 1932 one can imagine Globke setting down his life-story to date, emphasising his conservative leanings and admitting to a certain impatience with the sterile party politics of the Weimar republic. Globke belonged to the Centre party and he would have shared that party's view that Hitler should be given a chance to prove his claims and step down if he failed. In the subsequent years, as Hitler's autocratic rule was established, Globke, the keen civil servant, would have accepted the Third Reich as a political fait accompli, even though he did not approve of it in every respect. He would not even have voted for Hitler, but he served him in the conventional manner of the civil servant. There is no evidence whatever for any note-worthy resistance to Hitler from the Centre party in 1933, but there are plenty of signs of their approval. Globke's life story is meaning-less unless one realises that by 1935 the senior civil servant, for all his reservations in detail, regarded Hitler's Reich as an institution worthy to be served.

The German civil servant, for centuries accustomed to obedience, countered any doubts which might have arisen at that time by his faith in the absolute validity of law and higher authority. Both have always had a reassuring effect on a German. In his curriculum vitae written in 1935 Globke would certainly have mentioned the laudatory minute, referring to his "constant readiness to take responsibility" which Frick, the Minister of the Interior, appended to Globke's request for promotion. To the same man writing in 1945, however, the truth seems to have been quite different. Now he emphasised his Catholic allegiance and his old days in the Centre party. On 18th January 1946 Cardinal Preysing of Berlin certified that Globke, now in serious straits, had always had a kind thought for the persecuted Jews. Obviously the one does not exclude the other. But what is quite unacceptable is the "I-was-against-it-from-the-beginning" formula as claimed after the war by Globke and so many other Germans. If these three life stories were to be compared, the one written in 1945 would be easily recognisable as the most subjective since it was written in the greatest embarrassment.

After the war Globke claimed that his special job in the Ministry had been to prevent the worst from happening to the Nazis' victims and to pass on regular information to enable the Catholic clergy to combat Hitler. But the Churches were by no means entirely opposed to Hitler. Whilst some churchmen put up a courageous resistance others engaged in various forms of collaboration. Taken all round Globke was not in a position to prevent anything from happening, just as he probably did nothing to make matters worse. Basically he was just one of the little cogwheels in a dictatorship which can be replaced without any noticeable effect on the machine. After discounting the dishonest accusations made by the Communists and the untrustworthy attempts of the other side to defend him, we are left with a human being caught in the toils of evil—a German, in fact, like so many others. That the Communists of all people, who know what a dictatorship can do to a man of goodwill, should have been the loudest in their indignation over Globke is one of the greatest pieces of dishonesty of our age.

Nor has the truth about the Third Reich been revealed by the copious books of memoirs which began appearing on the German book market around 1950. The majority of their authors, figures of the recent past, were to a certain extent using their memoirs as another form of 'questionnaire' with the aim of putting themselves in the best possible light. The accent was less on the facts than on their personal innocence. Busy pens bent the past into the required shape. Certainly much that was written was true; but not everything was mentioned which went to make up the reality of the Hitler era.

Political memoirs have of course always tended to show up the author in the best possible light. In his four-volume *Memoirs* ex-Reichs Chancellor von Bülow produced a model of this particular art. His opponents considered that in order to buttress his posthumous reputation he had indulged in a great deal of questionable self-exculpation at the expense of others. There was in any case a notable difference between the post-World War I and the post-1945 memoirs. The most of which von Bülow could have been accused was a lack of foresight in his execution of imperial policy, whereas all those who wrote memoirs of the Hitler period were suspect of having been more or less closely involved in the mass-murders committed by a lunatic dictatorship. To avoid the stigma of this infinitely more damning accusation the memoir writers of post-1945 were quite disproportionately concerned to stress their own non-involvement in the events.

Only two of the more readable works from the pile of post-war memoirs will be mentioned here, namely the memoirs of two senior officers of the Foreign Service, the former State Secretary Ernst Freiherr von Weizsäcker and the one-time ambassador Erich Kordt. They are an example of the recurring difficulty experienced by a German in facing up to his 'personal' history.

Weizsäcker is remembered by everybody who knew him as an honest man. His whole character made him seem incapable of ulterior motives. Nevertheless he was accused of having lent his hand to the inhumanities of the Nazi regime. During the Nuremberg trials the judges of the victorious powers faced him with incriminating documents which seemed to point to a knowledge of the greatest of Hitler's crimes. In his *Memoirs* (1950) Weizsäcker claimed that under a dictatorship it meant nothing if a person signed a document or made use of the brutal phraseology of the time. Because of the need to deceive the Gestapo, documentary and oral statements made under Hitler's regime had little or no value as evidence. According to Weizsäcker one was always obliged to speak in a code language, so that even private letters are not good evidence of a man's real opinions during the years from 1933 to 1945.

But the most incomprehensible aspect of the Third Reich was the very fact that in it so many Germans were induced to do things and to say things which in the light of what was revealed after 1945 must have seemed inconceivable to the very people who had committed them. Supposing that the most unlikely contingency had been realised and Hitler had turned moderate and had stayed in power—we can be absolutely certain that those who had drawn up these documents in their alleged 'code' would not have recanted a word of them, but would have let them stand as a valid expression of their viewpoint. The conditions of the time undoubtedly demanded a certain skill in dissimulation and juggling with words. That juggling and dissimulation are a component of every dictatorship is an inescapable fact. But if the validity of every documentary statement of the time is disputed, the question then arises as to when, in the many changes of political systems, did any German ever come to the point of committing his real opinions to paper? It is, after all, equally true to assert that all the post-1945 memoirs too were written in a kind of private code. Since opinion today takes different attitudes from those adopted under Allied occupation, it is not unlikely that many writers of memoirs may yet be tempted to revise their version of events for a further edition which would be more in tune with the current mood.

The pitfalls inherent in the claim to be using a 'code' language in difficult times was sharply demonstrated by State Secretary von Weizsäcker when in May 1942 he welcomed the diplomats repatriated from America in the pompous and aggressive language typical of the Nazi era. Ulrich von Hassell, who was recalled as German Ambassador in Rome in 1938 and was executed for his part in the plot on Hitler's life in 1944, noted in his diary that after the State Secretary's Frankfurt speech he had disqualified himself for any future post in a free Germany.

Weizsäcker avenged himself in his memoirs with a reference to von Hassell's earlier attempts to ingratiate himself with Hitler. Weizsäcker claimed that von Hassell had been a partisan of Hitler even before 1933. He went on to describe the zeal with which von Hassell had arranged Hitler's meeting with Mussolini in Venice in 1934. Only when the Nazis began to interfere with his diplomatic work in Rome did von Hassell lose his sympathy for them. Here is an example of two Germans, both well-meaning after their fashion, who refused to recognise each other's 'personal code'. Each was only prepared to allow that his own utterances were meant to be understood as deceptive camouflage. Weizsäcker described his membership of the Nazi party and his honorary rank in the S.S. as an un-avoidable price to be paid for remaining in office and carrying on his work in the spirit of the Resistance. By contrast he considered that von Hassell's brown uniform made him suspect.

Weizsäcker built his defence on the axiom that he had only stayed in his job to do good and prevent the worst. It is significant that such claims, which are normally held to be self-evident in public service, should have had to be specially emphasised by a civil servant under the Third Reich. There is absolutely no reason whatever to assume that a diplomat such as Weizsäcker should have consistently opposed Hitler from 1933 onward. Until 1938 he undoubtedly approved of his foreign policy, even though he may have thought his methods questionable in detail.

Hitler had reckoned in advance on a certain resistance from the middle classes. It was literally impossible to build a state relying only on his uniformed rowdies. If he had ever been in a position to write his memoirs he would have reminded all those Germans who allegedly strove to prevent 'the worst' from happening that in building up his power the inwardly hesitant or recusant middle classes had been, with their ability and sense of duty, the most valuable of all his collaborators. This viewpoint has at least equal validity with the claim that this or that official had only stayed in office under Hitler in order to work against him.

In his perceptive memoirs *Not on the Files* (1950) Erich Kordt wrote, with winning frankness, that under a dictatorship any opposition could hardly be anything but equivocal. The ambiguity begins with the contradiction between the glittering facade of affairs and clandestine insubordination. Ability does not go unnoticed even in a dictatorship. Thus Kordt, even in the proximity of von Ribbentrop, soon began to climb the ladder of promotion. As a young diplomat Kordt was once detailed, as the sole other passenger in a special aircraft from Athens, to accompany von Ribbentrop, who wanted to hear his advice. Obviously this occasioned a certain pride in the notice accorded to him, no doubt enhanced by the glamour of the uniform and esprit de corps of the diplomatic service. Kordt soon became the Minister's chef de cabinet at the Foreign Office. He was given the task of conducting foreign diplomats to the Nuremberg party rallies. Ribbentrop does not seem to have gained the impression that Kordt was fundamentally opposed to the regime.

As early as 1933, writes Kordt, English friends had pressed him to remain in the service in order to do everything possible to prevent matters from getting worse. Kordt's later attempts to restrain Hitler's megalomania and bellicosity are documentarily attested. In the Czech crisis he advised the British government through his brother Theodor that to make Hitler see reason they must adopt a firm tone in dealing with him. The offering of such a piece of advice was, however one may condemn him in other respects, mortally dangerous. At one time Kordt carried a pistol to shoot Hitler, but he never managed to draw it. Let those who are sure that they would have possessed greater determination mock him; the events of 20th July 1944 proved how few people are prepared to sacrifice themselves.

Nowadays it is extraordinarily difficult to pass fair judgment in retrospect on those who as it were 'kept two sets of books' during the Third Reich—on the one hand the clenched fist in the trouser pocket and on the other the acceptance of promotion and decorations. The constant conspiratorial activity, the urgent talks in locked rooms, the cryptic telephone calls and coded letters, the making of plans and drawing up lists of ministers for a free German government—all this, however dangerous any stirring of opposition may have been, achieved in the end precisely nothing.

The fatal events took their course without the least regard to those figures who in reality or imagination tried to "prevent the worst". Hardly one of these attempts at self-exculpation has contributed anything to an understanding of the phenomenon that was Hitler. Without it necessarily being the author's intention, these memoirs merely perpetuate in a different form the suspicious implication that only the merest fools were taken in by Hitler.

Mistaken though it is to see Hitler as having been raised to power by dark figures such as the big industrialists, generals and megalomaniac diplomatists, it is on the other hand equally false to hand out a blanket acquittal for the entire German governing class. Hitler would never have come to power if so much opposition (as was claimed after 1945 to have existed) had made itself felt sooner or in other than literary form.

In 1945 Thomas Mann believed that he had evolved a clear pattern of behaviour, at least in the intellectual sphere, which a decent German should have adopted under Hitler. He should not have published a line. In his opinion everything published in Germany after 1933 was stained with blood and shame, although Mann actually modified this rigid attitude on a number of occasions. On 3rd

February 1936 he admitted in a letter to the *Neue Zürcher Zeitung* that German literature had only in part emigrated and that those who had stayed were not to be despised.

Thomas Mann's cry of 'blood and shame' was still remembered in 1961 when S. Fischer Verlag's anthology of articles from its much-respected journal *Neue Rundschau* simply ignored the volumes published in Germany between 1934 and 1944 because the publishers considered that during these years, when the only voices had been those of slaves and hirelings, the spirit of the journal had been in emigration. This angered the writers who had been published in the *Neue Rundschau* during those ten years—they included among others Theodor Heuss—but they were no more than delayed victims of the inadequate rules laid down in 1945, according to which a good German should have remained silent between 1933 and 1945. The stay-at-homes refused to accept Thomas Mann's reproach. They opposed their 'inner emigration' to his conventional emigration. There were also writers who wrote only for their desk drawers, but when the tyrant had fallen and they were opened not much was revealed. The emigrés mocked: it was clear that in those years intellectual Germany had emigrated.

Yet in spite or because of the obtuseness of the official censorship there did exist in the Third Reich a tolerated literature of conscious detachment. Even the technique of writing between the lines could only be carried out with the tacit connivance of the rulers, whose intelligence in any dictatorship should not be underrated.

Berthold Brecht condemned all those who wrote under the Third Reich and claimed that "the womb from which they crawled is fertile still". Brecht, himself the voluntary or involuntary servant of a dictatorial regime (which in no way affects his value as a writer), cuts an odd figure as the judge of those who continued writing under the Third Reich. In spite of those who claim to find critical references to Soviet rule in his plays, he was nevertheless a valuable advertisement for the G.D.R. They had their troubles with him over details, but in general he provided the façade of intellectual respectability for the Ulbricht regime. We may assume therefore that those 'internal emigrés' of the Eastern bloc who have criticised the misdeeds of Communist bureaucracy are tolerated with a purpose.

Wilhelm Hausenstein, a man with entirely clean hands and the universally respected first post-war German ambassador in Paris, published in the *Süddeutsche Zeitung* on 24th December 1945 in answer to Thomas Mann a long list of books "free of blood and shame" which in his opinion showed that a lively intellectual activity had existed during the years of Nazism. Hausenstein praised a number of poets, writers and publishers who had remained in Germany as faithful servants of the truth in the face of Hitler's despotism. Hausenstein considered that overt resistance to the tyrant was possible. He heaped up whole piles of books which in his optimistic view implied "in every line a refutation of the whole Nazi swindle". Quantities of art books without the least Nazi slant, an astonishing range of works on theology and comparative religion, historical treatises and an imposing number of publications in the natural and humane sciences demonstrated, in Hausenstein's opinion, that the claim that the German intellect had utterly withered in those twelve years was a dubious over-simplification and a falsification of the real state of affairs.

Among a good hundred titles he specially singled out Ricarda Huch's *Age of Divided Faith*, Ernst Jüngers *Marble Cliffs*, Theodor Heuss' biography of Friedrich Naumann and in particular Werner Bergengruen and Reinhold Schneider. Besides these there was an abundance of literature in translation. Unlike Thomas Mann and others, Hausenstein approved of the fact that a great number of books were published at that time. Of course the dictatorship exploited the intellectual life of the country as camouflage, but writers cannot wholly leave their public disappointed.

How many doctors and priests stayed at their posts because they knew that their people needed them? Why should a writer not be allowed to feel the same calling? Similarly unjustified complaints are today being made against academics and professional men in the Soviet Zone: "Why doesn't Dr. X come over?" one hears people ask uncomprehendingly in the West and, because people are incapable of realising that he cannot simply abandon his colleagues, family and friends, does not want to abandon his patients, pupils or his flock, he is damned as a supporter or beneficiary of the Ulbricht regime.

One is appalled if one tries to imagine the volte-face and white-washing which would feverishly begin if ever—which God forbid—West Germany were overrun by Communism. Or let us rather assume that East Germany might somehow or other be liberated from bolshevist rule and incorporated into a free Germany. In both cases it would probably transpire that nothing had been learned from the last violent change of regime. There would certainly be new questionnaires, and searching questions about membership of the S.E.D. would be asked. Once again the new judges would estimate the character and proportionate guilt of the individual from his uniform, the organisation he had belonged to and his party member-ship—none of which, however many lies and distortions might creep into the answers to the questionnaires, would alter one jot of the historical reality of the two States of partitioned Germany, any more than did our postwar refusal to admit the truth about Nazism.

Once in a conciliatory moment Thomas Mann challenged the habit of dividing Germans into good Germans and evil Germans. Even under the Third Reich, he said, a good Germany had persisted even though temporarily defeated by the devil's wiles: the two Germanies form, in fact, a unity. Good Germany is as much to be found in the present-day Federal Republic as in the G.D.R.—as also is evil Ger-many. The rigid division of the two by a sharp line in time or space will never be convincing, particularly when it is too loudly invoked by those anxious to prove that they belonged to the good side.

So we are left with the question which in this particular form has been the unique dilemma of our history: where lies the true Germany —in Weimar or in Potsdam? In the Federal Republic or in the G.D.R., with the emigrés or with those who stayed on in silence, in the concert hall or the barrack square, with those who work with their brains or the manual workers? The Third Reich was contrasted with the 'other Germany', a formula still in use by the extreme left which claims that the Federal Republic is nothing but a continuation of the Nazi state. The truth that a nation, like every human being, consists of both good and evil elements which are inseparable is only being slowly realised in this land where history is all too easily for-gotten, rejected or falsified.

8

QUIS CUSTODIET . . .?

As if the severe criticism directed at the German character from abroad were not enough, the land of schools and schoolmasters produced at an early stage its own merciless brand of self-criticism. In July 1895 von Treitschke was moved to declare that the Germans had "done themselves positive harm with their boundless appetite for self-censure".

In a singular alliance German and foreign preceptors seized the Germans in a pincers' grip and turned them at times into the most reprimanded creatures on earth. There can be no other people which has produced from its own ranks so many bitter exponents of the faults in its own character. After every catastrophe the disregarded prophets would emerge and, like teachers lecturing rows of pupils on their behaviour, they would give the German people a resounding ticking-off. Index finger raised, they would demonstrate how much misfortune the Germans would have been spared if they had only listened to their warnings. Foreign criticism, self-criticism and the thunderings of frustrated prophecy combined to intensify each other and produced a state of contrition in a nation which would swear not to disregard these warnings next time.

Whoever makes a close study of German self-criticism will undoubtedly come to the conclusion that the German people have not always been very fortunate in their self-appointed Cassandras, though if no one paid attention to them they were themselves partly to blame. The German task-masters of the Wilhelminian epoch seem in retrospect to have been a curious mixture of wisdom and foolishness. They were seldom in agreement over what were the strengths and what the weaknesses of the Germans.

The best and the worst of German self-criticism are combined to an extraordinary degree in the figure of Friedrich Nietzsche, the bitterest critic that the German people has ever had. In a letter to his sister of 1858 he even rejected his mother: "How is it possible that we are blood relations!" To his mind Germany did not deserve Nietzsche, her greatest son, because she failed to appreciate him. This hatred became a torture which—in the great thinker's own words—poisoned his very entrails. Imperial Germany with its "sneering coldness" and its "rabid authoritarianism" (*The Gay Science*) seemed repulsive to the philosopher of the superman. In Bismarck's speeches Nietzsche found him "tactless and arrogant"; the tone of voice used by the German officer was unbearable. The Germans of his time were, he thought, "good-natured but sly".

In his *Twilight of the Idols* of 1888 he managed to produce a few words of praise for German industriousness, manliness and stamina; but their new-found power had merely stultified the Germans, their intellectual powers were being progressively crushed by a grotesque fever of economic and political activity. At the same time that Germany was waxing as a great power, "France is acquiring a completely different significance as a cultural power". Nietzsche's love for France developed at a distance. He delighted in witty French literature, but knew few Frenchmen personally. The Germans, on the other hand, unfortunately for them, he knew only too well.

In *Ecce Homo* Nietzsche's detestation of the Germans took on a pathological form. "The presence of a German" now actually disturbed his digestion. Intercourse with them was degrading: "The Germans are a canaille." Whilst his contemporaries were deriding the Germans' excessive class consciousness and their worship of rank, Nietzsche thought that the Germans had absolutely no feeling for rank, gradation and order in human society. He found them too pious, too democratic, too good-natured—the very qualities in which other critics found them lacking. Even physically Nietzsche thought his fellow-countrymen absurd, to the point where he laboriously searched his own genealogy for ancestors of foreign origin. But the acme of German vulgarity was for Nietzsche that they were not even ashamed "to be simply Germans and nothing else".

Nietzsche's express contempt for Christian compassion provided the Hitlerite state, together with the concept of the superman, with a certain, though meagre, veneer of philosophical justification. The sage himself would have been the first to be amazed at Hitler's endorsement of his ideas. On the evidence quoted above it is not difficult to guess what views he would have expressed on Nazi rule in the Third Reich. The superman of his imagining had little in common with the average officer of the S.A. or S.S. or with the leading clique of the Party itself. He would have been repelled by the brutish parade-ground tone and the suppression of the intellect under the orders of a semi-educated demagogue. Hitler never progressed beyond a crude misinterpretation of the framework of the elaborate philosophical structure which Nietzsche himself had tried to guard from abuse by his scornful remarks about the vulgar masses for whom his words were not meant. The Nazi bosses saw no further than the "glorious blonde beast thirsting for booty and victory". The philistine middle-class read no further than the passage in *Zarathustra* which reads: "Goest thou to women? Then forget not thy whip", a remark typical in its vulgarity of the Wilhelminian Germany in which it was written. The windbags of the Nazi era clung obsessively to the idea of the "master race". Gauleiter and Reichs Commissioner Erich Koch, for example, used the expression in a speech of 5th March 1943 at least half a dozen times. Otherwise, as he probably feared with good reason, no one with Koch's personality as their only evidence would have believed in his claims to mastery.

Following Nietzsche's example, there was no lack of schoolmasterly preceptors of the German people, such as Paul de Lagarde, to lash them for their faults and prescribe remedies for national regeneration, expressed in violent terms which were often a mixture of sharp insight and arrant rubbish.

We should be equally chary of accepting unreservedly the strictures of another German preceptor, who sternly declared during World War II that the German people would have been spared all their misfortunes if only they had paid attention to his—Thomas Mann's—warnings. Thomas Mann was after all forty years old when in 1918 he introduced himself to the German people as the brilliant expounder who would put the events of the war in perspective with his often astonishing work *Observations of a Non-Political Man*. He was at that time estranged from his brother Heinrich. In the *Observations* he dismissed him, with less than fraternal regard, as a lackey of the French and a near-traitor. With biting sarcasm Thomas mocked all those who, like his brother Heinrich, wanted to talk the Germans into becoming parliamentary democrats. He thought nothing of the "superstitious belief in majorities". He regarded the authoritarian German state as the "form of state most fitting and suitable to the Germans and fundamentally the one which they desired". So away, thought the Thomas Mann of World War I, with "the alien and repellent catchword 'democratic'".

After the war the author of *Buddenbrooks* did not like to be reminded that in his *Observations* he had praised the educative value of battle. Certainly in 1916 and 1917, when he wrote this work, war was for him in the language of the day a cleansing bath of steel. It was not to be assumed, wrote Thomas Mann, that "dear mankind would cut a better figure in an endless state of peace than under the sword". Fired by his own eloquence he went on to describe how he had heard that men who had been blinded were "of all the patients in field hospitals the most cheerful—they romp about and throw their glass eyes at each other". A Prussian ensign standing rigidly to attention was evidence for Thomas Mann then of a "heightened sense of purpose in life", and the custom in the easternmost provinces of Germany of "bowing to kiss the hem of the master's garment" he thought nothing more than "natural". Proud obedience was in itself something specifically German. Even the Imperial Germany of the day was too western and democratic for Thomas Mann's liking.

It is therefore not surprising if Thomas Mann put forward a very simple explanation for Germany's unpopularity in World War I: he saw Germany in the role of the persecuted innocent. In their unsuspecting good nature the Germans had been totally unprepared to find the hatred of republicans and freemasons "so shamelessly incited against our state structure, our honest militarism, our spirit of order, authority and duty". The "whining" of Edith Cavell, the British nurse shot by the Germans, he dismissed as "sentimental rubbish". Miss Cavell had misused her nurse's uniform by helping Belgian soldiers over the frontier and had thereby brought on her own death.

After World War I Thomas Mann, particularly when he recalled his brother Heinrich, saw himself as a prophet who had been cheated by history. In the political competition between the brothers Heinrich Mann was now indisputably in the lead. His novel *The Subject* was published too late to be of much use to the subjects of the Kaiser; understandably enough it was only published after the war but the author assured the public that it had been finished by 1914. Thus at a time when Thomas Mann in his *Observations* was expressing his admiration for "honest militarism", his brother Heinrich was depicting the Germans under Kaiser Wilhelm as repulsive lickspittles. Heinrich believed that in contrast to his brother's panegyric to authoritarian Germany, he was showing up the reality of that era in *The Subject*: the stultifying automatism of the parade ground, the swaggering pomposity of the Kaiser himself, the crushing power of the aristocracy and the monied classes. The "subject" in the novel is personified by the middle-class industrialist Dr. Hessling, a man who has never grown up since his student club days, seducer of a working-class girl whom he promptly leaves in the lurch—an incident of which he is painfully reminded when he suggests to an army officer who has seduced his sister that he should marry her and is kicked out with the contemptuous bellow of "dirty little shopkeeper". Whereat "the subject" springs to attention and accepts the God-given social ordering of things with resigned admiration.

The Subject was a brilliant caricature which combined once more all the dangerous and disagreeable characteristics of the Wilhelminian German: the beer-sodden student who thinks he is being stared at and invites his vis-à-vis to the gentleman's lavatory to arrange a duel; the nobleman who regards a middle-class girl as fair game; money-mad industrialists; a disreputable parson with his feeble-minded daughter; corrupt labour leaders; finally a wildly nationalistic German-Jewish lawyer who goes to a Paris cosmetician to have his physical appearance improved by surgery.

During the Weimar Republic the brothers Mann were reconciled and gave joint warnings against the danger which was threatening from the political right wing. They recognised the danger of Hitler at an early stage. Once the catastrophe had occurred the advice tendered by the brothers was not, admittedly, very enlightening. After his understandable emigration to America Thomas Mann did all that he could to spur on the democracies to arm against Hitler. In 1945 as a new American citizen he admonished the United States to treat the Germans sternly but justly. The Germans themselves he advised to hark to the voice of the great American democracy.

From 1950 onwards Thomas Mann began to doubt the Americans' leadership. Their rearmament of Germany made him uneasy. This marked the beginning of the brothers' attraction towards Soviet-dominated East Germany. In the "Goethe Year" celebrations in Russian-occupied Weimar in 1949 Thomas Mann praised the social achievements of East Germany—which he strictly refused to call communistic. The Germans noticed that Mann was not in fundamental opposition to every form of dictatorship. The dictatorship of the Soviet Zone, which proffered him a laurel wreath, displeased him a great deal less than Hitler's state. He praised Soviet Zone education because it inculcated "respect for intellectual achievements such as mine". Thomas Mann even felt then that he could call the G.D.R. a "multi-party state".

How changeable were Thomas Mann's views and opinions is emphasised by his remarks about Gerhart Hauptmann, one of the authors who had continued to publish books during the Nazi regime. In a speech on the occasion of Hauptmann's sixtieth birthday in 1922 Thomas Mann had praised him as the "most German of personalities" and the "intellectual leader of post-imperial Germany"— now all at once he found that Hauptmann was covered in blood and shame. Politically Heinrich Mann went even further than his brother. Even in 1933 he advised the German people, faced with the choice between Communism and Nazism, to vote Communist. At his own wish Heinrich Mann was buried in an East Berlin cemetery, whilst Thomas preferred the soil of his beloved Switzerland. For a long while the novel *The Subject* was the show-piece of the East German Communists: Heinrich Mann had no objections to the particular form of subjection exercised by the Germans of the extreme left.

Several of the swaggering, loudmouthed figures in *The Subject* were unmistakably influenced by the biting cartoons which appeared in *Simplicissimus*, a humorous magazine launched in Munich shortly before the turn of the century to satirise the leading figures of the age of Wilhelm II. After World War I *Simplicissimus*, in alliance with two of its contributors Thomas and Heinrich Mann, became one of those warning German voices to whom unfortunately no attention was paid.

For their attacks on conditions in Imperial Germany the editors of the magazine were subjected to fines and imprisonment for alleged lèse-majesté, but anyone who looks through the pre-World War I volumes will be amazed at what castigation was addressed with impunity at church and state. The form in which the editors of *Simplicissimus* saw the danger and stupidity of the Kaiser's Germany was most clearly expressed in the special issue of 1905–06 entitled "Peace with France". Once again Germany had beaten France— even if only in the imagination of the cartoonists who now demonstrated graphically the amazing consequences of a new German victory. The page entitled "If Germany were to win again" showed as the first consequence of war a total militarisation of German everyday life. From now on, it said, every civilian had to stand at attention in front of a soldier. A picture showed how the latest victory produced a rash of medals all over the country which even extended to dogs. Three stenographers developed rabies from the strain of writing down the ceaseless victory speeches in shorthand. *Simplicissimus* excelled itself in inventing the comically grotesque consequences of an imagined German victory: to inculcate patriotic sentiments with mother's milk wet-nurses were to be daily fed with a mixture of rifle oil and metal polish; for the enormously growing number of ex-servicemen's associations room would have to be found on distant islands; the great monument to victory would have to be erected in Morocco, because every possible space in Germany was already occupied by imposing figures. For *Simplicissimus* the German was a man who did not even take off his uniform in bed. The whole of German life was regimented. The magazine built up the bone-headed German officer, his world bounded by the inanities of the officers' mess, the racecourse or the casino, as the dominating figure of Imperial Germany. Recruits were nothing but raw material for drilling, which provided the officer caste with an outlet for its aggressive arrogance.

Two of the main targets for satire were the Kaiser and the Crown Prince, surrounded by a ruling class made up of a bullying military; a shamelessly worldly church; the financially ambitious junkers from east of the Elbe; conniving judges and barristers; brash, nationalistic students and a brutal police force as the strong arm of the powers-that-be. As in *The Subject*, Jews too were marginally referred to as supporters and beneficiaries of the imperial regime.

According to *Simplicissimus* the Kaiser's Germany was doomed to failure in foreign policy. The magazine once posed the riddle: "Why are English diplomats so successful and German diplomats so unsuccessful?" Answer: the English were charming and utterly civilian, the Germans were like bullet-headed sergeant-majors or scarfaced students. The contrast was emphasised in the illustration, showing the Germans with bloated, stupid faces and the Britons with faces that were kindly and humorous. Englishmen were frequently shown as good examples. British sports were tennis and running, the German sport: beer-swilling, with the two different types of figure juxtaposed—repulsive corpulence beside athletic slimness. Hardly a number of *Simplicissimus* went by without some cartoon of bull-necked, scarred students lurching through the streets and squandering their fathers' hard-earned money; drunk every night, they only knew the streets of the university quarter of the town from hearsay. Prussian policemen might zealously pursue cheeky workers and arrest people for dancing the tango in public—but the swaying students, as future judges and attorneys, were never touched.

A few Jews appeared as marginal figures in the cartoonists' grotesque vision of Germany. Jewish features were frequently to be seen in caricatures when a case of fraudulent bankruptcy occurred. The Wertheims (Jewish department store owners) decorated a Christmas tree to thank the Saviour for the good Christmas business. The theme was continued in the post-war inflationary period: then the great cartoonist Olaf Gulbransson showed Jewish-looking profiteers enjoying winter sports at Partenkirchen. *Simplicissimus*' Bavarian brand of anti-semitism was more than half humorous, especially since one of its most famous cartoonists, T. T. Heine, was himself a Jew. Bitterness was tempered by wit, since for circulation purposes the publisher must have taken certain anti-semitic tendencies among his readers into account.

The German as satirised by *Simplicissimus* has been treated at some length because it has influenced the foreigner's image of Germany to an extraordinary degree. Its drawings were internationally popular and were frequently reproduced and imitated. In World War I the Frenchman Henriot used *Simplicissimus* cartoons for his book *Têtes de Boches*, an anti-German propaganda work printed in huge editions. The cartoons spoke for themselves. They also inspired a horde of other Allied caricaturists whose job it was to help the Allied cause by propagating the idea of German beastliness. In foreign cartoons the German still exhibits features orginating from old *Simplicissimus* cartoons. The bull-neck, the belly, the duelling-scars, the grotesque uniforms and the faintly cloddish cast of features have remained as a memorial to the comic archetypes immortalised by the magazine in pre-World War I days. When German wartime cartoonists looked for similar home-grown caricatures of Frenchmen, British or Americans in order to oppose corresponding Allied types to *Simplicissimus*' Germans, they soon realised that no other country had produced from its midst such an implacable graphic satire of its own character.

After World War I, in which incidentally *Simplicissimus* adopted a markedly patriotic attitude, the Munich cartoonists considered that they had given timely warning of the catastrophe that overcame imperial Germany but had unfortunately been paid no attention. Even this claim to prophetic stature seems dubious if one recalls how for years the *Simplicissimus* cartoonists had mocked Wilhelm II for showing such courtesy and kindness when he had received President Theodore Roosevelt or other leading Americans. In both world wars the magazine, without many changes in its staff, exhibited an astonishing enthusiasm for the war. To these changes of policy, which were only partially due to force majeure, was added a certain blindness towards approaching danger. Like most Germans, *Simplicissimus* was taken by surprise by the events of 1914, 1918 and 1933. When taxed with the paper's lack of foresight in the years 1930 to 1932, Dr. Sinsheimer the editor-in-chief admitted: "We were . . . poor prophets". T. T. Heine the virulent cartoonist spoke of "satire that misfired". Even after 1933 not a few of the contributors stayed with the magazine. The cartoonist Schilling, who had courageously opposed the Nazis, yielded to them after Hitler's seizure of power. In 1945, unable to face yet another switch in political allegiance, he committed suicide. His death was a symbol of the bewilderment in which *Simplicissimus*, along with the majority of Germans, had become enmeshed.

In early 1963 there appeared, in the line of succession of the great German self-critics, a new attack on the Germans in the form of Ulrich Sonnemann's *The Pliable People*. Elements of the same critical points which had been made by Nietzsche, the brothers Mann, and *Simplicissimus* reappear here in modern dress. Sonnemann demands that the nation of subjects should turn into a nation of the disobedient. He considers it typical of the whole unfortunate course of German history that recently in a Bavarian village a whole company of the Bundeswehr, on the order of a sergeant, simply jumped into a dark pit, as a result of which two soldiers were killed. "Everything in Germany must start by our unlearning obedience and this . . . cannot be taken too literally."

Sonnemann considers that the German passion for imitation is degrading. Yesterday the Germans were spreading terror throughout the world, today they are aping "whatever the others do". Specially repulsive is the complacency of German politicians when they return from Washington or Moscow to Bonn or East Berlin and are congratulated for their total subservience to the policies dictated by the Powers of East or West—sickening examples of typical German pliability. Sonnemann appeals for an "open conspiracy". It must come from the left, because in his view the political right has nothing to show for the last hundred years but failure. The mental legacy of the past must finally be cast off by an act of liberation—away with the musty powers-that-be, the dim and corrupt little men who rule us! A further reason to include Sonnemann in the succession of classic German Cassandra-figures is his vagueness when it comes to practical matters. He mocks the pedantically raised German index finger, which has never yet succeeded in having any effect on the truly besetting German sins, but when he tries to be constructive his own advice is impossibly vague. The great freedom which the Germans are supposed to win for themselves is not much more than wishful thinking if seen in the context of the real world of today. A journey from East Berlin to West Berlin is an impossibility for most Germans. To go from Munich to Chemnitz means as much trouble and as many formalities as were once needed to go round the world.

Sonnemann's vision of the future is not remarkable for its practicality. He urges the Germans to cease modelling themselves on the animal kingdom: "Yesterday the blonde beast of prey, today the ant, that model of industriousness. The Federal Republic of Germany should earn itself a proud and unique place in history by being the first state in the world to bear a man on its coat of arms"—instead of a bird—"however hallowed by tradition this device may be."

Since the amateur preceptors and critics have had small success in Germany, it may be asked how the Germans have fared with their professional teachers. Unlike the amateurs they can hardly be absolved of responsibility for the vicious aspects of the German national character; they cannot simply be dismissed with the remark that the Germans might have been better off if they had paid attention to them. Anyone who was a teacher under the Nazi regime was linked with the dictatorship by the very textbooks that he used, however upright a personal life he may have led. All textbooks published after 1933 spoke an unmistakable language. Whoever taught pupils at this time in the so-called new spirit, whether voluntarily or through necessity, will hardly wish to sit in judgment on the foolishness or the mistakes of others, if only from the merest considerations of good taste.

German teachers have experienced changes of political system with particular intensity. They are the constant targets for reproach by those zealots for whom the past cannot be damned loudly and often enough. The teachers' hesitation to decry what they or their predecessors were recently required to praise is understandable. Four times in the past fifty years they have been required to repudiate the past. For a miserable stipend the Kaiser demanded that they should propagate the ethos of Imperial Germany. The Republic expected them to proclaim the virtues of the Weimar constitution and the errors of the Monarchy. Hitler subsequently poured his scorn equally on teachers of both royalist and republican views; in his opinion they were mere repositories of dead knowledge. He spoke of their "mania for objectivity"—of which they soon cured themselves without overmuch resistance. After 1945 the same teachers had to accept new curricula, new flags and yet another view of history and simultaneously to swallow the reproof of having until then taught a distorted impression of Germany's past. In 1945 as in 1933 many of them hesitated to accept the wholesale condemnation of the recently overthrown regime.

Whenever the sins of the Nazi era are discussed the German teachers are invariably heavily criticised. This was particularly the case during the Eichmann trial. On 20th January 1960 the Bundestag exhorted them to be more vigorous than ever in cleansing the "relics of error" from our history. The sins of the fathers were to be forcibly brought to the attention of their sons. Questionnaires reveal that the only aspects of the Third Reich which many school-children could recall were the autobahns and the elimination of unemployment. Soon, it was feared, the only thing which they would know about Hitler would be his moustache.

Unmoved by the noisy posturing of those who hope to exorcise the past by drowning it in abuse, serious teachers are engaged on introducing into the curriculum an objective and exact course of study on the period of 1933–1945. According to the view expressed by Max Brauer, Lord Mayor of Hamburg, 95 per cent of Germans either inwardly or outwardly accepted Hitler's regime and in his opinion the remaining 5 per cent was neither sufficient material on which to build a new state nor competent to be entrusted alone with a revision of the history of Germany from 1933 to 1945. No teacher and no pupil can avoid the fact that the Third Reich was, for better or worse, a part of German history. It includes, besides the solution of the unemployment problem and whatever else people may try to adduce in its favour, the murder of the Jews, the responsibility for starting the war and the destruction of the Weimar Republic as a consequence of the inadequacy of its defenders and the ruthlessness of its enemies. It is above all highly inadvisable to apply to the Germans the drastic method of education used with cats, that of rubbing their noses again and again in their own dirt. It was once suggested that it should be compulsory to show in all schools a terrible film which some sadistic German soldier had made of the murder of some Jews during the last war. Films such as this were shown to the Nazi leaders during the Nuremberg trials, which made sense, but the forcible confrontation with the evil side of human nature is not a proper subject for teaching in schools. One cannot imagine a French teacher demonstrating to his class the tortures used on the natives during the war in Algeria, just as British schools refrain from elaborating on some of the more brutal practices of the colonial past. The teaching of history should not deprive a people of its self-respect—this, at least, is the opinion of many nations whom the Germans regard as good examples.

The Germans have not yet regained the ability to take a candid and impartial view of their own history in those instances where it bears a Communist or Nazi tinge. At international congresses of historians the representatives of West Germany are conspicuous in regarding objectivity in history as something almost indecent. A bad conscience makes them always tend towards moralising, of a kind more suited to religious instruction than to the teaching of history. They offer moral conclusions based on hindsight instead of a chronicle of events. As might be expected, the attempts of the older generation to explain Germany's and their own immediate past have run into critical opposition from young people. In view of the ruins of 1945 it did not require much to prove that their fathers had failed. In any argument with their elders, young people always have the advantage of simply having been too young to have borne any of the guilt of Hitler's regime. The theme of parental failure is not a new one. After 1945, in addition to the normal conflict between generations, this theme acquired the attraction of an unanswerable political argument in which the young could enjoy a reversal of the usual roles of teachers and taught. The parents were always perplexed when asked to explain the causes of Germany's utter defeat. In the great school of history they were clearly the dunces, and it would have been a miracle if politically-minded youth had not exploited this state of affairs to the full.

1960 saw the emergence in West Germany of a highly subjective literature of condemnation and personal exculpation, whose authors based their competence to judge their parents on their own natural innocence due to their age. A notable example was Christian Geissler (born 1928) with his novel *The Inquiry*. He put his parents' entire generation in the dock. When Hitler came to power Geissler was in his kindergarten—a convenient, if somewhat limited, vantage point. According to Geissler Germany's fathers were guilty of double failure—once in the Third Reich and once after 1945. In the first case they allowed Hitler to unleash his violence and destruction, in the second they refused to admit their guilt and complicity. In Geissler's novel the father, incidentally, is dead; over his grave the son calls him to account for having belonged to the S.A., for not having made a public protest against the Nuremberg Laws and for having done nothing to prevent the outbreak of another war.

Among those who 'got away with it' Geissler castigates with particular virulence people such as Hans Globke; the priests who once blessed Hitler's armies; and the leaders of the various East German refugee groups. He asks a teacher why he allowed a Jewish schoolboy to be expelled from his class. He calls the refugee rallies "orgies of forgetfulness". War for him was nothing but "barbaric murder and arson". The farmers expelled from East Prussia are asked whether they wept when Polish or Russian women and children were crushed by the German war machine. Anyone wearing a medal issued under the Third Reich is for this angry young man nothing better than a post hoc apologist for Hitler's crimes. It is no use quoting the Allied bombing of Dresden to him: "Dresden is the end of a chain whose links we ourselves forged." Which is, of course, no more than the harsh, inescapable truth.

Whilst the hero of Geissler's *Inquiry* could not forgive his dead father, the thirty-five-year-old Gudrun Tempel is prepared to show her family a certain degree of leniency. In spring 1962 she published *Speaking Frankly About the Germans* which aroused a great deal of attention as a voice of the younger generation. Gudrun's father and mother voted for Hitler and the mother was one of the first to join the Party. In their daughter's opinion both meant well; neither of them—in common with most Germans—had the least notion of politics. Gudrun Tempel's life as she describes it is fairly confused. Her name itself prompts the first question: is it her own or is it assumed? She herself "quite voluntarily" joined the B.D.M.[1] But then came the violent clash between the fourteen-year-old girl and the

---

[1] B.D.M. =Bund Deutscher Mädel (League of German Girls), the Nazi female youth organization corresponding to the boys' H.J. (Hitler Youth).

headmaster of a high school—a beast in S.S. uniform. Ideologically —and, clearly, in another way too—he made a bid for this teenage girl, demanding that she should inform against her parents, who had meanwhile turned away from Hitler in disillusion. Revolted, Gudrun turns her back on the Nazi regime and becomes an outsider in a world of enthusiasts or fellow-travellers. (One is slightly surprised to learn later in the book that during the war she carried the national colours in international ski championships and fencing matches and broke in horses for the Wehrmacht.)

In the tradition of Nietzsche, Gudrun Tempel reveals to us that she is disgusted with the Germans. She first published her views in the London *Sunday Times* and received many letters from readers agreeing with her. Her remark that most Germans (including her parents) had no inkling of Hitler's extermination policies was the only point on which her British correspondents refused to believe her; from such a ruthless critic of her own fellow-countrymen they had expected a verdict of total guilt. Gudrun Tempel sees the Germans of today as a people whose life is bounded on one side by J. S. Bach and on the other by the latest model of Mercedes, whose only wish is not to be disturbed in the enjoyment of the pleasures of life. What is there to be done about it? The authoress deals out a few pieces of advice, but in view of her own decision to repudiate the Germans none of them sounds very convincing.

After her traumatic experiences at the hands of the Nazis, she was not spared a terrible epilogue with the Russians. In 1945 she was in Saxony. Her experience is hinted at rather than described. The lesson which she learned from it was that a German cannot excuse his own crimes by pointing to the crimes of others. Her father is dying of hunger and rape is the order of the day. The daughter goes through an appalling period of arrest in a cellar. None of these horrors prompts in her the obvious thought that the evil in the world, without overlooking the evil present in one's own people, is less a German than a universal evil. Gudrun Tempel considers her fellow Germans capable only of the worst and most degraded forms of behaviour. Behind the ridiculous German industriousness and efficiency she sees nothing but a gaping void.

Sitting in judgment on Germany, neither Gudrun Tempel nor Christian Geissler concede the slightest mercy. There can be no objection to their urge to reveal the truth, but one may be allowed to ask whether they would have had the courage to try out their un-

exceptionable principles on real, live dictators and their henchmen—
in East Germany, for instance.

The pupils have set themselves over the teachers and accuse them
of incompetence. The trick consists in deriving the right to direct
moral censure at their elders from the accident of the date of their
birth, through which they were no more than children under the
Nazi regime. The parents, burdened for various reasons with a
guilty conscience, only encourage the younger generation's tendency
to mock the material comforts of life in today's Federal Republic,
even though they may be enjoying these very comforts to the full.
The traditionally dogmatic German index finger, once reserved for
schoolmasters, is today often raised by young people who now, in a
reversal of past roles, claim the roles of preceptor, task-master and
prophet. Impractical as were the proposals of the old-style Jeremiahs,
the advice of the young critics of today is equally useless by itself.
In a novel which is typical of this whole trend the hero commits
suicide and lays the blame on his father, because he—the son—
cannot go on living in the corrupt world which his parents' generation
have created. The father is invited to transfer the son's savings to the
'Freedom from Hunger' campaign. With this brilliant notion the
author imagined that he was contributing something to human
understanding and an improvement in the moral climate of West
Germany.

The contrast between young and old exists in every country, but in
Germany it has been raised to the status of a sort of philosophy. With
every reversal of the pattern of events the professional young people
appear with their condemnation of their parents' failure. In his
Doktor Faustus Thomas Mann ridiculed this "perpetual adolescence"
of the Germans. Youth as a self-sufficient and permanent state of
mind was practically unknown in other nations; they were amazed at
the behaviour of young Germans who never regarded themselves as
a link in the chain but as something entirely new. During the Third
Reich Professor Jaensch coined the expression "adolescent type" to
describe the Germans—a people who never entirely grew up. Being
always obliged to disassociate itself with the past, modern German
history always gives an impression of dislocation and instability. It
is only in Germany that whole age-groups consciously repudiate the
past and act as though they were disconnected from it.

Traditionally Germany has always placed exaggerated hopes in
'Youth'. Angered at his brusque dismissal, Bismarck dedicated his

memoirs (with emphasis) to his "Sons and Grandsons". The Weimar Republic, despairing of ever gaining the loyalty of deep-dyed monarchists, saw its salvation in the young—but the young failed to fulfill these expectations and turned instead to the rebels and the dissatisfied. In the Third Reich they felt themselves appealed to once again as the hopeful generation; only they could be expected to realise fully the glories of the new age. On 24th April 1933 Gottfried Benn was carried away in a radio speech, which he was later to regret, and addressed himself to "this youth", which had "rejected the carefully prepared traps and fetishes of an intelligentsia turned defeatist" and were right in showing "little respect" for their elders.

After the defeat of 1945 it became the fashion once again to talk about a hopeful "new" German youth. In Germany "youth" seems never to progress beyond being "new". It was now being said that henceforth the new younger generation would never again be misled by slogans. Everybody assured each other that they had become wide awake, meaning sceptical. Similar declarations were made by young people after 1848 and 1918: unfortunately youth seems to be doomed to be deceived by catchwords at the very age when it considers itself particularly enlightened and rational. It would be a real sign of intelligence amongst the young if instead of clumsily painting the entire older generation black they were to strive for a balanced assessment of the great German crisis with all its shades of grey.

It would be a further indication of really new thinking in Germany if the younger generation, instead of demonstratively leaving the ranks, were finally to see themselves as one of many links in the chain of their country's development, however much they may disapprove of the deeds of their parents—the youth of yesterday—and however much they may have the right to condemn their crimes and failures.

9

THE NEW SOBRIETY

Like people who have fled from a violent explosion and gradually return to the scene of the disaster as the smoke disperses, the Germans are slowly groping their way back to their own past and beginning to realise that they are part of it. The difference in make-up between the Germans of 1933-1945 and the Germans of today is minimal. Some are the same people, some are their children. Whoever damns one cannot expect much good of the other.

A worthy attempt to put German history back into proper perspective was undertaken by Federal President Theodor Heuss with his biographical anthology, *The Great Germans*. This was a brave undertaking, since a predecessor to the book with the same title had been published in 1935 and 1936, edited by Wilhelm von Scholz. Scholz saw the men and women whom he singled out as forerunners, in their fashion, of the Hitler era. After the fashion of the time he only aimed to pay attention to figures "of Germanic origin and German blood", as was stated in the introduction. Jews were consequently excluded from the gallery of Great Germans. In spite of this concession to the powers of the day Scholz strove in his first edition of *The Great Germans* to achieve continuity, honesty and a high intellectual level. Twenty years later, allowing for the removal of purely time-serving elements, Heuss was able to resume the work begun by Scholz. Until late in the nineteenth century Scholz and Heuss were in broad agreement over their choice of German notabilities, although with Heuss several military figures were replaced by intellectuals. Heuss strove to avoid any form of hypocrisy, regardless of the political beliefs of the subjects. He entirely rejected the contention of the victor powers that German history, from Martin Luther by way of Frederick the Great and Bismarck to Hitler, was mainly populated by criminals. Heuss achieved a sense of historical proportion by wisdom and generosity. He refused to allow foreign disapproval to prevent the inclusion of Alfred Krupp, the man who had brought his Essen works to fame. An equal generosity was apparent at the other end of the political spectrum: after some hesitation Berthold Brecht was added as the final entry. Heuss realised that after so much upheaval and confusion the Germans needed an opportunity to recognise the diversity and contradictions in their own character and in those of the great personalities of their history. The new edition of *The Great Germans* contributed much to reconciling the Germans with their history and ceasing to regard it as nothing more than proof of German corruptibility.

In the years that followed, the argument over what constituted greatness in a German continued. In the spring of 1962 the Federal Post Office was obliged to drop the plan of including a portrait of the physicist Albert Einstein in a series of "Great Germans" because Einstein's executor opposed the suggestion. He objected to Germany using a postage stamp to lay claim to Einstein, who as a Jew had been forced to flee his country. Although Scholz did not include the Nobel prizewinner in his volume, he was naturally honoured in the new edition of 1956, in keeping with the principle enunciated in the introduction that the adjective "German" was not intended as a narrowly geographical or chauvinistic limitation. Einstein himself, incidentally, had foreseen the controversy which he was later to arouse: if the theory of relativity stood the test of time, he declared mockingly, the Germans would claim him as a German and the rest of the world as a Jew. If the theory were disproved, the attitudes would be reversed.

The shock of 1945 had a thoroughly sobering effect and brought about a cool reappraisal of some of the stock figures in standard German history text books. The disturbed relationship between the German people and their history began to return to normality. The habit of seeing Germany's past, as Paul Sethe expressed it, "solely in terms of gas chambers and wars of aggression" gave way to the recognition that fundamentally German history, like the history of mankind itself, is made up of a struggle between good and evil. The pitiless confrontation with their own past which the Germans experienced in the first post-war years had the effect of a cleansing bath. When the past centuries were soberly weighed up it was impossible to see them as nothing but a catalogue of Germany's national vices. The German regained self-awareness by identifying himself with his history—without presumption but also without constant self-flagellation.

The unpredictability of the Germans, which once caused their neighbours so much concern, seems as a result of this process of introspection to have given way to an admirable openness. The Germans, according to a current diagnosis as remarkable for its element of truth as for its inadequacy, are a people who, after the shattering upheavals of the last decade, want simply to have a good time. Their goals are now the international holiday resorts instead of the Urals to which Hitler once wanted to drive them.

The contrast between the mass of ruins which was Germany in 1945 and the reconstructed cities of the '50s and '60s gave rise to the glittering phrase "economic miracle". Material well-being was by no means regarded as a mark of glory by historians of the old school with their particular notions of national greatness. Prosperity now began to count as a historically respectable achievement. The rate at which the misery of the immediate postwar years was overcome make up an impressive chapter of modern history which gains its full significance when compared with the effect which hardship and unemployment had on the Weimar Republic. At the end of World War II German industry was only capable of producing nappies for every fifth baby and coffins for every third corpse. Men scrambled like animals over refuse dumps to seize a discarded crust from the kitchens of the occupation forces. The greatest migration of history vividly demonstrated the total disruption of the Reich, whilst a fearful toll of millions of dead and murdered weighed on the German conscience.

In the first hard years of peace the people showed the same incredible toughness which they had exhibited in war. The family as the basic unit of survival stood the test. Beside much that was sad there was much that was good and uplifting; people talked, argued, hoped, pulled themselves up and helped one another—the body and the mind hungered after better things and grew more sensitive and receptive than in times of abundance. In those days Germans were free of many of the ills which plague them today: enforced moderation had its good side. Abroad, attitudes varied. The view was even widely held that Germany's hardship was too mild a punishment for the crimes of the Nazi era. On the other hand poverty and destitution aroused sympathies of a kind unknown in the days of might and brilliance. In those years Germany was probably regarded with more liking and far less suspicion than in the years of plenty. The parched land was covered with a tide of aid and comfort. But whilst much was forgiven the Germans in time of hardship, the rapid reconstruction of her economy revived the memory of old scores. The war was not forgotten. With the spread of new riches, weighty voices abroad were heard declaring that the Federal Republic should have achieved her revival less provocatively and with less ostentation.

The urge to eat well again, to have a roof over one's head and to be decently dressed gave a gigantic impulse to the German economy after the currency reform. By 1953 a New York travel agent was advertising trips to Germany by informing Americans that this would be the last chance to see the ruins. The much admired—or envied— upsurge of the German economy is the result of hard work and good luck. The Allied dismantling policy, regarded with indignation by the Germans, was in fact responsible for removing little but outdated and inefficient machinery from German factories: re-equipment with new machinery gave post-war German industry a flying start, whilst the Allied countries gradually found their confiscated German machinery a hindrance to efficiency. The old German machines were the losers in competition with the new. A similarly beneficial effect was felt from the flood of refugees from the Russian zone and the former eastern provinces. At first these millions seemed to be stifling German economic life, but these men from the eastern provinces soon proved to be an excellent and indispensable labour force. Having lost everything they had, they brought to West Germany a firm determination to build a new life and became one of the most vital and constructive elements in the re-activation of the economy. By the time that the Federal Republic had been in existence for ten years foreigners were either favourably impressed, amazed or shocked at what the Germans had achieved. The productive capacity of Federal Germany had surpassed the output of the Greater German Reich of 1938; in steel production West Germany had moved into third place after the United States and the Soviet Union and, incredible as it may sound, had reached second place in world trade and third place in overall industrial output. Where in 1938 there were 10 million houses in the area bounded by the Federal Republic, there are 15 million houses today. The population has, of course, risen too—but not in the same proportion.

Other statistics, however, reduce the much-discussed economic miracle to rather less sensational dimensions. In 1961 the average employed person's income was 465 DM per month (= £40 2s. 6d.), and the wages of 80 per cent of workpeople fell below this figure. The West German consumes an average of 50 kilograms of meat, 20 kilograms of imported fruit and smokes over 1,200 cigarettes annually. 2 million cars in West Germany in 1950 had become 8 million by 1961. Compared with neighbouring countries the German standard of living is above average. France and West Germany have a roughly equal daily intake of 3,000 calories per person; the French eat more meat than the Germans who in turn eat twice as much meat as the Italians. For all the differences the statistics show the inhabitants of the Federal Republic as typical west Europeans, the material conditions of whose lives are growing increasingly similar—a fact which even seems to lead to similarities of character.

Externally the economic miracle manifests itself in the bad German habit of ostentatious display of one's possessions. The Englishman may drive an old car, a thing that would never be done by a German of equivalent social class, but the Englishman has more money in the bank. The German drives the latest model, but it is not always paid for. Big cars, luxury restaurants filled to bursting and the concierge's wife wearing Persian lamb may have become symbols of the economic miracle but are certainly not typical of the broad masses. They live much more modestly than the television aerials, the big cars and the other conspicuous phenomena of the '60s might lead one to suppose.

1960 was a peak year for the number of civil servants brought to trial for corruption. All of them had felt that in comparison with the rewards available in the private sector of the economy their incomes needed improvement. Officials in control of building contracts were bribed with furniture, cash and liquor and the size of the bribe corresponded exactly to the influence which the official exercised over the allocation of building contracts and to the expectations placed in him. Corruption was joined by fraud in the charges brought before the courts, another consequence of the get-rich-quick urge. The month of January 1958 alone produced the following cases: the Stuttgart nitrite swindle, the case of adulterated wine at Johannisberg, the milk and honey racket in Bavaria and the sale, running into millions, of condemned American cigarettes and foodstuffs. After this series of trials the Germans ran true to form again when the thundering voice of the Bench made itself felt. Backsliding civil servants pulled themselves together and a self-pitying comparison of their earnings changed to the excuse that they had not received gifts from the various firms because of their official influence but from personal esteem. Those who were dismissed from office soon discovered, however, that their patrons of yesterday now cut them in the street.

One of the severest critics of the shortcomings of his fellow country-men was Dr. Adenauer, although in general his particular brand of democratic paternalism and economic freedom exactly fulfilled the deeply-felt needs of post-war Germany. Politically today's German is passive rather than active. Looking back over the last few decades of his history he feels that he has had more than his share of the consequences of great-power politics. Three changes of regime, two currency devaluations, the division of the country, the loss of a quarter of the national territory, the destruction of the expansionist dream in the Russian winter—this was enough. Equally shattering for the Germans was the realisation that the harder they had striven the deeper they had fallen into the abyss. The Soviet contention that Germany is still intent on aggressive eastward expansion is positively grotesque in its misreading of the situation.

In the eyes of the numerous critics who were disturbed, or pre-tended to be, by the situation in Germany, the sobriety of life in the Federal Republic was of course seen as no more than a consequence of satiety, complacency and indifference. After the "Hindenburg German", who in their view had handed Germany over to Hitler, they coined the expression of the "Adenauer German", the target of a wave of polemical writing which attained its greatest volume around 1960. Whilst the Germans were enjoying an ever-increasing standard of material well-being, to such an extent that the govern-ment felt obliged to exhort people to moderation, all the Cassandras were convinced that German life had never been more contemptible. This criticism was concentrated in two books, *I Live in the Federal Republic* (1961) and *Stocktaking* (1962), two collections of articles of varying plausibility. They took as their main target the political aims of Adenauer's administration. He was found guilty of having perpetuated, or at least prolonged, the division of Germany by his policy of military alignment with the Atlantic powers, whilst his sterile policy towards Russia had wilfully jeopardised every chance of German reunification. Under him the Federal Republic had been turned into the advance guard of an ideological crusade against the Eastern bloc. A further theme of the what's-wrong-with-Germany school of criticism consists of the so-called missed opportunities. The well-known journalist Paul Sethe declared that all chances of a German foreign policy had been ruined by Adenauer's senile obstinacy.

Proof: the Russian note of March 1952, which had offered the Germans unification but had not been given serious study because the man at the helm in Bonn had been more concerned with welfare of the western half of Germany than with the fate of the Germans in the Soviet Zone. It requires a remarkable stretch of the imagination to see Uncle Joe Stalin as the father of German unity, but in the generally peevish mood which the incident created not a few Germans of considerable standing subscribed to the thesis of 'missed opportunities', missed through a combination of selfishness and indifference. However, as soon as the critics of the Adenauer line proposed alternative policies they became much more subdued. The recognition of the Oder-Neisse Line and a formal renunciation of any claims to our eastern provinces were repeatedly demanded, whilst entry into diplomatic relations with Warsaw and Prague was held to be long overdue. More attention in general should be paid to eastern Europe. The basic error of German foreign policy was seen as being the German's desire to have everything and have it all at once: unification, return of the eastern provinces, power, fortune and prosperity. Whether any other policy would have brought these a single step nearer realisation remains unproved and unprovable.

The Italian film *La Dolce Vita* started a lively discussion among the numerous critics of West German society: Does it exist here? The answer was a unanimous No. A social stratum ostentatiously dedicated to doing nothing does not exist in the Federal Republic. The Germans' spare time is much rather taken up with proving how little time they have. In fact, whilst their many critics are still labelling the post-war Germans as crass materialists and egotists, ten years after the currency reform, in the full flush of avid consumption there are increasing signs of a return to sobriety and moderation. Consumption has, after all, its natural limits; the champagne-swilling capitalist, in an age when the man in the street can afford a bottle of champagne for 5 marks on any suitable occasion is in any case an outdated stereotype of class warfare.

A person who has everything that his heart could desire feels like a child in an overfilled nursery. He returns to the old tattered rag doll. Five years ago there were industrialists who stuffed themselves with noodles to look fat, hence wealthy and impressive. Today they are much more concerned with slimming pills. Similar tendencies are observable in consumer goods. Top people no longer find a Persian carpet desirable when it is available in a department store.

When working-class people, in their clothes and furniture, are striving to be as middle class as possible, the class that they are imitating discovers the attraction of farmhouse furniture and loden coats, just as when the beaches of Capri or Mallorca begin to overflow, Bavaria and the Rhineland suddenly seem oddly attractive. After an orgy of too much of everything, it is now becoming smart to have less, do less, travel less or eat less. The immediate urge to fill stomachs underfed from years of privation was replaced by a concern for health and restraint. It has long been doubtful whether the Germans are still among the world's heaviest eaters and drinkers. Thick, rich soup, *the* typical German dish, is on the decline, as is the consumption of potatoes and alcohol. Doctors are prescribing increasingly strict diets and health food shops, with their vegetable fats and their fruit extracts, are booming. In the soberness following satiety people are rediscovering books, music and the pleasures of simple living.

Against the scepticism and ill-will directed at the German Federal Republic from various sources there has been no lack of official attempts to disseminate a favourable image of this young post-war state. In the Brussels World Fair of 1958 this truncated Germany showed itself as it hoped to be seen and judged by others. Chancellor Adenauer had decreed that modesty was to be the keynote of Germany's appearance at Brussels. The German fondness for vast proportions would have been out of place in a small country like Belgium, which since the occupation had unhappy memories of German 'efficiency' and thoroughness. We were to demonstrate the very opposite of all the unpleasant characteristics of which we were commonly accused. The gigantic eagle which glowered down from the top of the huge tower of the German pavilion of the 1937 Paris World Exhibition shrank in Brussels to the proportions of a canary. The threatening, brooding and aggressive German, symbolised by "le goût allemand pour le colossal", was no longer to be the dominant impression of the German pavilion; instead he appeared as a nice, tidy, modest, life-affirming creature. The Teuton had finally cast off his bearskin and was behaving himself.

The German buildings at Brussels were gracious and represented, in the words of the Düsseldorf architect Dr. Hans Schwippert, "regardless of the surroundings a new lightness, a new gentleness and grace". No pomposity, no delusions of grandeur: the neat, disinfected present-day German, with his postage stamps and his bookshelves, was anxious that everybody should forget how much trouble he had caused in this century. Anything but Deutschland über Alles! German heavy industry spared foreign susceptibilities with charming, airy metal spirals instead of slabs of cast iron. Beautifully arranged flowers formed an apologetic complement to the photographs of industrial might. Not a car, not a camera hinted at the size of German industry. In the effort to avoid any hint of boasting everything was reduced to a scale of such modesty that it was even slightly irritating to those who were aware of the true dimensions. The Soviets showed an oil painting of a German officer whipping prisoners. The Israelis showed German gas chambers, whereas the Germans kept their difficulties in the background: the disturbing problem of the division of Germany was relegated to a wooden relief map which harmed no one's feelings, and the fate of the refugees was carefully hidden from foreign eyes. This shop-window Germany did not seem entirely credible: somehow everything was too packaged, too sterile, too rosy and too neatly rounded off. The attempt to reduce German heavy industry to the scale of an advanced but small country was applauded but not believed. Even divided Germany has a certain weight among the industrial giants which cannot be conjured away by false modesty.

The German professors who were responsible for the exhibition were able to claim at least *one* undisputed success: the majority of foreign visitors were pleasantly surprised. However, the short-lived nature of the show's effect was shown by the fact that the same newspapers which gave the German pavilion a few lines of praise continued on their political pages to thunder at the Germans for being a menace. Once back in the maelstrom of international tensions, "Operation Modesty" at Brussels was of little avail to Germany.

The Germany west of the Oder-Neisse covers an area of no more than 222,000 square miles. The Germany against which the misunderstood Nietzsche inveighed was 337,500 square miles in extent. Hitler doubled the area of the Reich, which collapsed in pieces on defeat. Materially speaking the Federal Republic is perhaps viable, but if it is to be regarded as a true "Germany" it will first have to be united with the G.D.R. At the moment no one can see how this is to be achieved. Many people declare that the present situation cannot last forever, but if they say so aloud they immediately re-create the image of Germany as an incalculable threat: a country with millions of refugees who were only assimilated thanks to economic expansion; a people, a third of whom are under Communist rule; a state continually under Soviet scrutiny—all of these are grounds enough for uneasiness. After the loss of the areas of agricultural surplus West Germany must import 30 per cent of her food, and the export drive to pay for this creates ample opportunities for friction in an age of acute competition. The West German has grown up in prosperity. The great seduction of the German people occurred in the destitution and despair following 1930. Nobody knows how the Germans, spoiled by the recent years of plenty, would behave if serious unemployment were to return. Order and prosperity are mutually supporting: opinions differ as to whether the one would persist if the other were removed. A high standard of living may intensify the impact of a sudden crisis. Both literally and metaphorically the Germans have put on too much fat—their reserves of stamina are low.

A new Hitler is most improbable. In theory the next possible stage in German history is subjection to Communism: one of the nightmares of the West is that of a Germany aligning herself with the Soviet Union out of expediency or despair. It is as a potential cause of war that Germany arouses such feelings of unease among its neighbours, rather as a barometer is blamed for indicating changeable or bad weather.

In 1962 the West German boom began noticeably to slow down—the German miracle was about to be put to the test. Whilst the Federal Republic still kept up a healthy outward appearance, doubts nevertheless increased as to the strength and durability of this façade. As the lights of the economic boom started to flicker many people began to recall how much explosive material was stacked up within the makeshift structure of postwar Germany. The average German might withdraw into his shell and try to look as harmless as possible, but he could never be sure that international politics, in which he had once played so dangerous a part, would now leave him alone.

10

HAVE THE GERMANS CHANGED?

In its number for April 1960 the German magazine *Magnum* examined the question: Have the Germans changed? Twelve well-known figures of public life in the Federal Republic—politicians, scholars, writers, journalists—gave their views on this question. The consensus was remarkably favourable. Those thought most competent to judge attested that the Germans had shed a number of their most unpleasant characteristics, although, of course, only Germans (some were emigrants who had acquired another nationality) had been asked. The same questionnaire put to students of Germany in France, England or the U.S.A. would probably have produced a different picture. Official and private conversations with foreigners have shown again and again that clichés about the Germans are still widespread, clichés which might perhaps have been applicable twenty, forty or sixty years ago but which are meaningless today "because those particular warts have disappeared from the German face" (*Magnum*).

"The Germans are finally determined to be at peace with themselves and the rest of the world wants to be at peace with the Germans. So we have now decided on contented mediocrity," so runs Klaus Harpprecht's essay entitled *The Urge to Normality*. This radical change to a more sober collective outlook has been labelled opportunism by sceptical observers, but "opportunism is after all hardly a fault—it is a talent which enables the underdog to survive". The Germans have exploited this fact; following the example of the Italians, as Harpprecht goes on to say, they have tamed the wrath of the victors by embracing them. Professor von Salis even claims that the Germans have never found 180-degree swings particularly difficult. "They [the Germans] have in the past successfully been all things to all men: South German and Catholic in the heyday of Imperial Vienna, Prussian and Protestant in Berlin, franco-phile and cosmopolitan under Frederick the Great, cultured and internationalist in Goethe's Weimar, militaristic under Moltke, nation-alistic under Bismarck, a maritime world power under Wilhelm II, aggressively racialist and anti-semitic under Hitler, European with American leanings under Adenauer and Russian-oriented Communists under Ulbricht." The most positive assessment of the 'new' Germans comes from Golo Mann. They are today, he says, "one of the quietest, most matter-of-fact, most civilian of peoples and one of the least susceptible to collective hysteria in the world. . . . And the young people? I can only speak for young people at university, of whom I have some knowledge. They are critical, unprejudiced, polite, cosmopolitan, keen to work and lacking any trace of national-ism, hatred or of the dark side of misty romanticism. They are pro-foundly different from the student generation of thirty years ago and if things were to take a wrong turning again, this time it would not be their fault." Hendrik van Dam, general secretary of the Jewish organisation in Germany, comes to the conclusion that the Germans "have made an effort to change themselves. They cannot afford to remain the same". The writer Erich Kuby claims however, to find that the Germans have grown "mouldy"; they "no longer think". Kuby misses "the German voice in the chorus of nations. It simply is not there. The people are disturbingly silent. But I am con-vinced that this phase of dumbness is nearing its end. . . . The great disillusionment is beginning which needs must lead to a re-awaken-ing of the political instinct in the Germans."

At the end of 1961 the weekly newspaper *Die Zeit* put two questions to a varied selection of prominent Germans: "What do the Germans like?" and "What attracts you personally?" A glance through the mostly witty and sarcastically phrased replies shows clearly that the six classic German defects are today considered just as typical as they were half a century ago. The first question received inter alia the following replies—*The Germans Like:* "Their unshakeable conviction of their own efficiency, which neither a lost war nor the most glaringly obvious diminution of their potency and significance can diminish; capacity for suffering in obedience to orders, followed by a tendency to boast about it. . . ." (Professor Werner Haftmann, art historian); *The Germans Like:* "Themselves, me, everybody" (Ernst von Salomon, author); *The Germans Like:* "Long conferences, big crosses of The Order of Merit, the popping of champagne corks" (H. M. Ledig-Rowohlt, publisher); *The Germans Like:* "Order, Gemütlichkeit, leader-types" (Professor Walter Jens, author).

Gustaf Gründgens declares that the Germans want "a quiet life"; Bundestag member and publisher of *Die Zeit*, Dr. Gerd Bucerius thinks that they love peace "because they are afraid". The people who were questioned showed themselves up—naturally in a flattering light, by admitting a preference for things and pastimes of a strongly romantic and aesthetic nature—as just as typically German as the 'masses'. They were attracted by "a picture, a verse, a song . . . mountain, lake and tree . . ." (Haftmann), they would like to "glide sleeping over the water like a swan" (Ewald Mataré, sculptor), "listen to the mating call of birds" (Ledig-Rowohlt), they liked "a big city, rain and beautiful, intelligent women" (Ernst Wilhelm Noy, painter) and "Mozart, young people and Mozart" (Gründgens)—chiefly pleasures which, in their opinion, 'ordinary people' did not appreciate.

It seems from all these diverse views that the Germans of today largely elude definition—and no doubt fortunately so. Perhaps the most striking sign of a change in character may be that they will now put up with a great deal more derision and criticism than before. The German no longer feels obliged to challenge his real or imagined critic to a duel. If it is reprovingly suggested that the 'old spirit' is still abroad in the land the average German will join with the chorus of foreigners in finding this regrettable. It is really hardly surprising that foreigners, with certain laudable exceptions, are nowhere inclined to regard any of the six classic German faults, here listed, as superseded:

1. Their critics still find the Germans crude, noisy and tactless. As tourists they stand out by their bad manners. Isolated acts—particularly those of the police against demonstrators and harmless rowdies—are held sufficient proof that one must always be prepared for a recrudescence of German brutality.

2. German nationalism is nowadays expressed in the government's inflexible attitude towards the Eastern bloc and their continual demands for guarantees from the West. The Germans still believe that no move will be made with sufficient vigour until they are in charge.

3. German territorial greed, even after the defeat of the last war, is betrayed by their refusal to recognise their new frontiers and by an overt or secret longing for a return to their former size and power. Purchases of land abroad by individual Germans is regarded in a similar light: the German is at heart an

incorrigible expansionist. In economic affairs his competitive methods are unfair.

4. The hard core of the German menace is still militarism, now striving to compensate for the weakness of conventional forces by the acquisition of nuclear weapons. East and West are equally apprehensive of being dragged into war by Germany.

5. The traditional German tendency to genuflect to authority has not been removed by the superficial Americanisation of life. The Germans have shown themselves to be incapable of "true democracy". The nation will continue to accept dictatorial measures provided they are imposed in a sufficiently draconian fashion.

6. Even though the boom has reduced the Germans' urge to sweat and slave, they worship material success as much as before. Materialism has made the Germans into a nation of tightfisted egotists, from whom every million for aid to developing countries must be extracted by bullying or wheedling.

Are we therefore to assume that everything is as it was before and that the numerous links of friendship which we have built up abroad are only the result of the coolly utilitarian reasoning that they and we are all in the same boat? Nowhere in the free world is the German as such unwelcome. Many may perhaps regard him with condescending sympathy, like a discharged convict or a convalescent who is in danger of a relapse. This tends to be the line taken by the mass media, press, film and television, who continue to present the German as a distinctly questionable figure. The largely well-intentioned overtures of friendship from the West and the excellent contacts across the frontiers between young people and intellectuals are being overshadowed and distorted by a busy stream of propaganda which still pictures Germany as a potential menace. Sometimes genuine fears are being expressed, but often the motivation is commercial— the beastly German is good box-office—or food for petty politics. Every critic knows from experience that a juicy piece of destructive criticism is easier to write and much more amusing to read than a page of eulogy. The sinister German is a much more rewarding subject for his detractor than the dull, honest citizen of the Federal Republic. In the guise of education or moral indignation, constant reference to Nazi atrocities panders to the persistent human interest in cruelty.

The most repulsive kind of film German is largely an invention of the last few years. France and Italy have been particularly active in creating this figure. In spring 1962 the French film *The Eye of Evil* showed a German writer called Hartmann, a typically successful man of the era of the economic miracle, with all the material trappings, including a luxury villa in Upper Bavaria. To complete his enjoyment he imports from France not only champagne and brandy but also a wife. The trouble begins when a charming but unscrupulous Frenchman intrudes into his well-organised German existence. He seduces Hartmann's wife, the husband thereupon seizes the bread-knife and despatches his unfaithful French spouse. In his own words the French director was trying to show that "in certain situations a German can only act in a certain way". He may be efficient, success-ful, musical, athletic—none of this alters the nature of the "German beast", which since 1871 French intellectuals have been analysing with a mixture of admiration and disgust. So, the argument runs, when under stress the German reaches for the breadknife. German orderliness, coldness, grossness are contrasted in the film with French refinement and savoir-vivre. The Frenchman is the villain of the piece, but the audience is never left in a moment's doubt as to which character has or should have their sympathies.

In the film *The Three Truths* by François Villiers a German tourist couple in Paris buy up rubbishy junk at astronomical prices, an illustration of German lack of taste in accordance with Point 1 of the list of German defects. The Germans still have a weakness for the colossal, judging beauty by size and weight and using their wallets as their main criterion. In Louis Malle's film *Lift to the Scaffold* a well-heeled German enthuses over United Europe, but his enthusiasm is an obvious device to reverse the result of the war and turn defeat into a German ascendancy in Western Europe.

The most consistently anti-German have been Italian films. In March 1961 no fewer than sixteen films were being shown with Germans in the role of villain. Any difference between Nazis and good Germans was barely detectable. Vittorio de Sica, declared in July 1962, when he was in Germany making a film of Sartre's *Huis Clos*, that he was treating it as "an anti-Nazi film about present-day Germany". In an interview with the politically ultra-leftist magazine *Vie Nuove* he stated that the German film technicians had been "pale with nostalgia and pride" when they had heard a recording of Hitler's voice which had been included in the sound-track of the film. De Sica's attitude is typical of the country that was the birthplace of fascism, much more concerned with setting other people's past to rights than their own. Sweeping their own doorstep is usually done in the form of a joke. Italian national pride does not leave a film producer with much room to manoeuvre, as ruthless self-criticism is always bad for the box-office. An anti-German attitude, on the other hand, is always a money-making formula, the more so since various German bodies are always ready to praise the Italian film producers for their enthusiasm for spreading democratic ideals whenever they show sequences of German torture and gas chambers. A German film producer who tried to redress the balance slightly by reminding the Italians of their fascist past would be bound not to cover his production costs. It cannot, of course, be denied that the catalogue of German sins is much more extensive than the Italian.

In March 1962 the film *Ten Italians for One German* was given its premiere in Rome before an invited audience of a thousand; the title is concerned with Point 2 on the list of German defects—arrogance. The film deals with an attack by a Communist partisan on a German marching column somewhere in Rome, in which 32 South Tyrolese who had been conscripted into the German police were killed. In revenge and as a deterrent a German S.S. general had 335 Italian hostages shot. Before doing this he had attempted to avert his act of vengeance (personally ordered by Hitler) by inviting the ringleader to surrender himself, but this call evoked no response. The film fails to mention this not unimportant detail.

When in late 1962 the Italian film *The Four Days of Naples* provoked an official German protest, the writer Indro Montanelli declared that the Italian partisans' struggle against the Germans was now "the only aspect of World War II, which we not only lost but largely didn't even fight, capable of bolstering up our deflated national pride". The representation of partisans fighting German soldiers was "the only way of showing the world that as soldiers and as a nation the Italians had something of which they could be proud". It was not a question of hatred, but simply that Italy in a sense imported her patriotic tragedies from Germany just as the Germans imported fruit and vegetables from Italy. Not everybody will feel inclined to give such a light-hearted answer to the question of whether one nation should be denigrated simply to bolster another's national self-confidence. Films with anti-German themes grew in time to be such a safe commercial proposition in Italy that it became worth their while for blond young Germans to take up permanent quarters near the film studies of Rome, such was the demand for suitable 'Nazi' extras. Some extras, who to Italian eyes looked particularly German, were able to earn up to a thousand marks a week.

The preconditions for an outburst of Italian resentment against the Germans were created as early as 1944, when Italy broke away from Hitler's Germany. An understandable anger at the humiliations and blows suffered whilst allied with the Germans demanded an outlet. In August 1944 the Italian writer Curzio Malaparte published his ostensibly documentary book *Kaputt*, written in the first person singular and drawn from his own experience. He described how the S.S. introduced into their bestial training programme the cold-blooded gouging out of cats' eyes. Malaparte alleged that Ante Pavelic, the Croat collaborationist leader of the Ustasha, had shown him a basket containing twenty kilograms of human eyes—a present from his bodyguard. In the German edition *Kaputt* was presented not as a factual report but as a novel, in order to spare the feelings of the German readers and ensure good sales. The work which was now offered as a piece of macabre fiction had previously been read by millions of non-German readers as an indictment of the Germans based on authentic factual and documentary material.

William L. Shirer, annoyed perhaps by some German critics' hostile reception of his book, published an illustrated article in *Look* magazine under the title "If Hitler had won World War II". At a moment when Khrushchev was threatening the Americans with annihilation should war break out, Shirer was exerting his imagination to present his fellow-countrymen with the horrors of a fictitious German occupation, even though Hitler had not even been capable of conquering the British Isles. Whilst Shirer was at least able to lend his fantasies some plausibility by quoting historical parallels, his lead was followed by innumerable American writers of horror comics and pulp magazines who discarded all inhibitions. The German, thinly decked out as a Nazi, is used as a figure of bestiality to appeal to every degraded instinct—to the great financial advantage of authors and publishers.

The wave of trashy hate-and-horror writing even reached England. In May 1962 there was a British television production of a play by Robert Muller, whose climax was Hitler's return to Germany. First Hitler's son appeared on the screen and thanked the politicians of the

Federal Republic for having kept, despite considerable opposition, numerous trusty old Party members in office. A general was thanked for the reactivation of the Wehrmacht. After some hesitation the leading figures of the Federal Republic, including some calculating ecclesiastics, allow themselves to be persuaded to recall Hitler. Hitler appears and promises a new German Reich in all its old might and glory. All concerned are quite ready to consider another war and any lingering scruples vanish when Hitler convinces them that he is the only person capable of restoring German unity. In this ingenious play the six classic German vices are all represented in succession— clumsiness, chauvinism, insatiability, militarism, blind obedience and sweating industriousness.

The German as shown in the West on film and television bears a great similarity to the image put out by Communist propaganda. In the West the attacks are more imaginative, in the East they are more crude. In the West they contradict government policy, in the East they reflect it.

How rapidly East and West could concur in damning the Federal Republic was demonstrated by the *Spiegel* affair of Autumn 1962. The arrest of the publisher and a number of editors of the controversial news magazine was immediately seen as an attempt by the Federal government to rid itself of an irksome critic. Some of the arrests were carried out at night and the editorial premises were sealed off for weeks. Very soon the Bavarian-born Federal Minister of Defence, Strauss, became the main target of public criticism. He had been under attack from the *Spiegel* for years, generally in conjunction with a somewhat dubious construction project known as "Fibag". On 4th November 1962 he was still maintaining that the arrests had been carried out without the least connivance on his part. On 9th November Strauss was forced to admit in the Federal Diet that he had provided "official assistance" in the arrest of Ahlers, one of *Spiegel's* editors, in Spain: the Spanish police had been put on Ahler's trail thanks to a nocturnal telephone call to the German military attaché in Madrid.

The cause of the arrest was an article which had appeared in *Der Spiegel* on 10th October 1962 concerning a N.A.T.O. military exercise known as "Exercise Fallex". In the article the state of German defence was shown up, in shocking detail, as being nothing short of catastrophic. The entire military policy of Federal Defence Minister Strauss, based as it was on the assumption of the Bundeswehr receiving atomic weapons, was represented as a failure. On 26th October, nearly three weeks after the publication of the article, the Federal Attorney General proceeded to make the arrests.

The spokesman of the Federal government countered the immediate wave of public indignation with a plea not to give gratuitous propaganda material to the Communists, but the protesters of all political colours were not to be fobbed off with such a warning. It is of particular interest, in a study of foreign views of Germany, to observe the interaction between domestic German criticism and the indignation aroused abroad. It was Germans who first drew a parallel with the Gestapo, a German newspaper which was the first to write that the Federal Republic was no longer one of those states whose citizens could be sure it was only the milkman if there came a knock on the door in the early hours of the morning. German newspapers were the first to make the daring comparison with Hitler's methods of hustling off his opponents at dead of night. The indignation shown abroad was frequently only an amplified echo of German voices.

Communist newspapers adopted the pose of defenders of the freedom of the press. A German could not help noticing the grotesque contrast between the way the Communist papers reported the *Spiegel* affair and the years of suppression of the press in the Soviet Zone— a fact which incidentally worried many a western champion of freedom a great deal less than the action against the editors of the *Spiegel*. The curious situation arose in which commentaries in eastern and western newspapers were almost inter-changeable, both sides adopting nearly the same turns of phrase in criticising Germany.

"The most reliable West German magazine," said *Pravda* on 29th October 1962, "has fallen victim to Bonn's strong-arm men." The blow at the *Spiegel* was regarded by the Moscow newspaper as a new piece of West German "war-mongering". On 1st November 1962 *The New York Times* declared that the knock on the door at midnight "unmistakably recalled the methods of the Gestapo"; the freedom of the press in the Federal Republic was clearly in danger.

Even someone who may be sharply critical of the circumstances of the proceedings against the *Spiegel* will realise, on the other hand, how wrong were the conclusions drawn by many foreign publications about the affair. It was simply nonsense for foreigners to claim that Germany had reverted to incorrigible servility towards authority, capricious police action and autocratic government. Granted that the government had acted foolishly and clumsily: there can, howev:r, be no comparison of their action with the methods of Hitler's Gestapo.

The whole affair demonstrated the Germans' remarkable gift for showing themselves in the worst possible light. Unfortunately this impression seems to be little affected by personal contact between Germans and people of other countries, however pleasant the individual encounters may be.

Because visits abroad are usually short and language difficulties hinder any meaningful dialogue, tourists and natives generally see each other as little more than curiosities and pass on after no more than superficial contact. The German, for example, remembers little more than that the Italians are noisy, the Italian that the Germans behave badly.

The Germans, of course, are by no means unwelcome as tourists. Many foreign hoteliers consider them their best customers. The average German is not excessively fussy, which hotel-keepers like. He is generally alive to his surroundings, is disposed to be friendly and accommodating when on holiday and generally tips well. Nowadays it is far from being true that Germans abroad are conspicuous for their loud and boorish behaviour. Their previous manners, often based on feelings of insecurity, improved with practice.

However, the friendly 'Auf Wiedersehen' with which the foreign host speeds his parting German guests is by no means synonymous with a real increase in international sympathy and understanding. Travel agents have always propagated the well-meaning theory that nothing improves international relations and removes prejudices so well as extensive foreign travel; in fact, however, these kinds of mass-migratory encounters have little to do with improved inte:national relations. Nations are like people—too much close contact can easily turn affection into dislike. Whatever the travel agents may say, invasion by busloads of strangers has seldom done much for any peoples' reputation. The acquisition by Germans of property and real estate abroad, in particular in countries such as Switzerland, Ireland, Spain and Italy, has more than once provoked hostile re-actions of an intensity quite out of proportion to the relative strength of the Germans among foreign landowners of all nationalities.

True to form the Communist press has constantly tried to draw a parallel between German property purchases abroad and the desire to regain the provinces beyond the Oder-Neisse which they allege to be the policy of the Federal German government. The aim is to produce the impression that every German activity abroad is merely an aspect of their incorrigibly aggressive expansionism.

This rather ridiculous and far-fetched attempt to compare a perfectly natural wish to buy a villa in a sunny climate with German revisionism is, in fact, only another proof that all forms of anti-German feeling tend to be lumped together under the common denominator of the 'German peril'; and this is only another name for German militarism. In other words—the German image only begins to brighten when German armed forces are not regarded as a potential menace. Astonishing as this may seem in view of the comparatively modest number of Bundeswehr divisions, German militarism has become the main source of all current mistrust and dislike of the Germans. As the attitude of the Communist-bloc states shows, all the previous accusations of boorishness, nationalism, pan-Germanism, blind obedience and work-mania have been merged into the single bogey of German militarism. In concrete terms, this is expressed in the constantly reiterated fear that the Bundeswehr could be used by 'Nazi' generals to restore the old German frontiers by force.

It is arguable that the re-arming of a Germany divided and still obsessed by the recent past was carried out too soon. The verdict of Nuremberg, that militarism and blind obedience were to be eradicated in Germany "for all time", was still ringing in the Germans' ears. A number of German generals had been sent to the gallows, whilst those who were spared execution were vouchsafed no clear ruling on the limits of obedience to orders. Soviet judges at Nuremberg claimed in all seriousness that it was normal in the Red Army to protest against an unlawful command and that Soviet military law made allowance for conscientious objection and safeguarded every Red Army soldier against any caprice of his superiors. This claim led at Nuremberg to a clash between Rudenko, the Soviet prosecutor, and Field Marshal Keitel. Keitel, notorious among his colleagues during the Nazi regime for his spineless attitude to Hitler (his nickname was 'Keitel the lackey'), maintained at Nuremberg that any head of state and commander-in-chief, be he Wilhelm II, Ebert, Hindenburg, or Hitler, must be able to rely unconditionally on the obedience of his armed forces. When Rudenko accused the Field Marshal of carrying obedience to criminal lengths, Keitel interrupted him, saying: "I doubt whether there are any generals in the Red Army who did not obey Marshal Stalin unquestioningly." After his death on the scaffold,

Keitel's remarks were confirmed, albeit posthumously, from an unimpeachable source: Khrushchev declared that Soviet generals were forced to obey Stalin even when from sheer maliciousness he ordered them to squat down and dance the gopak.

Hardly had the Germans had time to learn that the best way of avoiding another catastrophe was to renounce all kinds of armed force for ever than the cry was heard from abroad that German soldiers were needed again.

As a result of the rapidly growing tensions of the cold war, General Eisenhower, who had meanwhile been appointed Commander-in-Chief of the N.A.T.O. forces, felt prepared to retract the unfavourable verdict on German soldiers which he had delivered in his book *Crusade in Europe*. In this book Eisenhower described how he had refused, when a high-ranking German officer capitulated, to "observe the custom of bygone days and allow him to call on me". He went on to state that "there grew within me the conviction" . . . that the German forces represented . . . "a completely evil conspiracy with which no compromise could be tolerated".[1]

On 23rd January 1951 Eisenhower declared that he now realised "that a real difference existed between the German soldiers and officers on the one hand and Hitler and his criminal accomplices on the other". Personally he was not of the opinion that the German soldier "as such" had forfeited his honour. The "great majority of German soldiers and officers" had had nothing to do with the despicable and dishonourable acts of "certain individuals".

This was the official end of the theory of collective guilt. The statement was an obvious example of expediency, which would certainly not have been made with such promptitude had the West not been in urgent need of German troops. The Soviets, consistent with their policy, declined to issue any such statement. In countless notes they maintained that the old and new generals of the Bundeswehr were revanchists, war criminals and mercenaries who had sold themselves to Hitler. Doubting western politicians were energetically assured that the modest number of West German divisions was no obstacle to the German generals' urge to plunge into new and disastrous military adventures: the aggressors would present the Americans with a fait accompli and drag them unwillingly into another war. The constant Soviet warnings

[1] Dwight D. Eisenhower, *Crusade in Europe*, Heinemann, London 1948, pp. 172–173.

about the German military machine have not been without effect. The careful division of command in N.A.T.O. headquarters was instituted to pacify any of the Allies who might have felt threatened by independent German action. In spite of Moscow's claims to the contrary, the Federal Republic is incapable of taking any significant unilateral military action: the very success of Allied efforts to de-militarise Germany proved an embarrassment when the time came to raise a West German N.A.T.O. contingent: a sceptical refusal to return to uniform after the recent debacle, genuine pacifism, unwillingness to leave well-paid civilian jobs and serious doubts about the validity of obeying orders that might conflict with conscience—the latter a direct result of Allied strictures which were given categorical expression at the Nuremberg trials—all combined to make the Germans unwilling to join the newly-formed Bundeswehr.

One of the most hotly debated issues was the question of whether escape from one side to the other of divided Germany should constitute desertion and whether a German was justified in firing on his own countrymen from the other side of the Iron Curtain. In the meantime official sources in the G.D.R. have clearly stated that the troops of the Bundeswehr are to be shot at without qualm if the command is given, as being aggressive capitalist mercenaries. When President Lübke was required to give an answer to the same question to a group of officers in Hamburg on 11th October 1961 he came, after careful weighing of the issues, to practically the same conclu-sion. In spite of his obviously sincere attempt to resolve a potential crisis of conscience among West German officers, Lübke was unable to deny the tragic implications in a situation in which Germans might be called to fire on Germans.

When raising the Bundeswehr the Federal Government introduced extensive reforms in order to allay the inevitable unease attendant upon the re-activation of a German army. A figure such as the vicious Sergeant Himmelstoss made notorious in Remarque's novel *All Quiet on the Western Front* could never be allowed to reappear. When the first recruits reported for duty in March 1957 they were assured of sensible and humane treatment. The salient features of recruitment to the Bundeswehr could not fail to be noticed by foreign observers. There was no trace, for example, of the rush to join up which many had expected of such an allegedly military-minded people as the Germans. Military service was rather seen as a necessary evil. Copying American recruiting methods, the authorities did their utmost to make the service sound attractive. In spite of cleverly worded inducements it was clear from public opinion polls that the affluent civilian took precedence over the soldier in popular estimation.

The Social Democratic party, whose ingrained suspicion of the Reichswehr had added to the problems of the Weimar Republic in achieving a proper relationship between military and political authority, now behaved with a notable sense of responsibility in ensuring that the question of military service would not become a party political issue. The Federal Republic was also spared other difficulties which had plagued the Weimar Republic. There were no para-military formations such as the Freikorps nor an illegal force such as the "Black Reichswehr" and no recurrence of the 'stab-in-the-back' legend which had given force to the argument of the incorrigible militarism of the German officer corps. Finally, the Federal Republic was not undermined by the monarchist nostalgia which had caused such friction between the Reichswehr and the Weimar government.

On the ever-vexed question of the validity of superior orders, the Federal Government finally agreed that no soldier could declare with finality whether or not the cause for which he was required to fight was beyond all doubt a just one. Whilst officially exonerating the bulk of the German armed forces in World War II of involvement in criminal activities, the new German soldier was enjoined to relearn obedience without too much questioning. The Nuremberg dogma of a purely personal sense of duty, which could be revoked at any moment at the dictates of conscience, was now found to be over-subtle and unusable in practice. The Western powers were frankly afraid that any further attempts to analyse and relativise the concepts of giving and obeying orders would put their forces at a hopeless disadvantage in face of the rigidly disciplined Soviets and their allies. The Soviet Union, of course, regards every military action of its own as self-justifying and despite Rudenko's remarks at Nuremberg it forbids any member of its armed forces to question an order.

Whilst the Communist bloc continued to denounce the Bundeswehr as a hotbed of the German spirit of aggression, the West gradually accustomed itself to the sight of German uniforms, particularly since they had been designed to be as unobtrusive as possible. The changed attitude to the German forces was underlined by a thoughtful article in *Le Monde*. There was a time, declared the paper, commenting on the Hirschdorf disaster when German soldiers had been drowned in obeying an order to wade through a river, when blind obedience of orders had led to criminal action. Now it resulted in suicide. Then, with a glance at the war in Algeria, where French troops were subject to an equally rigid command system, came the final key sentence of the article: "Poor Germans, we are just like you!"

The Soviets were alarmed at the speed of West German rearmament. The Americans, on the other hand, considered that the Federal Republic was taking far too much time over it. By 1960 they were complaining with increasing sharpness at the Germans' inadequate and half-hearted allocation of funds for defence expenditure to relieve the American tax-payer. The complaints applied equally to defence and to aid for developing countries. The Germans, it was said, once so proud of their 'economic miracle', were now trying somewhat nervously to play it down—not out of modesty but out of fear that their reputation for affluence might cost them dear.

Thus the outside world is equally critical of German extravagance and German meanness. Foreign politicians are, of course, impressed above all by the outward appearance of prosperity which the Federal Republic exhibits. No success greeted attempts to explain to foreigners that West Germany was poorer than it looked and that especially where problems such as the shortage of school and hospital accommodation, the permanent state of emergency in West Berlin, the frontier regions deprived of their natural economic hinterland etc. were concerned, it might itself be counted as an underdeveloped country. Under President Kennedy's administration the German contribution to western defence was weighed in the balance and found wanting. Bonn's reaction was to start giving out funds with demonstrative generosity. *Simplicissimus* caricatured this type of 'aid' in the person of the anonymous desert sheikh who ordered a thousand W.C.s in Bonn even though no plans existed in his country for a sewerage system.

Nevertheless German enthusiasm for development aid brought out the best in their national character. Here at last was a constructive ideal which corresponded both to Erhard's demands to trim some of the fat off the economy and to the psychological need for an acceptable outlet of energy that would compensate for Germany's disastrous excursions into great-power politics in the past. It has now proved in retrospect to have been a piece of good fortune for Germany that the Treaty of Versailles deprived her of her colonies. She has been freed of the stigma of colonialism in the eyes of Asians and Africans, and provided Germans carry out their development aid with tact and sympathy they have the chance of making a positive contribution towards redressing old wrongs and incidentally helping to clear their own name abroad.

Have the Germans changed? Eugen Gerstenmaier gave an answer to this question in Rome on 14th January 1963 in the following words: "The Germany of today does not present a very exciting image to the world. But it is a fundamentally different image from that of the past. It shows a nation that wants to enjoy peace and prosperity to the full, yet is fully aware of the dangers of our age." This nation was now prepared to take full responsibility for the burden of its past. The aim of all Germans was to be "a reliable partner to anyone who believed in freedom under law"

There are of course opponents of the Germans who refuse to hear a good word spoken for them; all human imperfections are simply attributed to them en bloc. Nevertheless Germans must exercise patience and restraint when they have to listen to the verdicts of others: they are, after all, themselves considerably responsible for the distorted views held about them. But an equally heavy responsibility rests with those whose summary damnation does little but dishearten those Germans of goodwill who strive to make amends.

"Germany, my beloved fatherland, of whom I am so proud"— after the crushing blows of the recent past there can hardly be a single German who has the will and candour to make such a declaration as this, which Mozart wrote in one of his letters. National pride was permissible in those days and no one believed that the Germans stood beyond the pale of mankind—indeed, for many, Germany was synonymous with the best in mankind itself. Now the Germans stand isolated and much of the world sees them as the source of its misfortune. There is, God knows, enough evidence in support of this view.

In the face of every sort of prejudice the present-day German is nevertheless bound to point out (generally in vain) that to accuse him in the same breath of materialism, money-grubbing *and* militaristic aggression simply does not make sense. A nation which, it is claimed, has turned wholeheartedly to the worship of Mammon is hardly likely to want to precipitate an atomic war.

It can do nothing but good, therefore, if the Germans themselves can gradually come to realise that the German character has not been indelibly marked and moulded by those dates in heavy print which used to fill the school text books, dates of battles and coups d'état, dates of triumph and disaster. For centuries the Germans have lived their private lives as ordinary men and women aside from the mainstream of fame and national tragedy, a view which is no less true because it is banal. The honest businessman, the university professor, the village schoolmaster, the inventor in his laboratory, the poet's garret, the peasants and work-people, family life—who dares say that they should not be taken into equal account with the villains and monsters when judging the German people?

However rooted one's antipathy to the Germans may be, it is impossible with honesty to overlook the fact that the Germans, however great their past guilt, have now been reduced, in terms of international politics, to impotence. In the past one made 'hereditary enemies' of every sort and kind responsible for all this world's evil —the French, the Russians, the Germans, the Jews, the Protestants, the Catholics or the Treaty of Versailles. There is no denying guilt that has been established by the verdict of history, but it is absorbed with the years into generalisations and overlaid with other, newer manifestations of guilt. With time, the old cries ring hollow. Instead we are gradually beginning to realise that good and evil are not confined by time or frontiers and that they are not to be found in one nation alone.

INDEX